Securitisation in the Non-We:

C000115259

The concept of securitisation has gained increasing prominence in the past decade. Initially developed in Copenhagen, the term has been used to describe the broadening of the security agenda and the framing of particular issues as existential threats across the world. In spite of this prominence, very little work has been undertaken that questions the extent to which the concept can be applied beyond the Western world. This volume engages with these questions, providing a theoretical overview of issues with using the concept beyond the West, along with empirical papers looking at its use in a number of different contexts.

The chapters in this book were originally published as a special issue of *Global Discourse*.

Simon Mabon is a Senior Lecturer in International Relations at Lancaster University, UK, Director of the Richardson Institute, UK, and a Research Associate at the Foreign Policy Centre, UK. He is the author of *Saudi Arabia and Iran: Soft Power Rivalry in the Middle East* (2013), co-author of *Hezbollah: From Islamic Resistance to Government* (2015), *The Origins of ISIS* (2016), and co-editor of *Terrorism and Political Violence* (2015), amongst a number of other publications pertaining to Middle Eastern politics and International Relations.

Saloni Kapur is currently a PhD candidate at Lancaster University, UK. Her work interrogates international society's responsibility towards instability in Pakistan. She employs the English school's concepts of great-power responsibility and regional society to conduct normative research on international counterterrorism cooperation, drawing on aesthetic sources and treating terrorists as social actors.

Securitisation in the Non-West

Edited by
Simon Mabon and Saloni Kapur

Routledge
Taylor & Francis Group
LONDON AND NEW YORK

First published 2019
by Routledge
2 Park Square, Milton Park, Abingdon, Oxon, OX14 4RN, UK

and by Routledge
52 Vanderbilt Avenue, New York, NY 10017

First issued in paperback 2020

Routledge is an imprint of the Taylor & Francis Group, an informa business

© 2019 Taylor & Francis

British Library Cataloguing in Publication Data
A catalogue record for this book is available from the British Library

ISBN 13: 978-0-367-58650-8 (pbk)
ISBN 13: 978-1-138-31495-5 (hbk)

Typeset in Myriad Pro
by RefineCatch Limited, Bungay, Suffolk

Publisher's Note
The publisher accepts responsibility for any inconsistencies that may have arisen during the conversion of this book from journal articles to book chapters, namely the possible inclusion of journal terminology.

Disclaimer
Every effort has been made to contact copyright holders for their permission to reprint material in this book. The publishers would be grateful to hear from any copyright holder who is not here acknowledged and will undertake to rectify any errors or omissions in future editions of this book.

Contents

CONTENTS

Citation Information

The chapters in this book were originally published in *Global Discourse*, volume 8, issue 1 (March 2018). When citing this material, please use the original page numbering for each article, as follows:

Introduction
The Copenhagen School goes global: securitisation in the Non-West
Saloni Kapur and Simon Mabon
Global Discourse, volume 8, issue 1 (March 2018), pp. 1–4

Chapter 1
'It's not a Muslim ban!' Indirect speech acts and the securitisation of Islam in the United States post-9/11
Clara Eroukhmanoff
Global Discourse, volume 8, issue 1 (March 2018), pp. 5–25

Chapter 2
Recursion or rejection? Securitization theory faces Islamist violence and foreign religions
Mona Kanwal Sheikh
Global Discourse, volume 8, issue 1 (March 2018), pp. 26–38

Chapter 3
Review of 'Recursion or rejection? Securitization theory faces Islamist violence and foreign religions', by Mona Kanwal Sheikh
Saloni Kapur
Global Discourse, volume 8, issue 1 (March 2018), pp. 39–41

Chapter 4
Existential threats and regulating life: securitization in the contemporary Middle East
Simon Mabon
Global Discourse, volume 8, issue 1 (March 2018), pp. 42–58

Chapter 5
Review of 'Existential threats and regulating life: securitization in the contemporary Middle East', by Simon Mabon
John Gledhill
Global Discourse, volume 8, issue 1 (March 2018), pp. 59–61

For any permission-related enquiries please visit:
http://www.tandfonline.com/page/help/permissions

Notes on Contributors

Clara Eroukhmanoff is a Lecturer in International Relations at London South Bank University, UK. Her research is broadly situated in Critical Security Studies and explores the role of language, art, and emotions in securitisation processes. She is particularly interested in the ways in which Islam has been securitised since the September 11 attacks and the subsequent (counter)-radicalisation discourses and practices in the United States and the United Kingdom, as well as Islamophobia, and the affective responses of solidarity to victims of terrorism.

Edwin Ezeokafor is a Lecturer and Researcher on African Security at the University of Dundee, UK. He coordinates the module 'Terrorism: challenges to oil and gas industry'. He is an expert in development and governance.

John Gledhill is an Associate Professor of Global Governance in the Department of International Development, and a Fellow of St Cross College, at the University of Oxford, UK. In his research, writing, and teaching, he investigates conflict processes, non-violent protest movements, state formation and dissolution, peacekeeping and peacebuilding, post-conflict reconstruction, the politics of transitional justice, and transnational social mobilisation.

Mona Kanwal Sheikh is a Senior Researcher in the Department of International Security at the Danish Institute for International Studies, Denmark. Her main area of expertise is militant movements in Pakistan, especially the movements related to the Pakistani Taliban. Her research focuses on religious justifications of, and mobilization to, violence. She has also worked more broadly with Islamist ideologies related to Al-Qaeda, Hamas, and the Muslim Brotherhood.

Saloni Kapur is currently a PhD candidate at Lancaster University, UK. Her work interrogates international society's responsibility towards instability in Pakistan. She employs the English school's concepts of great-power responsibility and regional society to conduct normative research on international counterterrorism cooperation, drawing on aesthetic sources and treating terrorists as social actors.

Christian Kaunert is a Professor of Policing and Security, and Director of the International Centre for Policing and Security, at the University of South Wales, Wales. His research has a clear focus on Policing and International Security, especially in the area of EU Counter-Terrorism, including its external dimension; Terrorism and Counter-Terrorism; and International Relations more generally.

Mark Lacy is a Senior Lecturer in the Department of Politics, Philosophy and Religion at Lancaster University, UK. He is also an Associate Director of Security Lancaster. His current research focuses on cybersecurity and conflict outside of the West. He is an expert on critical security studies, European social theory, and digital geo-politics.

Simon Mabon is a Senior Lecturer in International Relations at Lancaster University, UK, Director of the Richardson Institute, UK, and a Research Associate at the Foreign Policy Centre, UK. He is the author of *Saudi Arabia and Iran: Soft Power Rivalry in the Middle East* (2013), co-author of *Hezbollah: From Islamic Resistance to Government* (2015), *The Origins of ISIS* (2016), and co-editor of *Terrorism and Political Violence* (2015), amongst a number of other publications pertaining to Middle Eastern politics and International Relations.

Daniel Prince is a Senior Lecturer in Cyber Security at Lancaster University, UK. He is also an Associate Director and Business Partnerships Manager for Security Lancaster. His specialties include network and systems security, risk management, service management, business development, business engagement, and knowledge transfer. He is a Book Series Editor at Routledge on Studies in Conflict, Security and Technology.

Juha A. Vuori is a Professor of International Politics at the University of Turku, Finland. His research interests include securitisation theory, security problems, regional security complex theory, surveillance studies, Chinese foreign and security policy, nuclear weapons, mass culture, and foreign policy ideology.

The Copenhagen School goes global: securitisation in the Non-West

Saloni Kapur and Simon Mabon

The theme of the International Studies Association's 2015 Annual Convention was 'Global International Relations and Regional Worlds', a theme that highlighted what Acharya and Buzan (2017) refer to as 'the American and Western dominance of [International Relations]'. Acharya and Buzan's (2017) contention is that whereas International Relations (IR) continues to refer to Western theoretical approaches and history, the world is moving into a phase in which Western dominance is on the decline, suggesting that it is time for IR to incorporate not just non-Western ideas and histories, but also a more holistic, global understanding of IR. At the same time, Acharya and Buzan (2017) argue that their advocacy of a Global IR accepts the mainstream theories of IR, but challenges them 'to accept the ideas, experiences and insights from the non-Western world' and 'expects them to give due recognition to the places, roles, and contributions of non-Western peoples and societies'.

Acharya and Buzan's work on non-Western and Global IR provides the ideological foundation for this special issue on Securitisation in the Non-West. Securitisation theory, or the Copenhagen School of IR, is increasingly being applied to cases outside the Western world to comprehend the role played by discourse and political actors in constructing something as a security threat (Acharya and Buzan 2017). In addition, a number of scholars have taken on the task of critically analysing securitisation theory's success in satisfactorily explaining security dynamics outside the West, and various suggestions have been made as to how the theory could be tweaked or broadened to allow for more accurate representations of security in undemocratic, illiberal and other non-Western settings.

Claire Wilkinson (2007), for instance, uses the case of Kyrgyzstan to posit that securitisation theory as put forward by the Copenhagen School is unable to sufficiently account for developments beyond the West for two reasons: First, she asserts, the theory takes it for granted 'that European understandings of society and the state are universal'. Wilkinson opines that theorists within the Copenhagen School must explicitly question normative concepts such as state and society. Second, the theory's emphasis on the speech act may be unsuited to non-Western contexts where limitations to speech exist, and where securitisation may take place through other means, including action. She criticises the linear construction of a speech act leading to an exceptional measure, stating that where speech is constrained, an extraordinary action could precede the speech act.

For Holbraad and Pedersen (2012), revolutionary Cuba provides a case of a non-liberal non-Western state where the liberal assumptions underpinning securitisation theory come into relief. While securitisation theory assumes normal politics to be clearly distinct from emergency politics, the liberal view perceives revolutionary regimes to be in a permanent state of emergency and, therefore, in a continuous state of securitisation where extra-political means are the norm. However, Holbraad and Pedersen point out, the liberal distinction between the state and society collapses in a revolutionary ontology, with revolutionary states assuming themselves to *be* the people. Thus, rules and exceptions cease to exist for a revolutionary state because the state *is* society. This renders problematic the Copenhagen School's assumption of a normal state of politics that can be distinguished from exceptional measures.

A third critique of securitisation theory has been carried out by Greenwood and Ole (2013), who test the theory in the context of Egypt during the Arab Spring. The Arab Uprisings separated regimes from societies in a number of states, toppling previously embedded authoritarian regimes in Tunisia, Egypt, Libya and Yemen. In other states, regimes framed protesting groups as existential threats, reconstructing the nature of political organisation amidst the conflation of domestic and regional, normative and geopolitical agendas. Greenwood and Wæver find that the theory assumes a basic level of stability and cannot therefore be applied to exceptional situations where there is no such thing as normal politics. They argue that the Egyptian revolution was such an exceptional situation and that this can be understood to be a Western bias in the theory, because Western states no longer encounter such exceptional situations.

In a time where state–society relations have frayed, amidst parabolic pressures from globalising forces and indigenous resistance to such forces, the need to offer context-specific explorations that are not solely based upon approaches predicated upon Western ontologies appears to be of paramount importance. Yet whilst the desire to move beyond Western approaches to IR is commendable, we must be careful not to throw the proverbial baby out with the bathwater.

Stemming from a workshop organised by the Richardson Institute and held at Lancaster University in the summer of 2017, this special issue seeks to engage with the application of processes of securitisation in a number of different non-Western contexts. With this in mind, across eight chapters and responses, the special issue tests the application of securitisation theory in a number of non-Western contexts. In the first article, Clara Eroukhmanoff (2018) introduces the concept of indirect speech acts, using the case of the securitisation of Islam in the United States. In the second article, Mona Kanwal Sheikh (2018a) explores the role of securitisation in engaging with Islamist violence, with a focus upon how securitisation can be used to capture the narrative structure of such violence. By engaging with empirical examples, Sheikh seeks to open the problems of an ontological nature stemming from Western-centrism with regard to both the application and design of the theory. In response, Saloni Kapur (2018b) focuses upon the importance of *political realities*, which can facilitate a greater and more accurate awareness of context-specific instances of securitisation, whilst also stressing that the conflation of religion and politics does not necessarily result in securitisation.

In the third article, Simon Mabon (2018a) considers the application of securitisation efforts in the Middle East, looking at Saudi Arabia and Bahrain. Mabon argues that amidst a complex and shared normative environment, securitisation processes often transcend state borders and thus have both intended and unintended consequences beyond state boundaries. Hence, concepts of the audience require greater theorisation. In response, John Gledhill (2018a) teases out aspects of the liberal ontology that Mabon focuses upon, whilst also placing emphasis upon colonial legacies and their impact upon the idea of 'normality'.

The fourth article by Kapur (2018a) engages with the securitisation of Pakistan by Indian actors, with a particular focus upon the so-called 'Line of Control'. Kapur argues that securitisation moves in India constitute a 'two-act play', which challenge the linear aspects of securitisation processes understood in a Western context. In response, Sheikh (2018b) posits that whilst this is a classical approach to understanding securitisation, it also allows for a focus upon the audience and the importance of popularity.

The fifth article by Ezeokafor and Kaunert (2018) looks at the role of securitisation in Africa and the nexus between securitisation and neo-patrimonialism. Ezeokafor and Kaunert use securitisation as a mechanism through which relations between leaders (elites) and societies can be better understood, arguing that a greater level of context and better synthesis between securitisation and neo-patrimonialism is required for an accurate understanding of political life across Africa.

The sixth article by Lacy and Prince (2018b) considers hyper-securitisation and the construction of cyber securitisation, moving beyond territorial and spatial dimensions. Lacy and Prince suggest that the speed of hyper-securitisation and technological change requires the re-examination of the spatial dynamics that shape policy, wherein risk and (un)intended consequences collapse into planning. In response, Juha Vuori (2018b) stresses the importance of focussing upon core values at the heart of both political projects and hyper-securitisation, which allows for a discussion of difference and also intent.

The seventh article by Vuori (2018a) explores Chinese efforts 'to prevent the securitization of China's rise in the US'. In doing this, Vuori draws upon ideas of de-securitisation within Chinese foreign policy towards the major powers, contributing not only to debates on (de)securitisation but also to understandings of Chinese foreign policy. In response, Lacy (2018a) considers the extent to which desecuritisation can be viewed as a tool of deception, suggesting that to get a more nuanced understanding of events – and indeed Chinese foreign policy – we should focus more upon infrastructural developments, where deeds reveal more than words.

In the final article, Gledhill (2018b) considers how securitisation can aid understanding of political life in Latin America, with a particular focus upon Brazil and Mexico. Gledhill argues that amidst the neoliberal agenda, political and social life has been securitised amidst the rise of 'political mafias' that have simultaneously become both guardians of order and victims of systems. In response, Mabon (2018b) suggests that this approach offers a powerful mechanism through which political and social life can be better understood.

Together, these articles highlight an array of areas for further exploration when taking securitisation theory beyond its Western domain. Whilst we should be careful not to repudiate all aspects of the theory in its application outside the Western world, it is clear that greater nuance is required beyond the West. This process has sought to identify areas through which the 'shackles of Westphalia' can be removed, creating space for further ontological and epistemological study, whilst retaining the utility of the Copenhagen School's approach.

Disclosure statement

No potential conflict of interest was reported by the authors.

References

Acharya, A., and B. Buzan. 2017. "Why Is There No Non-Western International Relations Theory? Ten Years On." *International Relations of the Asia-Pacific* 17 (3): 341–370. doi:10.1093/irap/lcx006. Accessed December 20, 2017.

Eroukhmanoff, C. 2018. "'It's Not a Muslim Ban!' Indirect Speech Acts and the Securitisation of Islam in the US Post-9/11." *Global Discourse* 8 (1): 5–25. doi:10.1080/23269995.2017.1439873

Ezeokafor, E., and C. Kaunert. 2018. "Securitization Outside of the West: Conceptualizing the Securitization-Neopatrimonialism Nexus in Africa." *Global Discourse* 8 (1): 83–99. doi:10.1080/23269995.2017.1412619

Gledhill, J. 2018a. "Review of Simon Mabon 'Existential Threats and Regulating Life: Securitization in the Contemporary Middle East'." *Global Discourse* 8 (1): 59–61. doi:10.1080/23269995.2017.1408269

Gledhill, J. 2018b. "Securitization, Mafias and Violence in Brazil and Mexico." *Global Discourse* 8 (1): 139–154. doi:10.1080/23269995.2017.1406679

Greenwood, M. T., and W. Ole. 2013. "Copenhagen-Cairo on a Roundtrip: A Security Theory Meets the Revolution." *Security Dialogue* 44 (5–6): 485–506. doi:10.1177/0967010613502573. Accessed December 20, 2017.

Holbraad, M., and M. A. Pedersen. 2012. "Revolutionary Securitization: An Anthropological Extension of Securitization Theory." *International Theory* 4 (2 (July)): 165–197. doi:10.1017/S1752971912000061. Accessed December 20, 2017.

Kapur, S. 2018a. "From Copenhagen to Uri and across the Line of Control: India's 'Surgical Strikes' as a Case of Securitisation in Two Acts." *Global Discourse* 8 (1): 62–79. doi:10.1080/23269995.2017.1406633

Kapur, S. 2018b. "Review of 'Recursion or Rejection? Securitization Theory Faces Islamist Violence and Foreign Religions,' by Mona Kanwal Sheikh." *Global Discourse* 8 (1): 39–41. doi:10.1080/23269995.2017.1411644

Lacy, M. 2018a. "China and Discourses of Desecuritization: A Reply to Vuori." *Global Discourse* 8 (1): 137–138. doi:10.1080/23269995.2017.1420858

Lacy, M., and D. Prince. 2018b. "Securitization and the Global Politics of Cybersecurity." *Global Discourse* 8 (1): 100–115. doi:10.1080/23269995.2017.1420858

Mabon, S. 2018a. "Existential Threats and Regulating Life: Securitization in the Contemporary Middle East." *Global Discourse* 8 (1): 42–58. doi:10.1080/23269995.2017.1410001

Mabon, S. 2018b. "Sovereign Implications of Securitisation Work." *Global Discourse* 8 (1): 155–156. doi:10.1080/23269995.2017.1410002

Sheikh, M. K. 2018a. "Recursion or Rejection? Securitization Theory Faces Islamist Violence and Foreign Religions." *Global Discourse* 8 (1): 26–38. doi:10.1080/23269995.2017.1411644

Sheikh, M. K. 2018b. "Securitization Analysis beyond Its Power-Critique." *Global Discourse* 8 (1): 80–82. doi:10.1080/23269995.2017.1414445

Vuori, J. A. 2018a. "Let's Just Say We'd Like to Avoid Any Great Power Entanglements: Desecuritization in Post-Mao Chinese Foreign Policy Towards Major Powers." *Global Discourse* 8 (1): 118–136. doi:10.1080/23269995.2017.1408279

Vuori, J. A. 2018b. "The Politics of Securitized Technology." *Global Discourse* 8 (1): 116–117. doi:10.1080/23269995.2017.1410370

Wilkinson, C. 2007. "The Copenhagen School on Tour in Kyrgyzstan: Is Securitization Theory Useable outside Europe?" *Security Dialogue* 38 (1): 5–25. doi:10.1177/0967010607075964. Accessed December 20, 2017.

'It's not a Muslim ban!' Indirect speech acts and the securitisation of Islam in the United States post-9/11

Clara Eroukhmanoff

ABSTRACT

According to the Copenhagen School, a political issue is prioritised, or 'securitised', when an audience accepts a speech act with a particular security grammar pointing to the dangerous nature of the threat and calling for extraordinary security measures. This article probes the opposite: what if not saying 'security' and instead saying 'friend' also contributes to the securitisation? I explore this logic with the ways in which Islam has been securitised in the United States from the Bush administration to the beginning of the Trump administration and offer an analysis of what this article calls the 'indirect securitisation of Islam.' Drawing on the philosophy of language of John Searle, an indirect securitisation is one that is successful through indirect securitising speech acts, that is, utterances that comprise two illocutions, one direct and one indirect, with the latter being the 'real' request of the utterance. Using covert forms of speech such as indirect speech acts enables elite speakers to 'deny plausibility' and claim they are not securitising (or 'the least racist person' as Trump claims), thereby 'saving face.' Indirect securitising speech acts are therefore an important strategic tool in elite actors' securitising playbook. The article seeks to make sense of a climate of American politics that seem ungoverned by conventional rules of speech by offering a timely study of how political leaders can 'have their cake and eat it too' in matters of national security.

Introduction

Securitisation theory draws attention to the selective use of language by politicians in the construction of security issues in the 'West' (Mabon and Kapur, this issue). According to Barry Buzan, Ole Wæver, and Jaap de Wilde (1998), the authors of securitisation theory, securitisation is a 'speech act': by invoking a security grammar, a state representative attempts to convince an audience and claim 'a special right to use whatever means are necessary to block it' (Wæver 1995, 55). This article probes the reverse: what if, by claiming that the issue is *not* security and by mobilising a language highlighting the peaceful nature of an issue instead, 'a state-representative moves a particular development into a specific area, and thereby claims a special right to use whatever means are necessary to block it'? Drawing on John Searle's (1975) indirect speech act theory, I argue that indirect speech acts can reveal a different type of securitisation, called 'indirect securitisation.' Direct securitisations are identified by an overt security grammar that labels an issue a threat, magnifies its dangerous nature, signals a point of no return and offers a possible way out, thereby lifting this issue 'above politics' (Buzan, Wæver, and De Wilde 1998, 32–3). By contrast, indirect securitisations are characterised by a covert security grammar where securitising actors avoid labelling the issue a threat, for fear of saying something gauche and be subsequently chastised. This article demonstrates that when it comes to securitising Islam, a religion perceived as non-Western, in a 'Western democracy' like the United States, elite speakers tend to use indirect speech to 'save face' since securitising religious minorities directly would be tantamount to a form of hate speech. Thus, I investigate the securitisation of Islam as a study *in* a Western context but *of* an issue that has been constructed as non-Western, or antithetical to the 'Western way of life.' Further, the indirect speech act approach may open a new line of inquiry into securitisations in the non-Western world insofar as covert securitisations are about the ability to mislead and to mask, rather than the capacity to speak per se.

To demonstrate this argument, the article first provides an analysis of speeches made by three presidents of the United States while in office in relation to Islam and Muslim communities. The analysis indicates that in these speeches, a direct security grammar with respect to Islam was not mobilised. George W. Bush and Barack Obama make sure that Islam is not associated with 'security,' or 'threat,' and instead frame Islam as a peaceful religion that is hijacked by an extremist fringe of extremists. Even newly elected Donald J. Trump (2016b), who during his campaign talked about a 'complete shutdown' of Muslims entering the United States, once in power, reassured the public that his executive order was 'not a Muslim ban' (2017c). The second section unpacks Searle's indirect speech act theory and lays the theoretical groundwork necessary for conceptualising the securitisation of Islam as an indirect securitisation. The implications of indirectness are explored in the third section, where securitising indirectly is considered a strategy deployed by elite speakers to thwart accusations of wrongdoings (such as racism). This is made possible because indirect speech allows securitising actors to deny plausibility by claiming that they never meant to securitise. Being able to save face is important for elite speakers for a failed securitising move can affect their political clout and in turn they can lose authority and legitimacy as security speakers. When President Trump has not respected the rules of covert speech and ventured outside of his speechwriter's text, for instance when he branded African nations and developing countries 'shitholes', these incidents have backfired and have invited responses that either ridiculed him or created diplomatic tensions (e.g. with South Africa) (CNN 2018). As Shogan (2006, 10) notes, one way to achieve credibility and maintain authority is to use rhetoric, which includes covert strategies such as indirect speech acts.

The concept of indirect securitisation provides an innovative twist to securitisation theory and is fundamental to how minority groups become securitised by elite speakers with the executive power to move issues 'beyond politics,' an issue that is relevant beyond the Western world. Indeed, when a securitisation constitutes a form of hate speech, such as saying that Muslims are a threat to the United States who need to be monitored, securitising actors securitise indirectly for fear of being accused of racism or discriminating against a minority group. This article speaks to philosophies of everyday language, in particular to covert forms of hate speech and racism, and offers a timely analysis of the indirect securitisation of Islam in the United States. Indirect securitisations illuminate the ways in which various American administrations, Democrat and Republican, can claim the war on terrorism is 'not a religious war' while at the same time target the Muslim population domestically and internationally. While covert language is not yet central to the philosophy of language (Saul 2017), how established speakers manipulate, lie and mislead their audiences is vital in the world and has become an increasingly pertinent area in International Relations since the rise of Trump and right-wing populism. Indirect securitisations can shed light on the nexus between the securitisation of minority groups and racism, notably how 'security' is intertwined with racist constructions, and how these practices reinvent themselves in the twenty-first century in the face of actors who claim they are the 'least racist person' (Trump 09/12/2015; Trump 15/09/2016; Trump 16/02/2017).

Framing Islam as a peaceful religion

On 17 September 2001, six days after the September 11 attacks, Bush travelled to the Islamic Centre in Washington DC to speak to American Muslim communities and reassured them that the United States was not at war with Islam. He declared that '[t]he face of terror is *not* the true faith of Islam. That's *not* what Islam is all about. Islam is peace.' Equally, on 20 September 2001 Bush asserted that the terrorists 'pervert the peaceful teachings of Islam' (Bush 17/09/2001, emphasis added). Offering an olive branch to the Muslim world, Barack Obama (04/06/2009) announced in Cairo that 'America and Islam are not exclusive,' instead, 'they overlap, and share common principles – principles of justice and progress; tolerance and the dignity of all human beings.' More recently, newly elected President Trump (2017c), from the Oval Office, claimed that the 'extreme vetting' executive order passed during his first hundred days in office is '*not* a Muslim ban.' Yet, Bush's 2003 invasion of Iraq, Obama's extensive drone programme and Trump's several attempts to ban individuals coming to the United States from a list of predominantly Muslim countries created by Trump's administrative team,[1] suggest that in the context of the war on terrorism Islam has been 'securitised,' meaning that security measures, exceptional and mundane, target the Muslim population.

This article is particularly concerned with elite speakers (such as the president of the United States) who have the executive power to trigger extraordinary measures like the PATRIOT ACT, the surveillance of 'Muslim neighbourhoods' and the assassination of American citizens by drones in territories with which the United States is not at war. To a certain extent, this article reinstates the elitist and exceptional understanding of securitising moves, which has been compared to the conceptualisation of politics by the German jurist Carl Schmitt ([1922] 2005), and rightly contested by a wide array of scholars, from the Paris School of Securitisation (Bigo and Tsoukala 2008; CASE Collective 2006; Diez 2007) to scholars working on the governmentality of security, technologies of risk and the securitisation of catastrophic events and trauma.[2] They argue that while the Copenhagen School has opened space for thinking of security beyond Cold War balance of power, the School has also closed it by merely exploring exceptional discourses of powerful actors, at the expense of everyday security practices and the 'little security nothings' (Huysmans 2011). Some have thus called to go beyond the 'spectacle of security' and instead investigate everyday experiences of (in)security (Lundborg and Vaughan-Williams 2011, 369).

I focus on presidents not because statesmen are the only actors shaping our understanding of what constitutes a societal and security issue. This would assume a top-down and overtly discursive understanding of how knowledge and meaning are generated. I focus on elite speakers for an important reason, namely, that these speakers contribute to the pervasiveness of covert forms of racism and hate speech, which remain unabated and unpunished because these actors can claim they never meant to securitise or that what they said is 'not racism.' This practice has become ubiquitous since the election of Trump, who has activated the securitisation of Islam in the United States, but has couched it under Executive Orders and the language of national security (Hassan 2017, 187–8). I do not suggest that actors other than the presidents of the United States have not securitised Islam or that practices other than speech do not contribute to seeing Muslims as threats. Securitisation is always manifold and includes a multitude of direct and indirect, discursive and non-discursive, exceptional and everyday *acts* performed by a variety of what the Copenhagen School calls functional actors, 'actors who affect the dynamics of a sector' and 'who significantly influence decisions in the field of security' (Buzan, Wæver, and De Wilde 1998, 36).

Functional actors like Fox News assert quite explicitly that the United States should be worried about the role of Islam in American society, but others such as the police have relied on more imagined and less explicitly means of communication, for instance explaining the radicalisation of Muslim individuals with metaphors of growing bad seeds and incubators (Eroukhmanoff 2015). These securitising moves constitute the background knowledge necessary for the indirect securitisation to be successful, as we will see later in this article. They are instrumental in the growing Islamophobic attitudes in the West, founded on the perception that Islam is a threat to the Western liberal-secular order and a threat to security (Mavelli 2013, 160–1). The election of Trump (2016b) has crystalised anti-Muslim prejudices by being overtly critical of Muslims during the 2016 election campaign, even calling for a 'total and complete shutdown of Muslims entering the United States until our country's representatives can figure out what the hell is going on.' Trump's Islamophobia is, as Hassan (2017, 188) notes, well documented. Still, prejudices about Islam and the role of Muslims in the War on Terror also stem from less overt iterations than Trump's 'Muslim shutdown' comment. Indirect speech acts are part of this covert construction and as such should be examined on their own merit, especially in the context of a Trump presidency which has been successful in maintaining Islam is at the centre stage of politics while simultaneously preserving the Bush and Obama administrations' official rhetoric that the war on terrorism is 'not a battle between different faiths, different sects, or different civilizations' (Trump 21/05/2017). Indirect securitisations can unravel the contradictory and unpredictable messages sent from a president that seem to defy any systematisation (Bentley, Eroukhmanoff, and Hackett 2017). This question matters even more precisely because there has been a constant effort on the part of each president to reassure the public that Islam is a religion of peace and a friend of America, paralleled by security measures that discriminate against this minority group like the 'Muslim ban.'

As such, the next section proceeds with an analysis of nine speeches made by former President Bush, former President Obama and the 46th President of the United

States, President Trump. The speeches were selected on the grounds that they fulfil the 'total speech act situation,' that is, the conditions necessary for the speech act to succeed, which depend on the appropriateness and authority of the speaker, and the context in which the speech is enunciated; for example, its location, if the speech takes place after or prior to an important event, or whether it is broadcasted. In other words, the total speech act situation relates to the sociological conditions external to the speech, rather than its internal grammar (Balzacq 2015, 5). The speeches selected represent significant moments in time, were scripted, were all televised, sparked a debate about the role of Islam in American society and in the War on Terror and about the choice of words made by the respective presidents. They include the first address after the September 11 attacks, the visit to the Islamic Centre in Washington D.C. on 17 September 2001 where Bush declared that 'Islam is peace', and the declaration of the 'Global War on Terror' on 20 September 2001. With respect to Obama's speeches, the article explores Obama's highly praised remarks in Cairo designed to improve US relations with the Muslim world by seeking a 'new beginning' during his first term, the address on national security and counterterrorism in his second term delivered at the National Defense University in 2013, and lastly, his remarks at the White House summit on countering violent extremism, in which he urges Muslims to not let ISIS hijack Islam in 2015. The next section also examines three speeches made by Trump that have been worthy of attention in his presidency so far, such as his victory speech of the 2016 US elections calling for American unity, Trump's first declaration as a president on combatting radical Islamist terrorism delivered in Ohio, and Trump's much-anticipated address to the Muslim world in Saudi Arabia on 21 May 2017.

These speeches were delivered both in the United States and in the Muslim world, thereby having been written for different audiences, but arousing global public interest. They symbolise(d) defining moments of a presidency, such as the President's first visit to a foreign country, or a declaration of war. Of course, the texts selected represent a slim number of speeches for each speaker, especially for Obama, who ran two terms. But what this article is interested in is not every iteration of these actors. Rather, this article explores those iterations that have avoided the connection between Islam and terrorism and those that have claimed that the war on terrorism is not a war against Muslim friends, in other words, this article is concerned with the absence of direct securitising language. These utterances, which are part of the macro-securitisation of Islam in the 'West,', are still securitising, albeit indirectly.

A. *President George W. Bush*

Bush's first move sought to securitise the Taleban regime. In his declaration of the War on Terror, Bush referred to the Taleban regime as 'threatening people everywhere' and demanded to be handed the terrorists responsible for the attacks. Bush frames justice in a Talionic understanding of 'an eye for an eye' that guarantees that '[w]hether we bring our enemies to justice or bring justice to our enemies, justice will be done' (Bush 20/09/2001). Afghanistan is categorised as a different and clashing civilisation to the one of America, where individuals are free to have beards as short as they wish and where women have equal rights in society. A Manichean divide is presented when he speaks about the bravery and 'the daring of our rescue workers, the caring for strangers and neighbours' as opposed to the destructive value of evil, 'the worst of human nature' (Bush 11/09/2001) and 'the enemies of freedom' (Bush 2001c).

Here, the direct security grammar is in place. Bush (20/09/2001) emphasises the existentially threatening nature of al Qaeda by arguing that al Qaeda 'hates' the American people, signalling a point of no return and offering a solution or a way out, lifting the issue 'above politics.' Indeed, terrorists hate American freedoms and 'kill not merely to end lives, but to disrupt and end a way of life.' Interestingly, the emphasis on al Qaeda's hatred for the United States as one of the core reasons for the attacks is reminiscent of George Kennan's telegram that warned the Harry Truman administration against the Soviet's 'innate antagonism' towards the United States. That this direct security grammar was available in 1946, when the famous Mr X's telegram was sent, attest to the existence of a securitising logic across time and space. Both Kennan and Bush's direct security speech acts were successful. Kennan's telegram alarmed the Truman administration and eventually led it to officialise the Truman doctrine of containment. Shortly after Bush's address on 20 September 2001, Congress voted in favour of the PATRIOT act, which extended the surveillance power of the state, and in favour of two wars, one in Afghanistan and the other in Iraq to deter global terror.

Bush's speech acts were also successful in securitising the Muslim population, yet in the absence of a direct security grammar. Indeed, six days after the September 11 attacks, Bush (17/09/2001) hastened to visit the Islamic centre in Washington D.C. to declare that 'Islam is peace' and that the terrorists are not the 'true' face of Islam. On 20 September 2001, Bush 2001c stated that 'Islam' should not be equated to 'terrorism' and should be separated from the terrorists by declaring that 'the terrorists are traitors to their own faith, trying, in effect, to hijack Islam itself.' Fierke (2007, 88) argues that apart from Bush's misguided reference to the 'crusade,' Bush's 9/11 address explicitly avoided reference to the Islamic identity of the attackers and a discourse of a clash with Islam. Indeed, for Bush (20/09/2001, emphasis added), '[t]he terrorists practice a *fringe* form of Islamic extremism that has been rejected by Muslim scholars and the vast majority of Muslim clerics, a *fringe* movement that perverts the peaceful teachings of Islam' and that 'those who commit evil in the name of Allah *blaspheme* the name of Allah.' The notion of a 'fringe' of extremists who pervert the 'real' teaching of Islam, whose essence is peaceful, was also echoed by Obama.

B. *President Barack Obama*

Ten years on in the War on Terror, Obama (04/06/2009) in Cairo spoke about a 'new beginning' between the United States and Muslims around the world, one based on mutual interest and mutual respect, and one based upon the truth that 'America and Islam are not exclusive.' The speech in Cairo was widely considered an olive branch to the Arab world, to reach out to Muslim communities in a region that gained stronger anti-American sentiments than during the earlier Bush administration (Guerlain 2014, 482–3). An emphasis on commonalities between the 'Muslim world' and the 'West' would be the basis for a new partnership. Obama talked about the American-Arab relationship in non-security terms and seized this moment to press the reset button. Indeed, according to Obama, 'in order to move forward, we must say openly to each other the things we hold in our hearts and that too often are said only behind closed doors. There must be a sustained effort to listen to each other; to learn from each other; to respect one another; and to seek common ground' (Obama 04/06/2009). At the National Defense University 4 years later, Obama (23/05/2013, emphasis added) reiterated that 'the United States is *not* at war with Islam.'

In addition, in a press conference on countering violent extremism, Obama (19/02/2015) went to great lengths to remember the 'good Muslims,' 'the more than one billion people around the world who do represent Islam, and are doctors and lawyers and teachers, and neighbours and friends.' He (19/02/2015) also makes reference to the 'good Muslim' policeman during the Charlie Hebdo attacks in Paris, 'who died trying to stop [the terrorists],' and to the Muslim worker at the Jewish supermarket who remarked that it was not a question of Jews, Christians or Muslims, and that 'we are all brothers.' More recently, Obama 2013, emphasis added) reiterated that 'the United States is *not* at war with Islam.' Instead, Obama stated that 'we are at war with people who have *perverted* Islam' (Obama 19/02/2015, emphasis added). Securitising speech acts that dehumanise 'terrorists' are not lacking.[3] Yet, these speeches often make terrorists 'traitors' to their own faith (Jackson 2005, 64) and are thus not directed at the Muslim community as a whole.

By doing so, Bosco (2014, 28) suggests that American discourse short-circuited the Clash of Civilisations from one of a clash between Islam and the West, to one *within* Islam. Bosco (2014) argues that the 'distorted' and 'extremist' interpretation of Islam, the one adopted by Islamist terrorists, was securitised in the United States, whereby the referent object for security—the object to be secured—was 'moderate' Islam, the 'true' meaning of Islam. The true threat was not religion. Rather, it was a twisted interpretation of Islam, whose peaceful essence was considered as eternal (Bosco 2014, 4). Indeed, terrorists were ideologues 'obsessed with ambition,' who distorted the harmony and peaceful nature of their religion and who must be stopped before their crimes multiplied (Bush 06/10/2005). This discourse allowed the Bush administration to use religion strategically, by avoiding framing the War on Terror as a religious war, and thus distant from the rhetoric of al Qaeda.

Still, this short-circuit made Islam take centre stage, and prevented a blowback from the neo-conservatives during the Bush administration for appearing 'too soft on Islam.' Overall, Western political leaders such as Bush moved away from the cultural and religious traits of the 'terrorists' in order to limit religious hostility by focusing on common values between the various communities in the West (Booth and Dunne 2002, 3). According to Bosco (2014, 28), 'if the War on Terror had a religious component, there was no reason why the Western state too could not harness religion as a weapon.' Yet, this strategic deviation and the official discourse that stated that 'Islam is a religion of peace' were unable to avoid the deployment of security measures that targeted the Muslim population and unable to caveat the antipathy toward those seemingly perceived as Arabs, Muslims and Middle Eastern (Ross 2014, 77).

While securitisations occur as a result of causal and non-causal, linguistic and non-linguistic, visual and non-representational elements, the constant effort by Obama to place Islam next to positive adjectives such as 'good,' 'virtuous' or 'peaceful,' or to place Islam in opposition to war, tells us what kind of realities and ideas the president of the

United States wishes to bring into being. In that respect, the reassurances that Obama kept offering could even be termed desecuritising moves, attempts to bring Islam back into 'normal politics.' This argument leads to the conclusion that these moves have failed, for Obama was unable to put an end to the drone programme in Somalia, Yemen, Pakistan, Afghanistan and Iraq, to the Guantanamo Bay detention centre, to the use of torture in 'black jails' of Afghanistan, or to the heightened surveillance of Muslims in the US. Presidents have significant institutional constraints that prevent them from radically altering the course of security policy, but the view of a failed desecuritising move gives too much power to structural forces. The president is considered a prisoner of a whole range of actors, factors and interactions and acts merely at the mercy of Congress (Guerlain 2014, 491). This lack of agency is untenable, especially in the case of Obama, who has made drones his 'weapon of choice' and generally preferred covert forms of counterterrorism. Obama's counterterrorism practices have reflected not only more continuity with his predecessor, but a more aggressive foreign policy towards Muslim countries that epitomises a gap between 'Obama the Orator' and 'Obama the Decider' (Guerlain 2014, 483). Desecuritising involves a return to the 'normal.' But Obama has maintained an exceptional logic by orchestrating a Central Intelligence Agency (CIA)-led drone programme in territories with which the United States is not at war. As Goldsmith (2009) notes, 'almost all of the Obama changes have been at the level of packaging, argumentation, symbol, and rhetoric.' The conciliatory rhetoric, though, abruptly ended in the run up to the 2016 elections and ultimately changed this non-securitising grammar.

C. *President Donald J.Trump*

On many occasions during his campaign, Trump promised to conduct 'extreme vetting' of all Muslims entering the American homeland. On 7 December 2015, Trump termed the extreme screening into a total shutdown of Muslims because the United States has 'no choice' (in The Telegraph 2016). In the same speech, Trump accused Obama of avoiding using the phrase 'Islamic terrorism,' confirming that Obama had been avoiding associating terrorism with Islam. According to Trump (2016a), anyone who cannot say the words 'Islamic terrorism' or 'radical Islamic terrorism' 'is not fit to lead this country,' though he himself avoided this term when he spoke in Saudi Arabia on 21 May 2017. Throughout the election campaign, Trump (15/08/2016) referred to radical Islam as a 'hateful ideology' and declared that the United States could not let 'its oppression of women, gays, children and nonbelievers – be allowed to reside or spread within our own countries' (point of no return). The United States must and 'will defeat radical Islamic Terrorism' by adopting a 'new approach' and 'all actions should be oriented around this goal' (solution of lifting the issue 'above politics') (Trump 2016a). Here, a clear securitising language is observable, one that points to the existentially threatening nature of 'radical Islam,' advances a point of no return ('we cannot let this ideology'), and a way out requiring extraordinary security measures ('all actions should be oriented around this goal').

Yet, once elected, Trump employed less inflammatory language, and even made a *couple* of linguistic U-turns. In his acceptance speech, Trump (2016a) declared that his movement was 'comprised of Americans from all races, religions, backgrounds and beliefs' and that it was time to 'come together as one united people.' Although this instance was an incident as he returned to a provocative language shortly afterwards, the acceptance speech was remarkably different from earlier speeches, giving a misleading hope of a future administration that would play down campaign rhetoric. Still, after his election victory, the video of Trump about the 'complete shutdown of Muslims' of 7 December 2015, disappeared from Trump's campaign homepage (Telegraph 2016). From the Oval Office, Trump then claimed that his executive order banning any individual coming from Iran, Iraq, Libya, Syria, Somalia, Sudan and Yemen, albeit excepting 'persecuted Christian minorities' in the Middle East, was 'not a Muslim ban.' While President Trump did not go as far as former President Bush and former President Obama in framing Islam as a religion of peace, Trump reassured his audience that his order was not a discrimination against one religion, a gesture that he had not extended during his campaign.

The purpose of the executive order was instead masked into a language of national security and the protection of the homeland to 'protect the American people from foreign nationals admitted in the United States,' as Secretary of Homeland Security John Kelly reiterated on 31 January 2017 (Department of Homeland Security 2017). A few days later, a federal court ruled in favour of the restraining order on the ban, putting an immediate halt to what Washington Attorney General Bob Ferguson (2017) called 'President Trump's unconstitutional and unlawful executive order.' In the courtroom, Noah Purcell, the Washington Solicitor General, argued that the executive order was in fact a ban based on religious discrimination. New York City Mayor Rudy Giuliani (2017) had confessed that Trump had asked him to 'put a commission together,' and 'show [him] the right way to do it legally,' confirms that Trump had sought to legitimate and legalise a 'Muslim ban' in the name of national security (Purcell 2017). But while the first ban was chaotically rolled out in January and blocked by numerous lower court rulings, a second – streamlined – ban unfortunately came into effect in the summer 2017 (McCarthy and Laughland 2017).

There are wider implications about rules of language beyond the legal framework that are worth exploring. Once elected, speakers such as Bush, Obama and to some extent, even Trump, are limited in what they can say out loud, that is, with a direct security grammar like Trump's call for a 'total shutdown on Muslims,' which has since been removed from his official campaign website. The examples indicating a lack of direct securitising move do not mean an absence of securitisation overall. On the contrary, the next section demonstrates that these speakers are informed by rules of appropriate language, supported by what Tali Mendelberg has called the 'Norm of Racial Equality,' when securitising minority groups. As President(s) of the United States, these elite speakers therefore resort to a covert securitising grammar, indirect securitising speech acts, to comply with the Norm of Racial Equality. To understand how indirect speech acts works, this article turns to John Searle's philosophy of language and lays the groundwork for situating the Presidents' speech acts as indirect securitising speech acts.

Searle's indirect speech act theory

A. *Indirect speech act theory*

The philosophy of Searle is situated in the philosophy of ordinary language. It echoes parts of Wittgenstein's *Philosophical Investigation*, in the sense that saying something engages in a rule-governed form of behaviour in ways that are similar to the rules of chess or football (Searle 1971, 40). This view challenges the logocentric view of the world in which language offers enough distance from the world that it can represent reality as it is, including our own selves in this world (Onuf 1989, 43). When Bush and Obama assert that Islam is peaceful or when Trump utters that 'it is not a Muslim ban,' specific rules of appropriate saying govern the ways in which these actors speak (even in the case of Trump). It is these rules and the practice they create that is of interest here.

Searle's philosophy of language sets him apart from other philosophers such as Wittgenstein because meaning is constituted in part by the *intention* of the speaker to produce certain effects in the hearer (Searle 1979, 31). In doing so, Searle distinguishes between 'speaker meaning' and 'literal utterance meaning.' This distinction allows Searle to differentiate between simple cases of speech acts and more complex ones like metaphors or indirect speech acts. In simple cases, 'the speaker utters a sentence and mean exactly and literally what he says' (Searle 1979, 30). A standard speech act situation is performed when the speaker utters something and believes that what she/he says is 'true' and intends to communicate this belief to the hearer. For example, if I say to a student, 'I have this book in my office,' for this utterance to be 'true'—meaning that the hearer understands my utterance—the book must be, in fact, in my office. However, if I say, 'I have a brother,' and on the contrary, I only have sisters, my utterance would have made sense grammatically, but would not have been 'true' in the sense of representing a 'true' state of affairs. Yet, my intent there was perhaps not to 'truly' communicate my genealogical tree, but to do something else. Perhaps I was singing the lyrics of a song I heard on the radio, perhaps I was learning English on an audiotape, etc. In this case, the meaning of the speaker and the meaning of the literal utterance are different, and for Searle, it is only by dissociating the two that one can make sense of indirect speech acts. In everyday life, not all cases of speech acts are as simple as the 'I have this book in my office' case. On many occasions, the speaker may mean what she/he utters, but also mean something more, which is not conveyed in the literal utterance meaning (Searle 1979, 30).

In cases of indirect speech acts, the speaker means what she/he utters, but also means another illocution with a different propositional content. Indeed, an indirect speech act is an act in which 'the speaker may utter a sentence and mean what she/he says and also mean another illocution with a different propositional content' (1979, 30). In other words, while the speaker means what she/he says ('Islam is not a threat'), she/he means something more ('but the only way to tackle the threat of terrorism is to securitise the Muslim population'), which is not communicated in the first illocution. A much-celebrated example offered by Searle is the dinner table situation. When someone asks: 'Can you reach the salt?' Searle argues that the speaker's meaning is a request to pass the salt, rather than a mere question about whether she/he can indeed reach the salt (Searle 1979, 30). What is interesting, or what constitutes a puzzle for Searle (1979,

31), is that the hearer understands the indirect request of passing the salt when what she/he hears is literally about something else. Indeed, the hearer passes the salt without answering the literal question that he or she can in fact reach the salt, without passing the salt. The literal sentence meaning here is one's ability to reach the salt, yet the speaker's sentence meaning is a *request* to pass the salt (Bertolet 2001, 335). The question about the ability to reach the salt is direct, but represents the second illocutionary act, serving the primary, indirect illocutionary act of requesting that the salt be passed (Bertoletss 2001, 336). Searle's (1979, 31–2) hypothesis about the success of the indirect speech act is that 'the speaker communicates to the hearer more than he actually says by way of relying on their mutually shared background information, both linguistic and non-linguistic, together with the general powers of rationality and inference on the part of the hearer.'

Indirect speech acts explain how powerful actors such as Bush, Obama and President Trump can maintain that 'Islam is peace' or that the executive order is 'not a Muslim ban' in public and simultaneously target Muslim communities domestically and internationally. While they mean what they utter—'Islam and America are not exclusive'—they also mean something more, 'securitising Islam is inevitable in times of war,' which is understood by the audience because they share background knowledge and are able to make inferences respective of this background. The leaders of the 'free world' convey a securitising message that is not literally spelt out in the literal utterance. Instead, a second illocutionary logic with a different propositional content—here securitising Islam—is communicated indirectly, in the same way passing the salt in a dinner situation is requested through a second illocution if one can *reach* the salt. The utterances 'Islam is peace,' 'our Muslim friends' or 'it is not a Muslim ban' and all the reassurances that former and current president of the United States have repeatedly uttered are thus direct illocution but serve the primary and indirect illocutionary act of requesting to securitise Islam. In this case, the audience understands the indirect request of securitising the Muslim population without having to acquiesce to the direct illocution that posits the peaceful essence of Islam. The direct and indirect illocutions seem not contradictory within the postulate of a war on terrorism that has at its heart an exceptionally racist and Orientalist logic. To understand the steps by which the audience infers the indirect but primary request to securitise Islam, let us reconstruct Bush's speech to Congress following 9/11 in the same way Searle reconstructs the dinner situation.

B. *Reconstruction of G.W. Bush's speech*

According to Bush (11/09/2001):

> Tonight, we are a country awakened to danger and called to defend freedom. [....] Whether we bring our enemies to justice or bring justice to our enemies, justice will be done [...] [Terrorists] are sent back to their homes or sent to hide in countries around the world to plot evil and destruction [....] The terrorists are traitors to their own faith, trying, in effect, to hijack Islam itself [...] The enemy of America is not our many Muslim friends. It is not our many Arab friends. Our enemy is a radical network of terrorists and every government that supports them [...] The search is underway for those who are behind these evil acts. I've directed the full resources for our intelligence and law enforcement communities to find

those responsible and bring them to justice. We will make no distinction between the terrorists who committed these acts and those who harbour them.

By following Searle's indirect speech act method, this quote above can be reconstructed as such:

Step 1: G.W. Bush told the hearers of Bush's address (the American public including the security practitioners and functional actors) that the nation has awakened to danger because of a radical network of terrorists that hijack Islam, and that justice will be done.

Step2: Bush is cooperating with 'us' and therefore his utterance has some aim or point (principles of cooperative conversation).

Step 3: The setting of the speech is not such as to only indicate that the country has awakened to danger, which is obvious (factual background information).

Step 4: Therefore, his utterance is probably not just factual information. It probably has some ulterior illocutionary point (inference from Steps 1,2,3, and 4). What can it be?

Step 5: A preparatory condition for any directive illocutionary act is the ability of the hearers to perform the act predicated in the propositional content condition (theory of speech acts).

Step 6: Therefore, Bush has told us something to which the preparatory conditions for how justice will be done will be satisfied (inference from Steps 1 and 6).

Step 7: The hearers are now listening to a speech by the president after the 9/11 attacks; they know that the search for terrorists is underway and that full resources have been given to the intelligence and law-enforcement agencies (background information). The hearers have also been prepared for the discourse of exceptionalism. In exceptional times like the attacks of September 11, exceptional measures are required.

Step 8: Bush has therefore alluded to the satisfaction of a preparatory condition. Bush wants to bring the end of terrorism, and this will be done through a consideration of all background information (inference from Steps 7 and 8).

Step 9: The security professionals have identified a category of individuals at risk of being radicalised, the Muslim population (background information).

Steps 10: Therefore, in the absence of any other plausible illocutionary point, Bush is probably saying that 'to give full resources to the law-enforcement and intelligence community' means that the security professionals are free to conduct surveillance operations on the population identified 'at risk' and that this means religious minorities can be targeted (inference from Steps 5 and 10).

Step 12: Bush is therefore asking to securitise the Muslim population (action).

The success of the indirect speech act securitising Islam is, of course, contingent on the background knowledge shared by the speaker and the audience, as well as on the powers of rationality and conversational implicatures demonstrated throughout this reconstruction. When G.W. Bush utters 'the enemy of America is not our many Muslim friends,' the sentence only makes sense in relation to a set of assumptions about the world order, the role of religion in society and the role of Muslims in the fight against terrorism. Equally, when Donald Trump retorts to journalists: 'this is not a Muslim ban,' this utterance activates old Orientalist myths about Islam which have been reinforced since 9/11 with the war against al-Qaeda and ISIS. Kumar (2012, 42–59) points to five different myths about Islam that have prolonged this discourse in the United States. She argues that common Orientalist myths have created and maintained the idea of an unchanging *homo Islamicus*, a 'Muslim mind' incapable of reason, rationality and self-rule, and thus antithetical to the 'Western way of life.' Kumar also notes that Islam is portrayed a sexist religion that subjugates and oppresses women, even when those who perpetuate this myth have a poor track record in gender equality. Lastly, Muslims are assumed to be ticking time bombs determined by their religion to inevitably act violently, now or in the future (Kumar 2012, 52). What is important for this article is that those myths constitute the shared background knowledge that will be activated when the words 'Islam' or 'Muslim' are uttered. Sentences pointing to the peaceful nature of Islam and the contribution that Muslims make to American society can coexist with descriptions such as 'Islamic terrorism,' which 'restick the words together and constitute their coincidence as more than simply temporal' (Ahmed 2014, 76).

Hence, the phrase 'Islam is peace' or, again, 'Muslims friends', acts as a dog-whistle, a coded word or formulation that will be invoked during a speech and that will resonate with the audience to mean something else. Such an indirect securitising move would appear on its face to be not securitising and innocuous, 'lending deniability if confronted with racism accusations' (Saul, forthcoming, 9). Still, the dog-whistle 'Islam is peace' actualises a series of social conventions that implicate the audience's pre-existing knowledge in the same way that saying, 'Could you reach the salt?' in the dinner situation actualises a web of meaning produced before the request is uttered, which, in turn, is necessary for the hearer to pass the salt. The utterance 'Islam is peace,' thus, does not create new meaning ex nihilo. Instead, the dog-whistle of the indirect speech serves to (re)mobilise particular framings about Islam and the role of Muslims in the war on terrorism, framings that precede the speech act and are articulated elsewhere, for instance, by functional actors like the media, counterterrorism agencies, or/and by Trump himself, during the 2016 campaign. Dog-whistles, as Saul (forthcoming, 2) observes, 'are one of the most powerful forms of political speech, allowing for people to be manipulated in ways that they would resist if the manipulation was carried out more openly—often drawing on racist attitudes that are consciously rejected.' Securitising actors thus rely on a more complex repertoire of securitising language than the overt security grammar originally developed by the Copenhagen School, one that may lend itself better to research in non-Western contexts. The next section demonstrates the strategic advantages, or 'benefits,' in indirectly securitising, and argues that indirect securitising speech acts are a significant tool in elites' securitising playbook.

Strategic advantages of indirect securitising speech acts

After unpacking Searle's indirect speech act theory and applying it to Bush's speech, this section highlights the strategic benefits of using indirectness in securitising processes. One reason for using indirect speech is that human beings are social animals, and as such, are often driven to explain *why* they have chosen certain path of actions, rather than simply describing them (Goddard and Krebs, 2015, 13–4). As social animals and meaning-making beings, human beings care about the reception of their proposition and about the impression they make on others (Goddard and Krebs, 2015, 379; Pinker, 2007). In cases where saying certain things could offend the hearer, jeopardise the speaker's social status or incriminate her or him (in the case of a bribe for instance), speakers will likely avoid direct speech. Avoiding direct speech may be a conscious move on the part of the speaker, or it may be a semi-conscious response of self-regulation. This is the perspective of Pierre Bourdieu, who argues that speakers often euphemise speech to shape utterances according to what is positively sanctioned in a field of practice. For Bourdieu, euphemisation is a form of 'censorship' that does not operate at the conscious level. Instead, these strategies are 'more or less conscious,' governed by the field of practice in which the utterance is placed (Bourdieu, 2001, 119). Moreover, they are embedded in the speaker's 'linguistic habitus' in the sense that speakers become socialised into speaking in a certain way (with indirect speech for instance). Presidents may first use indirect speech intentionally, but the repetitive use of indirect speech makes these strategies become habits rather than deliberate acts of rhetorical manipulation. The problem is that proving strategic intentions or knowing the 'true' motives of actors is methodologically intractable. Indeed, this would require having access to people's minds (Krebs and Jackson, 2007, 40). In any case, whether indirect speech acts are intentional or unconscious, using them has clear strategic *effects*. This article thus places greater emphasis on the effects of indirect speech in securitisation and thus on the perlocution of the speech act, rather than on the motivations of political leaders in employing indirect speech, and thus on the illocutionary act.

The reasons for using indirect speech have been explained by Lee and Pinker, who draw on Strategic Speech Theory. Strategic Speech Theory seeks to maximise the chances of success and avoid worst possible outcomes for each player in the game. Upon hearing the indirect speech act, the hearer has two choices: she/he can cooperate and accept the request or she/he can react adversarially and be uncooperative (Pinker S et al. 2008, 833). Cooperating with the speaker when she/he directly securitises leads to the success of securitisation, yet not cooperating with the speaker, meaning that the audience has rejected the securitising move, leads not only to a failure of securitisation, but to the breaking of Mendelberg's 'Norm of Racial Equality' and accusations of racism. However, the case of indirect speech offers a range of strategic benefits for: a) implementing security measures, which we will term 'benefits for the securitisation'; b) the speaker; and c) the audience.

A. *Benefits for the securitisation*

Indirect speech has a positive function insofar as it achieves better securitising effects, for instance, the ability to maintain two contradictory agendas, by explicitly supporting one idea—Islam is a peaceful religion—and indirectly conveying a request to increase the development of security technologies and surveillance operations on 'suspect' Muslim communities (Eroukhmanoff, 2015), security measures that are outside the normal political framework. Legitimacy matters not only for the speaker, but also for the issue or policy at stake. Indeed, legitimacy constitutes an essential part of how policy options are created and mobilised (Goddard and Krebs, 2015, 9). The greater the capacity of political leaders to maintain the legitimacy of security practices, as Balzacq (2015, 3) notes, the less resistance these will engender in the future. Viewed in this light, using indirect speech helps pave the way for security practices that would otherwise have been rejected. Indirect securitising speech thus heralds a change of policy, by setting the scene for future security practices. They are thus precursors and indicators of security practices.

B. *Benefits for the speaker*

Lee and Pinker (2010, 795) points out that:

> A speaker resorts to indirect speech when the relational model assumed by the speech act clashes with the model that currently holds between the speaker and hearer, avoiding the risk of awkwardness or shame in the same way that a briber avoids the risk of an arrest.

In the event the hearer is hesitant or antagonistic to a proposal (a securitising move), a direct securitising move can backfire and lead to serious repercussions for the speaker, one of which will be to acknowledge or even apologise for saying something gauche, or socially unacceptable. Since the civil rights and the counter-culture movement of the 1960s, Mendelberg (2001) argues that a 'Norm of Racial Equality' is established that guides how Americans and politicians address issues of race and minority groups in public. The Norm of Racial Equality has made overt forms of racism and hate speech unacceptable. Of course, the boundaries of the permissible in the Trump era have been pushed significantly (Saul, 2017), but Trump's denial that his executive order is a 'Muslim ban' victimising individuals of Islamic faith and his persistent claim that he is 'the least racist person' indicate that the Norm of Racial equality still plays a significant role in shaping how elite speakers speak. By using indirect speech, politicians avoid breaking the Norm of Racial Equality and the risks associated with doing so (embarrassment, the accusation of being racist, and a loss of legitimacy). This is because the speaker can claim she/he never 'meant' to securitise since the request (a form of hate speech) was not literally spelt out. According to Lee and Pinker (2010, 787), indirect speech 'allows plausible deniability of a breach of a relationship type and thus avoids the aversive social and emotional consequences that would be triggered by such a breach.' In other words, being able to deny the intention of a securitising act protects the securitising actor; it provides a convenient alibi that the securitisation was not 'his or her intention.' As newly elected Trump declared, his executive order is 'not a Muslim ban.' Bush, Obama and Trump can thus 'save face,' avoid a backlash with the population for attempting to securitise a religious minority.

Moreover, reacting unfavourably to an *indirect* request avoids the worst possible outcome, that is, the securitisation fails *and* the speaker pays the price of saying something maladroit or offensive. For the president of the United States, the risks of securitising directly the Muslim population by asserting that 'Islam itself is a threat' can not only be considered as discriminatory, but also lead to a possible loss of legitimacy, credibility and authority. Political leaders are in constant need of support, or 'political capital,' according to sociologist Pierre Bourdieu. Since political capital rests on symbolic power, political leaders such as Bush, Obama and Trump must constantly nurture their support by appealing to the electorate and the general population (Vuori, 2008, 70). Drawing on Wiberg, Vuori (2008) contends that 'legitimacy is perhaps the most significant element in the survival of any social institution and all governments must exercise a minimum of both persuasion and coercion in order to survive.' The use of indirect speech in circumventing the Norm of Racial Equality is an integral part of maintaining legitimacy as an elite speaker, even for Trump, who has to constantly backtrack from the offensive statements he has made at a prior time. Continuous coercive ruling is simply unsustainable, even in non-democratic contexts (Vuori, 2008). Likewise, direct securitisations that overtly discriminate against minority groups cannot be a long-term strategy for elite speakers, who are informed by the Norm of Racial Equality and can lose legitimacy if they repeatedly break it. In addition, indirect speech maximises the chances of success of a securitisation.

C. *Benefits for the audience*

Lastly, indirect speech is also advantageous for the audience, for they can accept or reject an indirect request without feeling embarrassed about their choice. Indeed, as Lee and Pinker (2010, 802) note, a 'gauche direct request can embarrass a hearer.' This is because the hearer is backed into responding to a request that will limit his or her options in the future and accepting a proposal that is distasteful. By increasing uncertainty, indirectness provides an 'out' for both the speaker, whose second illocution may be rejected, and for the hearer, who can simply respond to the direct illocution and pretend she/he did not understand the indirect request. In the same way as the dinner situation in which the hearer simply passes the salt when asked if she/he can *reach* it, the audience of Bush, Obama and Trump's indirect speech acts do not have to explicitly acquiesce to the indirect request to securitise Islam, but can simply do the deed, without having to spell out or consciously reflect on the deed. To a certain extent, indirect securitisations remove the audience from *feeling* that there is a securitisation taking place, since a language of amity rather than enmity is used.

The strategic advantages can thus be summarised as:

Type of Cooperation/ Speech acts	Cooperative	Uncooperative
Direct	– Success of securitisation – Security practices in place	– Failure of securitisation – Breaking the Norm of Racial Equality – Accusations of discriminating against a minority group and of racism – Loss of credibility and authority for the speaker
Indirect	– Success of securitisation – Securitising actor paves the way for security practices that would otherwise not be accepted. – Audience is removed from *feeling* the securitising work	– Failure of securitisation – Securitising actor 'saves face' and avoids accusations of racism and a loss of credibility and authority

D. *Problematising the negotiation between securitising actor and audience in indirect securitisation*

Indirect securitisation calls into question the process of negotiation between securitising actors and the audience. The goal of the 'total speech act' and the success or failure of a securitisation depends upon the persuasive competencies and authority of the speaker and the context in which the speech is enunciated. The securitising actor must argue the necessity of extraordinary measures by employing the 'right grammar of security.' In this case, the persuasion seeks to lift the normal political framework and introduce extra-ordinary security measures. This process often relies on a language of existential threats, point of no return and an (often militarised) way out (Buzan, Wæver, and De Wilde, 1998). However, with indirectness, the negotiation is sought on different grounds. With indirect speech, the securitising actor does not attempt to negotiate the breaking of normal procedure to tackle an issue, as the analysis of Bush, Obama and Trump indicated. On the contrary, these actors seek to reassure the audience that the securi-tised issue is 'not a security issue,' thereby mobilising a grammar grounded in solidarity, pacifism and inclusiveness.

Hence, *indirect securitising moves* are not so much about magnifying the dangerous nature of a threat to persuade an audience, but about negotiating the cooperation of the audience in accepting an indirect request that is not literally uttered (and that both speaker and hearer know cannot be spelt out). The success and failure of securitisation depend not so much on the arguments put forward in the construction of new emergent threats. Rather, it is how well speakers use covert forms of speech (with the use of rhetorical devices, gestures, power and emotions) and how elite speakers can dog-whistle key phrases that will bring into play pre-existing knowledge about the falsely 'dangerous nature of Islam.' Indirect securitisations thus call into question the type of cooperation negotiated between speaker and audience and highlight a different kind of negotiation, one that is less about the *content* of the securitisation than about the skills required of the speaker to obtain the cooperation of the audience. Indirect securitisations also call into question the honesty and accountability of the speaker and of the audience who, by expressing and agreeing to an indirect message, are removed from the securitising work. Concomitantly, the use of indirect securitising moves by actors such as Trump does not indicate an absence of securitisation altogether, nor that Trump is effectively 'the least racist person,' but merely that the securitisation of minority groups and racism have reinvented themselves in the post-9/11 landscape in more covert forms.

Conclusion

This article inquired into the strategic use of indirect speech and applied this theoretical framework to the securitisation of Islam in the United States, though more research could explore the securitisation of minority groups using indirect language in the non-Western world. This article is explorative in nature and recog-nises that many questions are still unanswered. Still, the notion of indirect securitisa-tion opens space to more robust conceptualisation of a strategic security practice in which the audience and context are key, and to how the nexus between covert construction of security threats and racism play out in non-Western contexts. Some caution needs to be exercised with indirect securitisations. The intent of this article was not to find ways by which securitising actors can securitise better, nor does it view indirect securitisations as a positive act. This article agrees with Waever (1995) that securitisations represent a failure to deal with issues democratically and are thus normatively negative, especially in the case of the war on terrorism, which has normalised an exceptionalist logic (Neal, 2012). What this article hoped to show is that security actors do not always need to invoke a security language of enmity to securitise. On the contrary, securitisations can be successful by mobilising a language of amity.

This has international significance in a context where far-right populism is rising across Europe, the United States, and beyond the Western world, and where leaders of those parties claim that they are 'not racist,' or not 'xenophobes.' When actors claim 'not to be securitising' in the same way Trump declared 'it is not a Muslim ban,' this article demonstrated that these utterances do not preclude a securitising move. Subversive politics of desecuritisation thus need to turn attention to instances where both speaker and audience can maintain that 'Islam is peace' and decipher covert forms of hate speech and securitisation. Moreover, since the request to securitise is indirect and the response does not need to be spelt out, speakers and audience are also prevented from *feeling* that they are part of a securitisation and remain comfortable in the idea that they are 'not racist.' Securitising indirectly thus provides an emotional cover that supresses any sense of responsibility and accountability in securitisation processes. While the Copenhagen School argued that the securitisation approach serves to underline 'the responsibility of talking security' (Buzan, Weaver, de Wilde 1998, 34), this article shows that indirect securitisations do just the opposite; they remove the securitising *act* from securitising actors and audiences. This unemotional type of politics of security intertwines with the idea that the Trump administration and moves to ban Muslims from entering the United States are about national security and not about race or religion, which permeates American politics since 9/11.

Notes

1. The first Executive Order banned individuals from seven predominantly Muslim countries but was suspended by a federal judge's order on in February 2017. A second was quickly issued, exempting green card holders and dual citizens. In June most of the second iteration of the ban was in effect. This second order was replaced in late September 2017, adding non-Muslim countries such as North Korea (Bbc News, 2017).
2. See the 2008 special issue of *Security Dialogue* on security, technologies of risk and the political.
3. See for example, Dick Cheney's (2009) assertion that Guantanamo prisoners are 'the worst of the worst' and that the only alternative to the Guantanamo naval prison was to kill terror suspects incarcerated there; see also his defence of waterboarding and torture at Guantanamo (Cheney 2009). See also Bush's (2001a and 2001c) reference to terrorists as 'evil' and as 'the worst of human nature.'

Acknowledgments

I would like to thank the editors of the Special Issue, Saloni Kapur and Simon Mabon, for organising a workshop in March as part of the Richardson Institute at the University of Lancaster, and for their feedback on the article. I would also like to thank Karin Fierke, Michelle Bentley, Thierry Balzacq and the reviewers for insightful comments and strengthening this research more broadly. The remaining mistakes are my own.

Disclosure statement

No potential conflict of interest was reported by the author.

References

Ahmed, S. 2014. *The Cultural Politics of Emotion*. Translated by. 2nd ed. Edinburgh: Edinburgh University Press.

Balzacq, T. 2011. "A Theory of Securitization: Origins, Core Assumptions, and Variants." In: *Securitization Theory: How Security Problems Emerge in Discourse*, edited by Thierry Balzacq. Oxon: Routledge.

Balzacq, T. 2015. "Legitimacy and the 'Logic' of Security." In: *Contesting Security: Strategies and Logics*, edited by Thierry Balzacq. Oxon: Routledge.

BBC News. 2017. *Trump's Latest Travel Ban Blocked by Second Federal Judge* [Online]. Accessed 16 Dec 2017. http://www.bbc.co.uk/news/world-us-canada-41668665

Bentley, M., C. Eroukhmanoff, and U. Hackett. 2017. "Trump's 100 Days: Foreign Policy and Security Implications: Introduction." *Critical Studies on Security* 5 (2): 166–167. doi:10.1080/21624887.2017.1355153.

Bertoletss, R. 2001. "Are There Indirect Speech Acts?" In: *Foundations of Speech Act Theory*, edited by Savasl Tsohatzidis. Oxon: Routledge.

Bigo, D., and A. Tsoukala. 2008. "Terror, Insecurity and Liberty: Illiberal Practices of Liberal Regimes after 9/11." In: *Understanding (In)Security*, Translated by. edited by Anastassia Tsoukala and Didier Bigo, Introduction. Oxon: Routledge.

Booth, K., and T. Dunne. 2002. "Worlds in Collision." In *Worlds in Collision: Terror and the Future of Global Order*, edited by Ken Booth and Tim Dunne. New York: Palgrave Macmillan.

Bosco, R. M. 2014. *Securing the Sacred: Religion, National Security, and the Western State*. Translated by. Ann Arbor: University of Michigan Press.

Bourdieu, P. 2001. *Langage Et Pouvoir Symbolique*. Translated by. Paris: Éditions du Seuil.

Bush, G. W. 11 Sep 2001a. "Address to the Nation on the Terrorist Attacks [Online]." Accessed 14 Feb 2014. http://www.presidency.ucsb.edu/ws/?pid=58057.

Bush, G. W. 17 Sep 2001b. "Islam Is Peace [Online]." Accessed 28 Jun 2015. http://georgewbush-whitehouse.archives.gov/news/releases/2001/09/20010917-11.html:TheWhiteHouse.

Bush, G. W. 20 Sep 2001c. "Justice Will Be Done [Online]." Accessed 14 Feb 2014. http://www.washingtonpost.com/wp-srv/nation/specials/attacked/transcripts/bushaddress_092001.html:TheWashingtonPost.

Bush, G. W. 06 Oct 2005. "Speech at the National Endowment for Democracy [Online]." Accessed 30 Jun 2015. http://www.presidentialrhetoric.com/speeches/10.06.05.html:ThepresidentialRhetoric.

Buzan, B., O. Wæver, and J. De Wilde. 1998. *Security: A New Framework for Analysis*. Translated by. London: Lynne Rienner.

Cheney, D. 2009. "Cheney: Gitmo Holds 'Worst of the Worst' [Online]". Accessed 13 Feb 2018. http://www.nbcnews.com/id/31052241/ns/world_news-terrorism/t/cheney-gitmo-holds-worst-worst/#.VUDVoK1Viko

CNN. 2018. *South Africa Formally Protests Trump's 'Shithole Countries' Remarks* [Online]. CNN. Accessed 08 Feb 2018. https://edition.cnn.com/2018/01/15/africa/south-africa-trump-diplomatic-protest/index.html.

Collective, C. 2006. "Critical Approaches to Security in Europe: A Networked Manifesto." *Security Dialogue* 37 (4): 443–487. doi:10.1177/0967010606073085.

Department of Homeland Security. 2017. *Transcript of Media Availability on Executive Order with Secretary Kelly & DHS Leadership* [Online]. Washington D.C.: The White House. Accessed 17 Feb 2017. https://www.dhs.gov/news/2017/01/31/transcript-media-availability-executive-order-secretry-kelly-and-dhs-leadership

Diez, T. 2007. "The Socio-political Effects of Securitising Free Movement: The Case of 09/11: Full Research Report." Esrc End of Award Report, Res-223-25-0055. Swindon: ESRC.

Eroukhmanoff, C. 2015. "The Remote Securitisation of Islam in the US Post-9/11: Euphemisation, Metaphors and the "Logic of Expected Consequences" in Counter-Radicalisation Discourse." *Critical Studies on Terrorism* 8 (2): 246–265. doi:10.1080/17539153.2015.1053747.

Ferguson, B. 2017. *Washington Attorney General Bob Ferguson Speaks on Trump Immigration Ban Restraining Order* [Online]. Youtube. Accessed 17 Feb 2017. https://www.youtube.com/watch?v=6GvFh-IUeJE.

Fierke, K. M. 2007. *Critical Approaches to International Security.* Translated by. Cambrdige: Polity Press.

Giuliani, R. 2017. Donald Trump Asked Rudy Giuliani How to 'Legally' Create 'Muslim Ban', Claims Former New York Mayor [Online]. *The Independent.* Accessed 17 Feb 2017. http://www.independent.co.uk/news/world/americas/donald-trump-muslim-ban-rudy-giuliani-how-legally-create-islam-us-immigration-entry-visa-new-york-a7552751.html.

Goddard, S. E., and R. R. Krebs. 2015. Rhetoric, Legitimation, and Grand Strategy. *Security Studies* 24 (Special Issue 1: Rhetoric and Grand Strategy):5–36.

Goldsmith, J. 2009. The Cheney Fallacy. p.03/04/17.

Guerlain, P. 2014. Obama's Foreign Policy: "Smart Power," Realism and Cynicism. *Society* 51 (Symposium: America in the World):482–491.

Hassan, O. 2017. "Trump, Islamophobia and US–Middle East Relations." *Critical Studies on Security* 5 (2 (Forum: 100 Days of Trump)): 187–191. doi:10.1080/21624887.2017.1355158.

Huysmans, J. 2011. "What's in an Act? on Security Speech Acts and Little Security Nothings." *Security Dialogue* 42 (4–5): 371–383. doi:10.1177/0967010611418713.

Jackson, R. 2005. *Writing the War on Terrorism: Language, Politics and Counter-Terrorism.* Translated by. Manchester: Manchester University Press.

Krebs, R. R., and P. T. Jackson. 2007. "Twisting Tongues and Twisting Arms: The Power of Political Rhetoric." *European Journal of International Relations* 13 (1): 35–66. doi:10.1177/1354066107074284.

Kumar, D. 2012. *Islamaphobia and the Politics of Empire.* Translated by. Chicago: Haymarket Books.

Lee, J. J., and S. Pinker. 2010. "Rationales for Indirect Speech: The Theory of the Strategic Speaker." *Psychological Review* 117 (3): 785–807. doi:10.1037/a0019688.

Lundborg, T., and N. Vaughan-Williams. 2011. "Resilience, Critical Infrastructure, and Molecular Security: The Excess of 'Life' in Biopolitics." *International Political Sociology* 5 (4): 367–383. doi:10.1111/ips.2011.5.issue-4.

Mavelli, L. 2013. "Between Normalisation and Exception: The Securitisation of Islam and the Construction of the Secular Subject." *Millennium – Journal of International Studies* 41 (2): 159–181. doi:10.1177/0305829812463655.

McCarthy, T., and O. Laughland. 2017. "Trump Travel Ban: Supreme Court Allows Enforcement as Appeals Proceed." *The Guardian.* Accessed 13 Feb 2018. https://www.theguardian.com/us-news/2017/dec/04/donald-trump-travel-ban-on-six-mostly-muslim-countries.

Mendelberg, T. 2001. *The Race Card: Campaign Strategy, Implicit Messages, and the Norm of Equality.* Translated by. Princeton: Princeton University Press.

Neal, A. W. 2012. "Normalization and Legislative Exceptionalism: Counterterrorist Lawmaking and the Changing Times of Security Emergencies." *International Political Sociology* 6: 3. doi:10.1111/j.1749-5687.2012.00163.x.

Obama, B. 04 Jun 2009. "A New Begining [Online]." Accessed 14 Feb 2014. http://www.whitehouse.gov/the_press_office/Remarks-by-the-President-at-Cairo-University-6-04-09:TheWhiteHouse:OfficeofthePressSecretary.

Obama, B. 23 May 2013. *Remarks by the President at the National Defense University* [Online]. Council on Foreign Relations. Accessed 14 Feb 2014. http://www.cfr.org/counterterrorism/president-obamas-speech-national-defense-university-future-our-fight-against-terrorism-may-2013/p30771

Obama, B. 19 Feb 2015. "Obama Tells Muslims: Don't Let Isis Hijack Your Religion and Identity" [Online]. *The Guardian.* Accessed 27 April 2015. http://www.theguardian.com/us-news/2015/feb/19/obama-tells-moderate-muslims-dont-let-isis-hijack-islam

Onuf, N. G. 1989. *World of Our Making: Rules and Rule in Social Theory and International Relations*. Translated by. Columbia SC: South Carolina Press.

Pinker, S. 2007. *The Stuff of Thought: Language as a Window into Human Nature*. Translated by. New York: Viking.

Pinker, S., M. A. Nowak, and J. J. Lee. 2008. "The Logic of Indirect Speech." *Proceedings of the National Academy of Sciences of the United States of America* 105 (3): 833–838. doi:10.1073/pnas.0707192105.

Purcell, N. 2017. *Washington V. Trump: Courtroom Highlights* [Online]. Youtube. Accessed 17 Feb 2017. https://www.youtube.com/watch?v=CfOSmXTaH1A.

Ross, A. G. 2014. *Mixed Emotions: Beyond Fear and Hatred in International Conflicts*. Translated by. Chicago: University of Chicago Press.

Saul, J. 2017. "Racial Figleaves, the Shifting Boundaries of the Permissible, and the Rise of Donald Trump." *Philosophical Topics* 45 (2): 91–116. doi:10.5840/philtopics201745215.

Saul, J. forthcoming. "Dogwhistles, Political Manipulation and Philosophy of Language." In: *New Work on Speech Acts*, edited by Daniel Fogal, Matt Cross, and Daniel Harris. Oxford: Oxford University Press.

Schmitt, C. [1922] 2005. *Political Theology: Four Chapters on the Concept of Sovereignty* Translated and edited by George Schwab. Chicago, IL: Chicago University Press.

Searle, J. R. 1979. *Expression and Meaning*. Translated by. Cambridge: Cambridge University Press.

Searle, J. R. 1971. "What Is a Speech Act?" In: *The Philosophy of Language*, edited by John Searle. London: Oxford University Press.

Searle, J. R. 1975. "Indirect Speech Acts." In: *Syntax and Semantics Vol 9.: Speech Acts*, edited by Peter Cole and Jerryl Morgan. New York: Academic Press.

Shogan, C. J. 2006. *The Moral Rhetoric of American Presidents* Translated by. College Station: Texas A&M University Press.

The Telegraph 2016. "Muslim Ban Statement 'Removed' from Donald Trump's Website." Accessed 13 Feb 2018. Available from: http://www.telegraph.co.uk/news/2016/11/10/muslim-ban-statement-removed-from-donald-trumps-website/

Trump, D. J. 09 Dec 2015. Donald Trump: 'I'm the Least Racist Person' [Online]. CNN. Accessed 12 Dec 2017. https://www.youtube.com/watch?v=XRDmWPAtHiA

Trump, D. J. 15 Aug 2016a. *Donald Trump Addresses Radical Islamic Terrorism in Youngstown* [Online]. Hill. Accessed 17 Feb 2017. http://thehill.com/blogs/pundits-blog/presidential-campaign/291498-full-transcript-donald-trump-addresses-radical

Trump, D. J. 2016a. "Transcript: Donald Trump's Victory Speech [Online]." Accessed 17 Feb 2017. https://www.nytimes.com/2016/11/10/us/politics/trump-speech-transcript.html

Trump, D. J. 15 Sep 2016b. "Donald Trump: I'm 'The Least Racist Person'." *CNN Politics*, p.12/12/17.

Trump, D. J. 2016b. "Trump Calls for 'Total and Complete Shutdown of Muslims Entering the U.S.' [Online]." Accessed 08 Feb 2018. https://www.nbcnews.com/video/trump-calls-for-total-and-complete-shutdown-of-muslims-entering-the-u-s-581768771855.

Trump, D. J. 16 02 2017a. *Trump Says He Is the 'Least Racist Person'* [Online]. Reuters. Accessed 12 Dec 2017. https://www.reuters.com/video/2017/02/16/trump-says-he-is-the-least-racist-person?videoId=371135921

Trump, D. J. 21 05 2017b. *Full Transcript of Trump's Speech to the Muslim World from Saudi Arabia* [Online]. Haaretz Online. Accessed 15 Dec 2017. https://www.haaretz.com/middle-east-news/1.790748

Trump, D. J. 29 01 2017c. *Trump Says Executive Order Is Not a Muslim Ban* [Online]. BBC News Online. Accessed 17 Dec 2017. http://www.bbc.co.uk/news/av/world-us-canada-38786462/trump-says-executive-order-is-not-a-muslim-ban

Vuori, J. A. 2008. "Illocutionary Logic and Strands of Securitization: Applying the Theory of Securitization to the Study of Non-Democratic Political Orders." *European Journal of International Relations* 14 (1): 65–99. doi:10.1177/1354066107087767.

Wæver, O. 1995. "Securitisation and Desecuritisation." In: *On Security*, edited by Ronnie D. Lipschutz. New York: Columbia Univeristy Press.

Recursion or rejection? Securitization theory faces Islamist violence and foreign religions

Mona Kanwal Sheikh

ABSTRACT

This article contributes to the larger debate on how to increase the cultural sensitivity in IR analyses, and particularly how the securitization theory can face some of the criticism relating to its embedded-ness in the West. The article shows that the expanding empirical application of securitization theory by scholars around the world, as well as the theoretical expansion (the opening of the religion sector) raise two important, but different questions, which are about potential a) limitations in the applicability of the theory on non-western cases, and b) west-centric biases in the design of the theory. This article sheds light on both types of criticisms by asking whether securitization theory is applicable to study the case of religious violence as I have done in earlier studies of the Pakistani Taliban, and by evaluating the assumptions and consequences of keeping with a west-centric concept of religion. The article makes three points: First, it shows that the theory's meeting with the Islamist case challenge the theory's conceptualization of securitization as a defensive narrative only. Second, it points at the limitations in the way religion has been conceptualized by the theory's proponents. Third, it argues that dealing with differences in the interpretations of political realities is an important element of the call to increased cultural sensitivity, and in this endeavour the securitization framework would gain from elements of world-view analysis.

I regard myself as a practitioner of securitization theory. During the past 10 years, I have taken the theory to the case of the Pakistani Taliban in order to explain *their* securitization processes: what they fear, what they claim to defend, and how they justify extraordinary measures such as violent attacks on civilians or suicide attacks (Sheikh 2016). My analyses have shown structural similarities and a security dilemma in the way values of freedom and secularism are securitized in dominant western discourses in the confrontation with 'the terrorist', and the way 'the terrorists' are reversely securitizing different dimensions of religion in the confrontation with the west.

With Ole Wæver, I have also taken the theory to study diverse manifestations of secularism in various western countries in order to show how the concept of secularism – one of the reference points in value-debates across the west – has a securitizing potential. And how the awareness of this can be an academic contribution to conflict-containment, when it comes to the conflict between secular and religious fundamen-talists (Sheikh and Wæver 2012). Finally, I have, together with my colleague Manni Crone, applied the theory to study different cases where Muslims, in a Danish context, have been securitized, and thereby expelled from 'normalcy' (Sheikh and Crone 2011).

All these appliances show the critical potential of securitization theory and its special ability to expose problematic power-practices where western identity is constructed in particular ways to 'talk something up' on the security agenda (intentionally or unin-tentionally, the theory does not care). However, in spite of this critical potential of the theory, it has not been immune to criticism that questions its own "western-ness" and the implications its liberal assumptions have for studying the non-west.

In this article, I will particularly focus on questions relating to the application of the theory to new types of cases non-western cases – where the securitization mechanism of justification seems to have resonance. This is done by discussing the theory's ability to capture the narrative structure behind Islamist violence. I will also focus on the pioneer-ing opening of a 'new sector' of security, namely the religion sector, in 2001, that illustrates some questionable implications of ontological west-centrism. The expanding empirical application of securitization theory by scholars around the world, as well as the theoretical expansion (the opening of the religion sector) raise two important, but different questions, which are about potential (a) limitations in the *applicability* of the theory on non-western cases, and (b) west-centric biases in the *design* of the theory. This article will shed light on both types of criticisms: One that asks whether securitization theory is suitable to study the case of religious violence (the applicability question) as I have done in earlier studies of the Pakistani Taliban, and one that more conceptually pushes the theory to work with less west-centric notions religion (the design question).

The article is organized as follows. First, I ask the question of how far the theory can be stretched by relating it to the case of the Pakistani Taliban. This section shows that the meeting with the Islamist case challenge the theory's conceptualization of secur-itization as a defensive narrative only. The second section turns to the question of a potential bias in the design of the theory and its main concepts, and particularly reviews the way religion has been conceptualized by the theory's proponents. The third section takes the religion debate a bit further asking how securitization theory could relate to the question of differences in the interpretations of political realities, which is an element of the call to increased cultural sensitivity. I suggest that the securitization framework would gain from considering elements of worldview-analysis (Juergensmeyer and Sheikh 2012; Sheikh forthcoming) in order to move beyond the idea of being neutral or 'blind to culture' (Valbjørn 2008) as well as being blinded by (one's own) culture.

How far can the theory be stretched?

It can never be a problem in itself, that human concepts, ideas and theories are embedded in some cultures more than other. Cultural contingency is a condition for science, also in cases where the study of 'objective' factors is a normative ideal. The cultural embedded-ness of theories pose a potential problem, when they are taken to places or contexts where they might not be the best suited one due to an inappropriate conceptual apparatus. The challenge emerge if the application of securitization framework in the non-west, risks ending up with west-centric interpretations of the security moves in the non-west, ultimately promoting a biased or 'selfish' policy interest of the west. Or as I will show in the next section, if it leads to wrongful diagnosis of what is at play (and what the formula for de-securitization should be), and hence reinforce orientalist notions of what for instance the Middle East is all about.

The popularity and wide scholarly applicability of securitization theory is partly based on the simplicity of the basic observations it is built on: When powerful actors are successful in their framing of something as an existential security concern, they can justify deviation from normalcy, and they can easier justify extraordinary measures. What they are doing 'by saying', the theory claims, is to lift something away from politics, where conversation and compromise is part of normalcy, to the realm of security, demanding some staunch measures addressing the existential threat (Wæver 1995).

With these basic observations, the founders of the securitization theory started (at least) two important conversations in the literature: One that had to do with the empirical reality 'out there', such as, who are the powerful actors e.g. is it always state actors? What about strong civil society actors in the non-west? Is security always a language of emergency, and when are extraordinary measures extraordinary (according to whose criteria, which culture, place or context)?

Another conversation that moved on the conceptual level, spoke to the disciplinary overweight of scholars occupied with identifying objective threats against order, the west, freedom, power balances etc. With the speech-act conceptualization of security, securitization theory developed a special ability to deconstruct threats that were represented as if their threatening nature was beyond question. While the first conversation pointed at some potential limitations of the theory, the last-mentioned conversation appealed to the non-west, perhaps due to the emancipatory potential (Amin Khan 2012; Bilgin 2011; Sheikh and Crone 2011). One could argue that securitization theory is particularly inclined to fulfil a political function due to its ability to make statements such as 'just because you say that Muslims are threatening liberal democracies, it is not objectively true, but if you convince your population of the existentiality of the threat, then you can take emergency measures that expand your jurisdiction as a policymaker'. As Bilgin (2011, 408) writes it makes sense to 'taking into account the political role of theories, theorists, and theorizing', which can explain why some theories travel easier than others.

The case of religious violence, however, is one that raises questions about the potential limitations of the theory. As I explain below it either calls for a revision of the securitization theory *or* leads to a conclusion that goes more in the direction of finding a theory that can better explain what the securitization theory can't. When I first started my study of the Pakistani Taliban movement, I wanted to know what happens when securitization theory is taken to study the securitization of violent religious actors in Pakistan. How does the empirical case reflect back on the theory and the concepts developed by the theory, and are the potential tensions or limitation an occasion for revising the securitization theory or should it rather be an occasion of finding another theory that explains the case better?

My case showed that religious securitizations reflect a different narrative structure than the 'structurally secular' securitization, which is embedded in a defensive discourse (Sheikh 2016). Following the description of a securitizing move (defined by Wæver 1995), the securitizing narrative that successfully establishes the need to take violent measures – in this case, militant jihad – consists of three main parts: designating an existential threat (X), a referent object (Y), and deriving appropriate action prescriptions (Z). Thus, in theory the archetypical securitization narrative reflects a storyline, which is constituted defensively and follows the direction $X \rightarrow Y = Z$. The logic of the securitization narrative, as it was originally formulated by the founders of the theory, is that the character of the threat and of the referent object established through a successful speech act generates the required justification for carrying through the extraordinary action directions.

It appears that religious claims of justification are in fact also embedded in a defensive narrative. But not solely. More often than not, a more offensive narrative accompany the defensive framing of why extraordinary action is required, in which religion plays a more aggressive role. In the offensive narrative the referent object (Y) gains a more agenda-setting role (Y1), while the threat or enemy (X) has a less triggering role than in the archetypical securitization. Instead, the threat/enemy takes on the position of an obstacle that must be overcome in order for the Taliban to follow their agenda. In this storyline, the action prescriptions (Z) are not 'just' a function of X threatening Y, and the urgency of defending Y is not only dependent on X, but Z is also conditioned by the religious claims of justification (Z1). Thus, in the offensive discourse the main storyline goes from $Z1 \rightarrow Y1$ but its success is conditioned by the elimination of the obstacle, and a more complicated narrative structure then appears: $Z1 \rightarrow Y1 = Z1 \rightarrow X$. The logic of this offensive storyline is that the necessity to struggle for Y1 stems not from the threat against it, but from what is interpreted as religious imperatives (e.g. to establish the rule of God). Similarly, according to this logic, the way the threat should be encountered ought to follow religious imperatives, which oftentimes stand in contrast to the security logic of sufficiency and proportionality.

The parallel reference to militant jihad as a faith-imperative under the given extraordinary circumstances plays out for example through the Taliban's frequent references to Quranic chapters [surat] and verses [ayat] in their communication and recruitment materials. These are interpreted a-historically and applied as religious claims of justification or 'evidence' when it comes to demarcating the enemies and legitimize uncompromising measures taken against them. Other ways the offensive discourse stands out is by representing jihad as a 'pillar' of Islam on par with the five orthodox pillars of Islam, providing religious jurisprudential arguments behind the necessity of undertaking jihad, or by representing the quest to implement sharia as a 'religious' duty for Muslims, One of the critical findings of this application of securitization theory to the case of religious violence is that the analysis rebut the oversimplifying claim that religious securitization moves are easier to make than non-religious securitization moves, and thus also the claim that religion has a special proclivity to violence. It appears instead that the religio-political actors related to the Pakistani Taliban have to strike a difficult balance between the religious claims of justification (which has an offensive narrative, but jurisprudence that puts restrictions on the exercise of violence), and the securitization claims of exception (which has a defensive reasoning, but a proportionality logic). In some places these different discourses merge, but there are remarkable examples of tensions that make parts of the Taliban narratives appear self-contradicting and inconsistent, and thus ultimately less convincing for a religious audience. One of the clearest examples of the problem this creates for the consistency in the Taliban narratives is the representation of God as existentially threatened when following the logic of the 'structurally secular' security discourse, while in the 'structurally religious' security discourse God is unbeatable since he is represented as the Almighty and the ultimate Sovereign.

On the other hand, the possibility of drawing on both offensive and defensive discourses enhances the mobilization capability of religio-political actors like the Pakistani Taliban, because they can simultaneously make (defensive) appeals to an audience that is chagrined at the imperialist policies of the 'West' and (offensive) appeals to those who actually agree with the Taliban interpretation of religious imperatives.

While the securitization theory has a formula for explaining the dynamics of the defensive reasoning, it has not theorized if/how offensive reasoning can be part of a securitization process, in fact boosting mobilization to extraordinary measures. The critical question however remains whether this difference between the offensive/defensive narrative structure and the secular/religious securitization is too radical to be contained within the securitization theory – that is, whether the case of the Pakistani Taliban still qualify to be treated within the securitization framework, which, both by its originators and by its users, has been defined as a framework illuminating the security dynamics of defensive framings. The answer will remain ambiguous and divide scholarship between those who accept the sociology of the theory i.e. that the application of it to new cases eventually reflects back on the theory, widening it. And those who take on a more essentialist/narrowing response that warns against the dangers of a laissez-faire application of a theory that in its original design might be best suited to explain defensive mobilization dynamics in liberal democracies.

Conceptual west-centrism

I now turn to the other question of a potential bias in the design of the theory and its main concepts. While finding an appropriate response to the applicability questions is a task that arguably lies mainly with the scholars who pick up securitization theory (rather than another theory) to explain new cases, there are also more foundational questions that have to do with the basic concepts of the theory or the imagery on which the theory rests.

Some of the conceptual critique that the securitization theory has already faced relates to the assumption of a harmonious relationship between state and civil society (within the political sector of security), and the implicit assumption of the state representatives being the 'senders' of securitizing messages and the civil society as the receivers/audience.[1] In the 1998 elaboration of the theory, the state and state representatives are central (though not always or exclusively), as the authors write that 'the invocation of security has been the key to legitimizing the use of force, but more generally, it has opened the way for the state to mobilize, or to take special powers, to handle existential threats. Traditionally, by saying "security", a state representative declares an emergency condition, thus claiming a right to use whatever means are necessary to block a threatening development' (Buzan, Wæver, and De Wilde 1998, 21).

Several appliers of the theory have shown, that when the theory travels to the non-west, the large gap between the politics of elites and the politics of the civil society emerge, questioning the role of the civil society as the audience of 'the states' securitization moves. Another, but related critique is aimed at the liberal assumptions (Holbraad and Pedersen 2012) of securitization theory. This particularly implies the dualisms of individual vs. the state, normal politics vs. emergency politics, assuming the existence of a normal rule based order.[2] Martin Holbraad and Morten Axel Pederson's analysis of the Cuban revolution, for example, point out that revolutionary regimes are in permanent emergency, and suggests a new concept to capture what they call 'revolutionary securitization', which pertains not to a passage from ordinary politics to the realm of emergency, but a fusion of the two (Holbraad and Pedersen 2012).[3]

They advocate a 'recursive' anthropological strategy to the question I posed above (how far can the theory be stretched?), where (new) data is used to transform the conceptual assumptions of the theoretical model. The Cuban Revolution hence becomes a way to extend the applicability of securitization theory, by suggesting a way to revise the basic concepts of the theory.

My critique (elaborated in Sheikh 2014) of the way religion was conceptualized in the article announcing the opening a new sector of security (the religion sector), also sets of a discussion, which has to do with west centrism in the concepts of securitization theory.[4] In my previous critique of the way religion was conceptualized when it was launched as a separate sector, I also elaborate on alternative ways to conceptualize religion, which makes it more widely applicable to both non-western cases, but also variations within the west. Here, I will summarize only those points in my critique that can illustrate the practical/normative consequences of west-centric conceptualizations.

Integrating religion into the theoretical framework was a pioneering step, which has allowed securitization theory to develop an ability to analyse new issues on the security agenda. However, the Millennium article (Laustsen and Wæver 2000) that launched the new sector of security adopted an ethno-centric concept of religion by relying too heavily on western theology/philosophy in its demarcation of religious discourse. This critique is important, I have argued, because of its repercussions for the thinking on de-securitization, and because the applied definitions of religion and religious securitization create a challengeable theoretical link between religion and violence.

Before the *Millennium* article published in 2000, religion was subordinated the societal sector as a source of communal identity. The same year, Laustsen and Wæver introduced religion as an independent sector, thus making faith its ultimate referent object by arguing that the treatment of religion within the societal sector was only able to cover the community aspect of religion and not religion as faith. This led them to define faith as the central element of religious discourse (drawing on Søren Kirkegaard) and faith as a distinctive quality of religion qua its distinction between transcendent and immanent, sacred and profane (drawing on Georges Bataille). The distinct trait of the religion sector of security is, they argued, that it defends not identity or community, but rather the true faith.

The defining distinction drawn between the sacred and the profane goes smoothly with respect to Protestant Christendom, but is very much a product of the way European religious thought has developed rather than a product of a universally applicable criterion for all religious traditions. Influential theoreticians like Emile Durkheim and Mircea Eliade, who are among the main proponents of the centrality of this dichotomy have been criticized by anthropologists who point out that the languages of many societies and cultures do not even have words that mean sacred and profane, thus indicating one of the limitations of this division.

The central role Laustsen and Wæver give to the concept of the sinful man in their demarcation of religious discourse illustrates why their definition is problematic. This concept upholds the distance between heaven and earth in Christian discourses, but in many other faith traditions the notion of original sin does not exist and for other interpretative communities the dissolution of the dichotomy between the sacred and the profane is the religious norm, hence part of normalcy. Eastern religions such as Zen Buddhism disapprove of cultivating dualism and the ability of monks to let go of all conceptualizations of good and bad, the sacred and the profane is, for example, the ultimate measure of their religiosity/piousness.

For other religions like Confucianism the sacred/profane dichotomy is far from the defining principle of faith, while Taoism emphasizes the balance of opposites (yin/yang), where neither part of the duality is subordinate to the other or has divine characteristics. Furthermore the idea of immanence – that the divine is incarnate in the world and not separate from it – appears in many traditions, often in competition with other theological/interpretational positions that make a sharp sacred/worldly distinction.

A graver problem with Laustsen and Wæver's definition of religious discourse, however, is the implications it has for how the securitization of religion is understood and that it leads them to conclude that those who securitize religion deny the gap between the transcendental and the immanent. Whether there is an unambiguous link between the dissolution of difference and securitization is challengeable as the above examples concerning various religious traditions demonstrate. Adding to this the dissolution of difference is characteristic of puritan and spiritually oriented interpretations of religion. For instance, some mystical interpretations of Islamic rituals challenge the desirability of upholding the transcendental/immanent gap based on discourses of fear and reward (heaven and hell). Instead they represent an alternative to what they perceive to be an artificial distance between the sacred and profane, and separation from the Divine is seen as an unnatural state for the human soul. While acting on behalf of God is indeed a central characteristic of violent religious movements, the dissolution of difference does not always lead to securitization.

The idea that the elimination of the gap conditions securitization also leads Laustsen and Wæver to argue that the formula for desecuritization of religion is 'acceptance of the fact that being in religious discourse is essentially being before a transcendental realm' since 'politics does something to religion'. This argument implies that the overlap of religious and political discourse condition securitization, ultimately violence, and if we follow this line of thinking it could accordingly be concluded that desecuritizing conflicts where religion plays a role would require an intervention to 'secularize' faith traditions that do not share a non-political concept of the religious or non-religious concept of the political. To take an example, orthodox religious discourse in relation to Islam concerns both deen (faith) and dawla (polity) and in this discourse the separation of politics from religion is often perceived as an artificial boundary. Policy analyses based on Protestant perceptions of religion would expectedly end up suggesting secularism or Protestant Islam as a solution to Islamist violence, as was the case when influential think tanks offered solutions to terrorism in the wake of the 9/11 attacks on the US.

The idea that the Islamic blend of religion and politics is problematic appeared, for instance as the conclusion in two reports published by the influential American think tank RAND after 2001: 'The Muslim World after 9/11' (2004) prepared for the United States Air Force and 'Civil Democratic Islam' (2003), prepared for the RAND National Security Research Division. The tendency to frame the values of the Enlightenment, reason and secularism in opposition to religion and traditionalism is apparent in both reports. In their representations modernity is grounded in the ability to separate religion and politics, while traditionalism is made antithetical to the basic requirements of a modern democratic mind-set defined by critical thinking, individual liberty and secularism. The way to confront terrorism and Islamism is to promote secularized versions of Islam, and as one report states, Islam must be influenced to adopt the values of the West, Christianity and secularism as, 'it is no easy matter to transform a major world religion. If "nation-building" is a daunting task, "religion-building" is immeasurably more perilous and complex' (RAND 2003, 3)

Making faith the sole referent object through a substantialist definition of religious discourse as advocated by Laustsen and Wæver also constitutes a problem for the applicability of the theory across different contexts. Anthropologist Benson (1993) argues that there is not necessarily an analytical problem in applying prototype definitions of religion informed by western culture and that on occasion theoretical parochialism can prove to be an advantage in illuminating isolated elements of larger phenomena. In this case, though, the narrowness constitutes an analytical limitation that could be overcome by relying on a less substantial definition of religion. The narrow and substantialist definition appears as a limitation since it does not enable the theory to capture the manifold dimensions of religion that religio-political activists claim in various parts of the world when they securitize religion. Empirical work on fundamentalism and radical religious movements shows that religious discourses that are drawn upon by religio-political actors in conflict not only defend faith, but also holy places (lands, temples, mosques etc.) or holy law. Hence the suggested unity of the referent object does not correspond with the comparative literature on religious violence (e.g. Marty and Appleby 1995; Juergensmeyer 2003; Jerryson and Juergensmeyer 2010; Sheikh 2016).

This suggests that the recursive strategy proposed by Holbraad and Pedersen (2012) is also applicable here. Research on the empirical reality in the non-west can be used to develop, revise and rebut west-centric concepts of the theory, which in the end can prolong the lifecycle of the theory.

The cultural turn hits securitization theory

The section above has shown that sensitivity to diversity (of state/politics/religion concepts) and 'empirical realities' around the globe is a potential challenge for the reach of securitization theory. State-centrism is a general critique of IR theories invented in the west,[5] and scholars have called for the discipline to differentiate between more forms of states than the modern European; and to consider other forms of sub- and supranational polities, which produces 'a diversity of forms of international behavior and rationalities' (Valbjørn 2008, 61)

Culture is a label that in its wider sense embrace more than variations in organizational forms. In this section I will address the question of differences in the *interpretations of political realities* – whether the state is weak or strong – which is another, but less treated, element of the call to increased cultural sensitivity (Chatterjee 2004). The increasing awareness of west centric biases in theory-building and appliances, naturally calls for more sensitivity to non-western settings, and in this endeavour the securitization framework would gain from worldview-analysis and insight into culturally specific inter-pretations of concepts.[6]

In the beginning of the 19th century, the Prussian philologist Wilhelm von Humboldt put forward the idea that there is a link between linguistic communities and their mode of apprehending reality. Humboldt is often described as the founder of the idea that language and worldview are inextricable, because he maintained that language gives us the concepts of history, destiny, nation, and morality. Anthropologists by disciplinary habit have been more disposed to take other people's perspectives seriously, and thus have accommodated more easily religious points of view. This has been true of well-known anthropologists such as Clifford Geertz, Louis Dumont, Mary Douglas, Stanley Tambiah, and Talal Asad. However, Anthropologists focus on worldviews to describe and compare certain ways of life (e.g. Hiebert 2008). They use worldview analysis to examine how groups acquire their most fundamental values and ideas of the good life and how they develop different customs and institutions.

In political science the interest in worldviews primarily reflects an interest in how ideas and beliefs condition particular political outcomes and action, including the use of overt physical force, violence or annihilation (Blyth 1997; Bottici and Challand 2010; Goldstein and Keohane 1993; Røislien 2007; Rowland and Theye 2008). Political Science has been very influenced by the Marxist way of approaching ideology and religion, and combined with the influence of the modernization narrative that created the dichotomy between religion and 'real science', it has only recently begun to take seriously the questions of how religion, as an interpretive frame, matters for the field.

For social sciences and global studies in general the relevance of studying worldviews is also its connection to action (Johnson, Hill, and Cohen 2011; Koltko-Rivera 2004, 23). Worldviews matters as they have an impact on human action, or because they can justify certain acts. In order for worldview analysis to be a useful tool in social sciences that can open up for insights relevant for questions of securitization, it needs to abstain from the simple causality questions that create straight lines from A (worldviews) to B (emergency/violence). Instead the goal should be to understand the subject's framework for thinking/speaking about reality and acting appropriately within it (Juergensmeyer and Sheikh 2012).

There are obvious overlaps between worldview-analysis in this sense, and securitization thinking. One of the basic claims of Worldview analysis is, that when actors have a combination of well-defined principled beliefs, in which notions of identity, justice and truth are very clear, and simple causal beliefs, in which the pathway to achieve their objectives is powerfully defined, they are in possession of a strong narrative. For example, narratives in which the world is seen through cosmic war images, and adversaries are identified as absolute enemies, while the subject is identified as part of a heroic vanguard, are more likely to have a stronger mobilizing capacity towards violent or confrontational action directions. Imagined singularities can be remarkably powerful and turn in to self-fulfilling prophecies, by imprinting images of a sharply divided world, where identities cannot be reconciled.

The narrative of a civilizational clash for example stages a dichotomous vision of the world – the cosmic war – with oppositions on an absolute scale (Juergensmeyer 1993, 2003). This image has not only imprinted itself in academic fields, but has successfully been adapted by both religious and secular zealots. Although Huntington's original idea of a civilizational clash has been strongly criticized for being too simplistic and scientifically inadequate (Bottici and Challand 2010; Sen 2006, 10), it can still be helpful if we apply it as cognitive lens that can display how some people perceive and organize the world and use it as a basis for action.

The literature that treats worldviews as a precondition for political outcomes, looks at worldviews as roadmaps for action. From this perspective it is interesting to study how the principled- and causal beliefs come to structure certain action preferences. In order to understand this approach, it is helpful to turn to Pierre Bourdieu's concept of classification struggles (Bourdieu 2004, 479). With this concept he focuses on the classification processes that characterize the struggles to classify the social world. According to Bourdieu classification struggles are struggles over the dominant 'principles of vision and di-vision' and it is through these processes of classification that social collectivities are formed and the world is divided (Bourdieu 2004, 1984, 483; Gorski 2013).

An analysis of classification struggles would look at how ones study objects engage in a definitional struggle to assert its truth about the social world itself and its opponents, how identities are evoked and how they gain a mobilizing capacity. Bourdieu moves his analytic lens away from predicting war between cultures towards looking at how cultural conflict is played out in a social political battlefield. His framework analyses the game of position takings, i.e. the ways in which vital players, representing opposed factions, project their own schemas, truths or dominance over others (Bourdieu 1984, 174–175; Gorski 2013, 243). These vital players or specialists as Bourdieu calls them, have the authority to speak for a social collectivity – to articulate its history, political opinions, needs, and demands and they therefore play a vital role in in the maintenance of group's boundaries and the mobilization of its members (Bourdieu and Thompson 1991, 173).

Such a position has a strategic lens on, but still represent an interesting aspect of worldview analysis. Like Bourdieu's approach, a worldview analysis can shed light on how worldviews become espoused, defended and disseminated in a relational context, and how they attain strong mobilizing effects, which has real political implications. Such an analysis does not reduce worldviews to be an instrument only, though it is interested in the effects they produce. The dynamic study of worldview entails that we study how vital players and members of the communities or groups we want to study, enter into conflict or competition with one another and simultaneously make both themselves and their opponents the object of classificatory practices.

Looking at interpretative frames is one way to embrace the turn towards a more culturally inclusive IR. Securitization theory would gain from recasting central concepts of its own identity as objects of classificatory practices. The cultural turn is not only about capturing larger bits of the reality out there, but also demands that IR theories develop a capability to move beyond what Valbjørn (2008) describes as being 'blind to culture' as well as being blinded by (one's own) culture.

Culture can be defined narrowly as collective identity (religious, ethnic, class, gender, etc.) or more broadly in terms of diversity in the meaning that different collective groups put into the collectivity, their context and their actions. As there is a general move among international relations scholars to increasingly draw on sociology, cultural and literary theory, media studies, postcolonial studies, gender studies, history and anthropology in order to understand the significance of culture (as identity, interpretative community and practice), securitization theory ought to take a deliberate move beyond a culture-blind identity.

Concluding remarks

The cultural turn was very late in hitting IR including the securitization theory, due to a variety of reasons. Some of these include the normative vision proposed by internationalist IR, stressing the need to focus on common human nature, more than differences, a main occupation with power as a champion concepts, a Marxist rejection of the 'reality' of culture on par with religion, and the more epistemological rejection of the non-scientific or subjective nature of culture (Valbjørn 2008, 58). Part of the critique that securitization theory faces is not particular to the theory (such as the centrality of the state), but applies to IR in general. Part of the critique might be wrongfully placed, since one could question whether the west/non-west schism really is one about the west/non-west or whether the schisms that these labels represent can actually be found within the west and the non-west, i.e. can we find liberal and illiberal tendencies both places, isn't there many western we's?

Regardless of this, I have touched upon three debates that are relevant to the endeavour of widening the global applicability of securitization theory. The first concerns the epistemological issue concerning the representation of otherness, which securitization theory has proven a special ability champion. The second is related to dealing with cultural diversity and different manifestations of the state/political power. I have discussed this aspect of the culture debate, by elaborating on the empirical case of religious violence and the theoretical case of the religion sector of the theory. A third, but still underdeveloped part of the debate, relates to the ability to deal with different *interpretations of political/religious reality* and potential differences in the logics behind emergency action. While securitization theory deals with these sort of differences *between* security sectors, it is increasingly clear that there can be variations *within* sectors that needs to be unfolded. Here, I have proposed that worldview analysis and its focus on classificatory practices contain elements that could be applied to 'outsource' the definitions of central concepts to the actors out there, instead of sticking to narrow concepts of religion or political authority.

Notes

1. One of the general critiques of securitization theory is its under-theorization of the concept of audience, see for instance Balzacq (2005).
2. I owe thanks to the summary provided by Saloni Kapur in her opening presentation at the workshop on securitization in the non-Western world, held at Lancaster University in March 2017.
3. See also Greenwood and Wæver (2013), who focus on the case of the Egyptian Revolution, asking what happens to the securitization theory if the whole situation is unstable?
4. Some of the points here are reiterated in that article.
5. See the 'Worlding Beyond the West' series, published by Routledge (2009–2013) and edited by Arlene B. Thickner and David L. Blaney (Tickner and Wæver 2009; Tickner and Blaney 2012, 2013).
6. See my forthcoming article on worldview analysis (Sheikh Forthcoming). Some of the points below are reiterated in that article.

Disclosure statement

No potential conflict of interest was reported by the author.

References

Amin-Khan, T. 2012. "New Orientalism, Securitisation and the Western Media's Incendiary Racism." *Third World Quarterly* 33 (9): 1595–1610. doi:10.1080/01436597.2012.720831.

Balzacq, T. 2005. "The Three Faces of Securitization: Political Agency, Audience and Context." *European Journal of International Relations* 11 (2): 171–201. doi:10.1177/1354066105052960.

Benson, S. 1993. *Conceptualizing Religion: Immanent Anthropologists, Transcendent Natives, and Unbounded Categories*. Leiden: Brill.

Bilgin, P. 2011. "The Politics of Studying Securitization? The Copenhagen School in Turkey." *Security Dialogue* 42 (4–5): 399–412. doi:10.1177/0967010611418711.

Blyth, M. M. 1997. "'Any More Bright Ideas?' the Ideational Turn of Comparative Political Economy." *Comparative Politics* 29: 229–250. doi:10.2307/422082.

Bottici, C., and B. Challand. 2010. *The Myth of the Clash of Civilizations*. Abingdon, Oxon: Routledge.

Bourdieu, P. 1984. *Distinction: A Social Critique of the Judgement of Taste*. Cambridge, MA: Harvard University Press.

Bourdieu, P. 2004. *In Other Words: Essays Towards a Reflexive Sociology, Repr. Ed*. Cambridge: Polity Press.

Bourdieu, P., and J. B. Thompson. 1991. *Language and Symbolic Power*. Cambridge, MA: Harvard University Press.

Buzan, B., O. Wæver, and J. De Wilde. 1998. *Security: A New Framework for Analysis*. Boulder, CO: Lynne Rienner.

Chatterjee, P. 2004. *The Politics of the Governed: Reflections on Popular Politics in Most of the World*. Delhi: Permanent Black.

Goldstein, J., and R. O. Keohane, eds. 1993. *Ideas and Foreign Policy: Beliefs, Institutions and Political Change*. Ithaca, NY: Cornell University Press.

Gorski, P. S. 2013. *Bourdieu and Historical Analysis*. Durham, NC: Duke University Press.

Greenwood, M. T. and O. Wæver, 2013. "Copenhagen-Cairo on a Roundtrip: A Security Theory Meets the Revolution." *Security Dialogue* 44 (5–6): 485–506. doi: 10.1177/0967010613502573.

Hiebert, P. G. 2008. *Transforming Worldviews: An Anthropological Understanding of How People Change*. Grand Rapids, MI: Baker Academic.

Holbraad, M., and M. Pedersen. 2012. "Revolutionary Securitization: An Anthropological Extension of Securitization Theory." *International Theory* 4 (2): 165–197. doi:10.1017/S1752971912000061.

Jerryson, M. K., and M. Juergensmeyer, eds. 2010. *Buddhist Warfare*. Oxford: Oxford University Press.

Johnson, K. A., E. D. Hill, and A. B. Cohen. 2011. "Integrating the Study of Culture and Religion: Toward a Psychology of Worldview." *Social Personal Psychologist Compass* 5: 137–152. doi:10.1111/j.1751-9004.2010.00339.x.

Juergensmeyer, M. 1993. *The New Cold War? Religious Nationalism Confronts the Secular State*. Berkeley: University of California Press.

Juergensmeyer, M. 2003. *Terror in the Mind of God: The Global Rise of Religious Violence*. 3rd ed. Berkeley: Comparative Studies in Religion and Society. University of California Press.

Juergensmeyer, M., and M. K. Sheikh. 2012. "A Sociotheological Approach to Understanding Religious Violence." In: *The Oxford Handbook of Religion and Violence*, edited by M. Juergensmeyer, M. Kitts, and M. K. Jerryson. New York: Oxford University Press.

Koltko-Rivera, M. E. 2004. "The Psychology of Worldviews." *Review of General Psychology* 8: 3–58. doi:10.1037/1089-2680.8.1.3.

Laustsen, C. B., and O. Wæver. 2000. "In Defence of Religion: Sacred Referent Objects for Securitization." *Millennium: Journal of International Studies* 29 (3): 705–739. doi:10.1177/03058298000290031601.

Marty, M. E., and R. S. Appleby, eds. 1995. *Fundamentalisms Comprehended: The Fundamentalism Project*, Vol.5. Chicago: University of Chicago Press

RAND. 2003. *Civil Democratic Islam – Partners, Resources and Strategies, RAND National Security Research Division*. www.rand.org/pubs/monograph_reports/2005/MR1716.sum.pdf

Røislien, H. E. 2007. "Living with Contradiction: Examining the Worldview of the Jewish Settlers in Hebron." *International Journal Confl Violence IJCV* 1: 169–184.

Rowland, R. C., and K. Theye. 2008. "The Symbolic DNA of Terrorism." *Communication Monographs* 75: 52–85. doi:10.1080/03637750701885423.

Sen, A. 2006. *Identity and Violence: The Illusion of Destiny*. New York: W. W. Norton.

Sheikh, M. K. 2014. "The Religious Challenge to Securitization Theory." *Millennium – Journal of International Studies* 43 (1): 252–272. Sage Publications. doi:10.1177/0305829814540853.

Sheikh, M. K. 2016. *Guardians of God – Inside the Religious Mind of the Pakistani Taliban*. Delhi: Oxford University Press.

Sheikh, M. K., and M. Crone. 2011. "Muslims as a Danish Security Issue." In: *Islam in Denmark*, edited by J. S. Nielsen, 173–196. New York: Lexington.

Sheikh, M. K. Forthcoming. "Worldview Analysis." In: *Oxford Handbook of Global Studies*, edited by M. Juergensmeyer, S. Sassen, and M. Steger. New York: Oxford University Press.

Sheikh, M. K., and O. Wæver. 2012. "Western Secularisms – Variations in a Doctrine and Its Practice." In: *Thinking International Relations Differently*, edited by A. B. Tickner and D. L. Blaney, 275–298. Abingdon, Oxon: Routledge.

Tickner, A. B., and D. L. Blaney, eds. 2012. *Thinking International Relations Differently*. London: Routledge.

Tickner, A. B., and D. L. Blaney, eds. 2013. *Claiming the International*. London: Routledge.

Tickner, A. B., and O. Wæver, eds. 2009. *International Relations Scholarship around the World*. London: Routledge.

Valbjørn, M. 2008. "Before, During and After the Cultural Turn. A 'Baedeker' to IR's Cultural Journey." *International Review of Sociology* 18 (Nr. 1): 55–82. doi:10.1080/03906700701823654.

Wæver, O. 1995. "Securitization and Desecuritization." In: *On Security*, edited by R. D. Lipschutz, 46–86. New York: Columbia University Press.

Review of 'Recursion or rejection? Securitization theory faces Islamist violence and foreign religions', by Mona Kanwal Sheikh

Saloni Kapur

This is a reply to:

Kanwal Sheikh, Mona. 2018. "Recursion or rejection? Securitization theory faces Islamist violence and foreign religions." *Global Discourse* 8 (1): 26–38. https://doi.org/10.1080/23269995.2017.1411644.

In 'Recursion or Rejection? Securitization Theory Faces Islamist Violence and Foreign Religions', Mona Kanwal Sheikh builds on her previous research on securitisation theory, the role played by religion in international politics and the Pakistani Taliban. In her latest offering, Sheikh considers whether securitisation theory is limited in its applicability to cases outside the Western world, as well as whether the theory contains a West-centric bias.

Applying securitisation theory to the discourse of the Pakistani Taliban, Sheikh finds that the theory tilts towards defensive framings, whereas the Tehreek-e-Taliban Pakistan employs a combination of offensive and defensive narratives to justify its resort to violence. For Sheikh, this suggests that either the theory needs to be widened to allow for this sort of a dynamic or one must accept that securitisation 'might be best suited to explain defensive mobilization dynamics in liberal democracies'.

On the more fundamental question of whether the theory is designed in such a way as to be inherently incapable of seeing the world in anything other than Western terms, Sheikh focuses specifically on Carsten Bagge Laustsen and Ole Wæver's (2000) attempt to introduce religion as a new sector of securitisation. Sheikh takes exception to Laustsen and Wæver's (2000, 710) core assumption that 'faith is coded through the distinction between transcendent and immanent'. She points out that while this distinction holds from a Protestant Christian perspective, it 'is very much a product of the way European religious thought has developed'. Sheikh draws attention to the Zen Buddhist rejection of dualism and the Taoist emphasis on the balance between yin and yang to undermine Laustsen and Wæver's assumption that the transcendent/immanent or sacred/profane dichotomy universally applies to religious experience.

In Laustsen and Wæver's (2000, 710) defence, they do proffer the disclaimer that their 'way to the universal (religion as such) goes through the particular (Christianity)'. However, they subsequently 'claim that all three levels of religion: faith as the principle of discursivation, *the distinction between transcendent and immanent as the principle of primary coding*, and mediation as the principle of secondary coding *will be found in all religions*' (Laustsen and Wæver 2000, 716, emphasis mine). This lends credence to Sheikh's claim that Laustsen and Wæver's conceptualisation of a religious sector of securitisation is predicated upon a Protestant understanding of religion.

Examples of exceptions to this assumption, in addition to the ones provided by Sheikh, include the Hindu Advaita Vedantic idea that 'self is the common factor at the root of all experience, the awareness in which everything happens', and 'there is nothing which is different from me. There is no duality' (Maharaj, n.d., 1). Sufi Muslim mystic Mansur Al-Hallaj likewise proclaimed, *'Ana al-Haq* (I am the Truth)' (Dawn, 2011). William C. Chittick (2011, loc. 1218) writes in his book *Sufism*, 'The stage of full human perfection is sometimes called 'being like unto Allah *(ta'alluh)*, which might also be translated as "deiformity" or "theomorphism"'. Similarly, American New Age author Wayne W. Dyer (2017) writes in his blog, 'The words *I am*, which you consistently use to define who you are and what you are capable of, are holy expressions for the name of God – the highest aspect of yourself'. Thus, there are multifarious strands of religious and spiritual thought where the distinction between the transcendent and the immanent is collapsed.

Dyer's presence on this list demonstrates that the bridging of the gap between the transcendent and the immanent is not limited to non-Western forms of belief, underlining Sheikh's observation that seeing the West and the non-West as a dichotomy is problematic. In her words, 'One could question whether the west/non-west schism really is one about the west/non-west or whether the schisms that these labels represent can actually be found within the west and the non-west, i.e. can we find liberal and illiberal tendencies both places?' Sheikh's challenge to the binary opposite of West/non-West echoes Appiah (2016), who asserts that 'the values European humanists like to espouse belong just as easily to an African or an Asian who takes them up with enthusiasm as to a European', and that 'they do not belong to a European who has not taken the trouble to understand and absorb them'.

Sheikh's questioning of the divide between West and non-West is pertinent not only for this special issue, but also for her empirical research area of Islamist violence. For as Richard Jackson (2005, 50) points out, the discourse surrounding the 'war on terror' has conjured up the image of a civilised, modern Western world fighting against pre-modern, non-Western, barbaric 'others'. Sheikh's problematisation of the West/non-West binary opposite paves the way for studies of Islamist violence that transcend the tendency to dehumanise Islamist militants as barbaric 'others', which could lead to a clearer comprehension of the reasons for Islamist violence and ways to address it.

Despite her reservations about unproblematically applying the labels 'Western' and 'non-Western', Sheikh accedes that political realities can be different in the West and outside it and calls for securitisation to make space for the existence of 'culturally specific interpretations of concepts'. She proposes that the insights offered by worldview analysis could fruitfully enhance the securitisation framework.

Sheikh's article provides considerable fodder for further research on securitisation and on Islamist violence. Her work suggests that there is much scope for further empirical studies of the securitising discourses of religious militant groups that could provide fascinating insights into securitising processes at the trans- and sub-state levels of analysis. Sheikh's writing opens the door to further work on securitisation and how it can be applied beyond the level of the state, something that is of great relevance as non-state actors, including but not limited to militant groups, play an increasingly active role in a globalising world order.

Additionally, Sheikh makes the vital point that it is erroneous to conclude that the overlapping of religion with politics must lead to securitisation and violence and that desecuritisation requires secularisation. Her observation suggests that important policy-oriented work could be conducted that problematises the idea that 'the way to confront terrorism and Islamism is to promote secularised versions of Islam, and … Islam must be influenced to adopt the values of the West, Christianity and secularism'. Her emphasis on the need for research to take cultural differences into account is relevant for scholarly work on Islamist violence in general – not only work informed by securitisation theory. Sheikh's insights call for more culturally sensitive work on Islamist violence, which steers clear of dehumanising discourses and facile distinctions between 'us' and 'them' and leads to deeper understandings of why militants act as they do and what can be done about it.

Acknowledgements

I am grateful to Dr Mona Kanwal Sheikh for her comments on an earlier draft of this review.

Disclosure statement

No potential conflict of interest was reported by the author.

References

Appiah, K. A. 2016. "There Is No Such Thing as Western Civilisation." *Guardian*, November 9. Accessed 10 October 2017. https://www.theguardian.com/world/2016/nov/09/western-civilisation-appiah-reith-lecture
Chittick, W. C. 2011. *Sufism: A Beginner's Guide*. Oxford: Oneworld Publications. Kindle.
Dawn. 2011. "The Story of Hallaj." November 10. Accessed 9 October 2017. https://www.dawn.com/news/672240
Dyer, W. W. 2017. "The Power of I Am." Wayne's Blog. Accessed October 9 2017. http://www.drwaynedyer.com/blog/the-power-of-i-am/
Jackson, R. 2005. *Writing the War on Terrorism: Language, Politics and Counter-Terrorism*. Manchester: Manchester University Press.
Laustsen, C. B., and O. Wæver. 2000. "In Defence of Religion: Sacred Referent Objects for Securitization." *Millennium* 29 (3): 705–739, December. Accessed October 9 2017. http://journals.sagepub.com.ezproxy.lancs.ac.uk/doi/pdf/10.1177/03058298000290031601. doi:10.1177/03058298000290031601.
Maharaj, S. N. n.d. *I Am That*. Accessed October 9 2017. http://advaita.com.br/wp-content/uploads/2010/08/1-I-Am-That-Nisargadatta-Maharaj-Resumo.pdf

Existential threats and regulating life: securitization in the contemporary Middle East

Simon Mabon

ABSTRACT

This article applies the concept of securitization to the Middle East with a focus upon the securitization of the Shi'a other. Such processes occur across time and space and are not restricted to state borders, escaping the Westphalian straitjacket. As a consequence, one must consider the construction of space and political structures across the region in order to understand the traction that such moves can find. It appears then, that in seeking to maintain short-term survival, regimes have sacrificed long-term stability, but the impacts of such moves transcend the typically linear constructed audiences within securitization moves. A key contribution of this article is to consider the extent to which audiences within the Middle East, both intended and unintended, transcend the linear audiences found within conventional processes of securitization. The article uses two case studies as a means of exploring the extent to which securitization can be applied to the Middle East. Such an approach helps us to identify the logics that are involved within the process of securitization, with consideration of the idea that we can populate a broad framework about the universal application of securitization to context specific cases.

As we move past the 6th anniversary of the Arab Uprisings, the dreams that had driven the protest movements, causing people to take to the streets and separating autocratic regimes from societies have been extinguished. In many cases, autocratic rulers remain in control having mobilized support bases and implemented coup proofing and securitization strategies to do so. In others, the battle rages and the space that was created from the fragmentation of the state has allowed for groups like Da'ish to gain prominence. As a mechanism of control, a number of Sunni regimes sought to securitize the Shi'a threat, framing minority groups as an Iranian 5th column and securing their place within the pantheon of Sunni Arab states opposed to Iran.

To this end, this article applies the concept of securitization to the Middle East with a focus upon the securitization of the Shi'a other. Such processes occur across time and space and are not restricted to state borders, escaping the Westphalian straitjacket. As a consequence, one must consider the construction of space and political structures across the region in order to understand the traction that such moves can find. It appears then, that in seeking to maintain short term survival, regimes have sacrificed long-term stability, but the impacts of such moves transcend the typically linear con-structed audiences within securitization moves. A key contribution of this article is to consider the extent to which audiences within the Middle East, both intended and unintended, transcend the linear audiences found within conventional processes of securitization. The article uses two case studies as a means of exploring the extent to which securitization can be applied to the Middle East. Such an approach helps us to identify the *logics* that are involved within the process of securitization, with considera-tion of the idea that we can populate a broad framework about the universal application of securitization to context specific cases.

There is, of course, a range of challenges to the application of securitization theories to the non-Western world. While a number of scholars have undertaken such efforts, including a number of luminaries involved within this volume, we must also be con-scious of a range of issues. To this end, this article seeks to contribute to these debates by asking to what extent we can learn about the logics of securitization, particularly within the non-Western context, by looking at case studies from the Middle East. It does this by employing a comparative framework, based upon a selection of *most similar* case studies. Such a decision facilitates awareness of key securitization processes across the Middle East and while they are by no means the only processes, the selected case studies help us to identify the logic that is involved within the more dominant processes of securitization in the Middle East. With the penetration of the region by hegemonic powers, we also consider the extent to which these actors are involved in processes of securitization. Given this, it is important to consider two processes of securitization that (1) are reflective of regional trends and (2) that share a similar logic of securitization, working across levels of analysis, transcending state borders. To facilitate this analysis I draw upon a number of diplomatic cables released by the Wikileaks organization. Although problematic ethically, they offer rich insight into securitization attempts, which would not be otherwise possible.

Debate about the process of securitization has become a central tenet of Security Studies and International Relations broadly. The broadening of the security agenda facilitated by the so-called Copenhagen School allowed for greater insight into the *construction* of security within the contemporary world. This article does not seek to offer an extensive analysis of the processes of securitization in the region, which have been argued elsewhere, including by this author (see Darwich and Fakhoury 2016; Mabon 2017). Instead, we will briefly reflect on the main stages of the processes, before populating the logic of these processes.

There are a number of concepts that must be noted before we can continue with our exploration. As Buzan, Wæver and De Wild argue, security 'is about survival. It is when an issue is presented as posing an existential threat to a designated referent object [...]'. The special nature of security threats justifies the use of extraordinary measures to handle them (Buzan, Wæver, and de Wilde 1998, 21). The article uses this brief definition of security along with additional developments that come with it. For the Buzan, Wæver and De Wild, security 'ultimately rests neither with the objects nor with the subjects but among the subjects' (Buzan, Wæver, and de Wilde 1998, 31). It is inter-relational and by identifying this we are better placed to understand it.

As Greenwood and Wæver articulate, the concept of securitization is rooted locally – as is suggested by its 'nickname', yet when it 'travels' beyond the West a number of conceptual problems emerge. Perhaps the most powerful is the idea that in the post-colonial world, concepts, such as politics, regime-society relations, and sovereignty are applied to contexts that bear little resemblance to their counterparts in the West, with vastly different contents. A prominent feature of the securitization move is that normal politics is suspended to allow for exceptional measures to be installed, but normal politics itself is a problematic concept.

Of course, when transferred across different contexts, definitions of 'normal' vary greatly, yet the fundamental aspect of such a concept is grounded in the idea of stability. As Wilkinson argues, inherent within securitization theory is the assumption that 'European understandings of society and the state are universal' (Wilkinson 2007, 5). To define a particular context as having the characteristics of normal politics, we must make a range of assumptions about the nature of society, about political situations, the role of religion in society, and about economic factors. These assumptions about the structure of state–society relations reveal the hegemonic Liberal ontology within the theory. Of course, all societies do have rules and perhaps the suspension of normal politics involves the suspension of particular rules within society.

The process of securitization generates sovereignty, by the articulation of what is deemed to be an extraordinary threat, *determining the exception* – and sovereignty generates securitization by virtue of the nature of the concept (Mabon 2016). Sovereignty is concerned with order and belonging, with security playing an integral part of efforts to create order. Yet as securitization moves take place across sovereign boundaries, drawing upon collective histories and experiences to provide justification, we must consider the extent to which we can refer securitization as a linear structure (Wilkinson 2007, 12).

Building upon this linear process, we must also consider the audience, to whom speech acts are uttered, which ultimately determines the success of the move (Buzan, Wæver, and de Wilde 1998, 25). Moreover, it is the audience that provides that context for the adoption of 'distinctive policies', which can be viewed as exceptional or not (Balzacq, Leonard, and Ruzicka 2016, 495). Typically, audiences are part of a linear process, yet when moves take place across sovereign borders to draw upon normative environments, we must consider the extent to which linear processes are in operation.

Politics, religion, and security in the gulf

Along with other regions of the world, security strategies in the Arab world were predicated upon a 'top-down' approach to understanding and framing security, simultaneously focusing upon the threats from external and internal actors. As such, while the focus upon security in the Middle East is often framed in 'traditional' terms, it is far more 'unconventional', with a strong focus upon regime survival, societal security, and ideological power. In many cases, we see the interaction of the traditional and unconventional, or the conflation of external and internal threats. To understand how this occurs we must provide some brief regional context.

In doing so, we must provide political and theological context within which actors are operating. The prominence of Islam within Middle Eastern states cannot be ignored, nor can its role in *the political*, the way in which events gain meaning. Within the Middle East, the site of the two holy places of Islam, the role of religion within both daily and political life is paramount. Religion also serves as a mechanism for regimes to secure their legitimacy – *and ultimately survival* – yet this is increasingly seen in zero sum terms across the region. As such, religion takes on an existential importance, as a prominent feature of securitization discourse, particularly so when located within political debates. Before we turn to our case studies, we must then provide a brief contextual overview of the regional security environment, which serves to underpin many of the perceptions and decisions that are made by actors in the region.

The rivalry with Iran has long dominated the security calculations of a number of prominent Sunni Arab states, notably Saudi Arabia (see Mabon 2013; Matthiessen 2013; Furtig 2006; Chubin and Tripp 1996; Keynoush 2016; Mason 2014). Within this context, since the revolution of 1979, Islam has played an increasingly instrumental role within what historically was a geopolitical rivalry, yet the Islamic rhetoric that was often directed at the House of Saud was seen to be an existential threat to the survival of the regime (Rubin 2014). Moreover, the provision of support to the 'downtrodden' of the Muslim world – typically held to be Shi'a Muslims – would be a cause for concern as these acts became increasingly politicized and identities over time would become securitized (Nasr 2007). With the fragmentation of states across the years following the revolution, this would provide space and sites for competition, vying for influence.

One of the key points of dissonance within the rivalry was over competing views of the US within the region. For Saudi Arabia, the US played an integral role in ensuring that regional security was maintained yet for Iran, regional security should be maintained by those operating within what Barry Buzan termed the 'regional security complex'. Of course, with its long and prestigious history of Persian Empire and conquest, Iran was 'uniquely qualified' to provide leadership over the Gulf region and to ensure its stability. Differences over the arrangement of regional security would be a regular source of contention, during the Iran–Iraq War, the Gulf War, the 2003 invasion and its aftermath.

Following the 1979 revolution, the regime in Tehran would establish a new constitution that explicitly located the Shi'a experience at the heart of its *raison d'etre*, particularly within the context regional security calculations, ushering in a period of rhetorical enmity seeking to demonstrate Islamic credentials to the wider *umma*.

Such comments were built upon with specific reference to the perceived impropriety of the Al Saud:

> If we wanted to prove to the world that the Saudi Government, these vile and ungodly Saudis, are like daggers that have always pierced the heart of the Moslems from the back, we would not have been able to do it as well as has been demonstrated by these inept and spineless leaders of the Saudi Government. (New York Times 1987)

The role of religion within the fabric of both Saudi Arabia and Iran means that religion plays an undeniably prominent role in shaping the nature of the rivalry between the two regional powers. Of course, when particular incidents occur, both states are keen to frame them within particular contexts, often to the detriment of the other. Direct targeting is also a prominent feature of the strategies of both states. Following the execution of the Shi'a cleric Nimr al Nimr in January 2016, Ayatollah Ali Khamenei predicted 'divine vengeance' for the execution of Sheikh Nimr (Fathollah-Nejad 2016).

In contrast, the Al Saud had previously framed the 1979 revolution as an example of 'Persian expansionism' (Fürtig 2006) along with being vocal about the interference within domestic affairs of other states (Mabon 2013). Indeed, prior to the *Hajj* of 1987, King Fahd attacked the 'hypocrites and pretenders who are using Islam to undermine and destabilize other countries' (Goldberg 1987).

Regime officials in Tehran were also vocal in their regional aspirations

> We will export our experiences to the whole world and present the outcome of our struggles against tyrants to those who are struggling along the path of God, without expecting the slightest reward. The result of this exportation will certainly result in the blooming of the buds of victory and independence and in the implementation of Islamic teachings among the enslaved nations. (New York Times 1987)

The politicization of religion and increased importance of faith within foreign policies of Gulf states meant that Islam took on an existential importance for regimes in the region. Within this context and given the plurality of religious views of actors with political agendas, sectarian differences took on an increasingly important role within the region, serving as a tool to divide protest groups and maintain the support of regional allies.

With the establishment of Hizballah, the Lebanese Party of God, in 1982 (El-Husseini 2010), and support for the Islamic Front for the Liberation of Bahrain during the 1980s (Alhasan 2011), it appeared clear to many Gulf rulers that Iran was putting its words into action. In 1996, the Khobar Towers residential complex was bombed, allegedly by Hizballah al-Hijaz with Iranian support (Matthiessen 2010).

In the post Arab Uprisings Middle East, a number of states have been characterized by serious tensions between regime and society, which have been furthered by external actors (Lynch 2016). The fragmentation of state sovereignty (Mabon 2017) across the region has provided a range of actors with the possibility to exert influence across the region, often seen in zero-sum terms. One such way that influence can be wielded is through reference to religious narratives, as a consequence of both the prominence of religion across the region and the spread of religious identity groups. Sectarian difference across the region leaves states open to external interference within state borders.

Amidst an increasingly contested region, there is a range of challenges to regime security, which erupted in 2011 with the onset of protest groups. The protestors raised concerns about the nature of political systems across the Middle East, along with demographic issues, economic factors and endemic corruption. Protests and counter protests followed as regimes and protestors sought to gain control of the situation and a range of tactics were used to this end. One such tactic was to strengthen the support base of the regime, achieved by securitizing a particular group. The decision to securitize actors, as a tool of solidification, would provoke serious divisions between protestors, changing the nature of protest movements and framing issues within broader regional dynamics.

In the years following the Arab Uprisings, regimes across the Middle East, threatened by the emergence of protest groups across the region, sought to ensure their survival. Regimes utilized a number of strategies, ranging from political reform to the use of force in an attempt to remove the threat posed by opposition groups. In engaging in such practices, regimes marginalized particular groups from civil society and, in doing this, the geopolitical environment across the Middle East began to shift. The severity of the threat facing largely autocratic regimes across the region quickly became apparent and caused Saudi Arabia – among others – to mobilize strategies to stave off domestic unrest, while aligning externally to maintain regional influence. The fragmentation of states across the region would provide scope for increased interference from external states in an attempt to increase their geopolitical standing.

When coupled with the recent history of the region, the fragmentation of states across the Middle East would increase concerns among Sunni Gulf states that Tehran would seek to increase its influence with Shi'a groups. To counter this, Saudi Arabia and other members of the GCC sought to strengthen ties across the organization, along with other Arab monarchies, with whom a particular set of characteristics are shared. Saudi Arabia also attempted to reduce Iranian influence in the region by supporting Syrian opposition groups in an attempt to topple Bashar al Assad, a long-standing ally of Tehran (Al-Rasheed 2012).

Furthermore, the manipulation of events in fragmenting states, Saudi Arabia had also sought to securitize the Iranian threat to actors in the US (Mabon 2017), yet Washington's reluctance to suspend 'normal politics' would provoke Riyadh to think carefully about its ability to rely on Washington as a security guarantor. Domestically, Saudi Arabia was seen to be a quiet reformer, offering a large economic package to placate domestic unrest while slowly embarking on a programme of reform (Mabon 2012), albeit on pre-decided issues, such as the role of women in politics. Riyadh also sought to diversify its economy away from reliance upon natural resources, yet such a move is in its infancy and could result in the emergence of tensions at the very heart of the Saudi state, with its Wahhabi clerics. Yet such tensions are for another article.

As a consequence of a number of exogenous factors, the rivalry between Saudi Arabia and Iran became increasingly fractious following the invasion of Iraq. In the following decade, distrust and enmity became defining characteristics of the rivalry, which was then exacerbated by opportunities presented by the Arab Uprisings and the fragmentation of regime–society relations. Independent of the uprisings, negotiations between the P5 + 1 and Iran were underway to resolve the Iranian nuclear crisis, and the agreement would increase Saudi Arabia's concerns about the ramifications of galvanized Iran, emboldened by the burgeoning rapprochement with the international community. By considering two cases of securitization we are well placed to reflect conceptually upon processes of securitization in the non-Western world, but also upon the changing nature of the Middle Eastern security environment.

Case study 1: the Iranian 'threat'

The threat from Iran

Our first case study allows us to consider how regimes have sought to cultivate – and maintain – support from regional actors, by focussing upon the securitization of Iran in the aftermath of the US led invasion of Iraq in 2003. As noted earlier, the establishment of the Islamic Republic in 1979 would dramatically alter regional relations and security calculations within many Sunni states, particularly those who possessed a Shi'a minority notably Bahrain, Saudi Arabia and Kuwait. In 2003, regional relations would be altered once again, with the toppling of the Ba'athist regime of Saddam Hussein in Iraq, leaving

Saudi Arabia and Iran as the two regional hegemons, seeking to shape the region in their image (Mabon 2013). At this time, Iraq had begun to fragment, leaving groups open to increasing influence from both states, however, given the shared religious ties between Iran and the Shi'a majority in Iraq, coupled with the assistance historically provided to Shi'a actors from Iraq under the Ba'athists, Iranian influence increased dramatically (see Haddad 2013; Tripp 2007). At this time, Riyadh sought to counter Tehran's burgeoning influence, building links both with regional states and the US, predominantly by attempting to securitize the threat posed by Iran.

Despite a burgeoning rapprochement between Saudi Arabia and Iran over the previous decade (Furtig 2006), increased hostilities between the two and the emergence of Iraq as an area of uncertainty – and later an arena of competition – would result in a dramatic shift in regional security calculations among Gulf states. The spread of religious minorities across the region, coupled with the complexity of security calculations in the Gulf, meant that security would become a prominent feature of politics broadly. Within this process, Saudi Arabia would frame Iran as a serious threat to regional security, directed at domestic, regional, and international audiences.

Regional security concerns as facilitating conditions

Such efforts to designate Iran as an existential threat emerge from both historical memory and contemporary events. The Islamic Republic's behaviour in the aftermath of the revolution had created a great deal of suspicion about Tehran's intentions across the Middle East, which became particularly prominent as state sovereignty began to fragment. Concern at Iranian support for Shi'a groups across the region was becoming widespread. King Abdullah of Jordan, referred to a 'Shi'a Crescent' (NBC 2008), wherein Shi'a populations across the region (mapped out in the shape of a crescent) were fifth columns doing the bidding of Iran.

Reflecting the growing power of Saudi Arabia after the 2003 invasion and alignment of Sunni Arab states and monarchies behind it, it was Riyadh that was able to best withstand geopolitical pressures and harness them to its advantage. Saudi Arabia would look to harness the currents of the uprisings and direct them in the direction of their national interest. Framing events along sectarian lines, as Riyadh would seek to do, provided states with the opportunity to frame uprisings within the context of broader geopolitical trends and with it, to discredit democratic and economic concerns. Ultimately, this approach can be understood as the mobilization of two sets of actions: the first, to mobilize a collective initially under the mechanisms of the GCC to ensure the survival of monarchical regimes across the region, and second, to respond to fears about Iranian penetration of a fragmenting region, resulting in the solidification of geopolitical alliances. In both cases, while other states also acted in response to these concerns, Saudi Arabia would take the lead.

At this time, one can easily see the extent to which Saudi Arabia sought to frame Iran as an existential threat to regional security. US diplomatic cables (later released by Wikileaks) recall the extent of Riyadh's paranoia at increased Iranian influence:

The King said he had "no confidence whatsoever in (Iraqi PM) Maliki, and the Ambassador (Fraker) is well aware of my views". [...] For this reason, the King said, Maliki had no credibility. "I don't trust this man," the King stated, He's an Iranian agent." […] Maliki has "opened the door for Iranian influence in Iraq" since taking power, the King said. (09RIYADH447_a 2009)

Saudi Prince Nayif bin Abdul Aziz also sought to demonstrate the importance of the American presence in Iraq, calling upon Washington not to 'leave Iraq until its sovereignty has been restored, otherwise it will be vulnerable to the Iranians' (06RIYADH9175_a). A later cable demonstrated the extent of Tehran's 'penetration' of Iraq by referring to the 'Iranian City of Basrah' (08BAGHDAD239_a 2008).

One consequence of Iranian penetration was to erode faith in the Iraqi political system, amidst suggestions that the Maliki regime lacked credibility and autonomy:

The King said he had "no confidence whatsoever in (Iraqi PM) Maliki, and the Ambassador (Fraker) is well aware of my views". […] For this reason, the King said, Maliki had no credibility. "I don't trust this man," the King stated, He's an Iranian agent." […] Maliki has "opened the door for Iranian influence in Iraq" since taking power, the King said. (09RIYADH447_a)

This sentiment was also shared by others, showing the lengths to which Saudi Arabia attempted to demonstrate the threat posed by Iran. A later cable recalled a conversation between the Saudi ambassador to the US, Adel Al Jubeir and the Charge, wherein Al Jubeir recalled a conversation to suspend 'normal politics':

the King's frequent exhortations to the US to attack Iran and so put an end to its nuclear weapons program. "He told you to cut off the head of the snake," he recalled to the Charge', adding that working with the US to roll back Iranian influence in Iraq is a strategic priority for the King and his government. (08RIYADH649_a 2008)

Diplomatic cables also noted concern about the influence that Iranian supported militias had across Iraq, stemming, in part, from the provision of financial support (Mabon and Royle 2017). At this time the level of sectarian violence increased dramatically, with casualties occurring as a consequence of fighting between coalition forces, Al Qa'ida affiliates, government actors, militias (Sunni and Shi'a) and tribal groups (Mabon and Royle 2017). Such concerns were not limited to Iraq and included Bahrain, Yemen, and Syria. In a meeting of the Organisation of Islamic Co-Operation, a communiqué was issued condemning 'Iran's interference in the internal affairs of the States of the region and other Member States (including Bahrain, Yemen, Syria, and Somalia) and its continued support for terrorism' (OIC 2016).

Audiences and success

From the designation of the threat and the facilitating conditions that gave rise to such moves, it is clear to see that a number of audiences were involved in securitization moves at different levels of analysis. Recognition of shared normative environments across state borders offers a number of challenges for securitization processes. Such environments are found through exploration of shared religious values across the Gulf and wider Middle East. They are also found with regard to perceptions as to the threat posed by Iran and as such, by framing Iran as a threat Saudi securitization efforts also speak to Israelis, those previously involved in the nuclear negotiations, and particularly the US. Of course, these two different approaches can – and do – overlap.

At a domestic level, securitization moves are designed to speak to the general Saudi citizens, a vast majority of whom are Sunni (around 40% of whom are Wahhabi). Such comments are also aimed at the Wahhabi *ulemma*, in an attempt to maintain their loyalty and to placate any concerns about deep-seated tensions between the Al Saud and clerics. Indeed, a vehement anti-Shi'a sentiment borne out of deep doctrinal differences is inherent within Wahhabi thought, seen in a fatwa calling upon the Shi'a to convert to Islam (Tietelbaum, p2). Such views impact upon both domestic and regional politics. Regionally, (the perception of) rising Iranian influence has ramifications for security calculations for Sunni states with Shi'a minorities, who are often perceived to be 5th columns. As a consequence, such groups are seen to be a threat to the stability of the state, both domestically and regionally by virtue of their alleged links to Iran.

Internationally, efforts to securitize the Iranian threat to US audiences demonstrate the importance of the US for Saudi Arabia's security. In addition to the speech acts document above, Saudi Arabia also sponsored a number of think tanks and universities in the US in an attempt to create a favourable narrative and environment for securitization moves to find traction (Fisher 2016). While the Obama administration did not strike against Iranian targets, we must consider that another understanding of the suspension of normal politics has fed into conditions that have left the Trump administration able to question the vitality of the nuclear deal. They also build upon long-standing Israeli efforts to securitize Iran, once again, stressing the complexity of securitization moves and their non-linear dimensions. It has also facilitated the emergence of a burgeoning relationship between Saudi Arabia and Israel, around shared visions of regional security.

Case study 2: the Shi'a of Bahrain

> We shall deport them to Howar, Jenan and Noon islands …
> With a shining and sharp sword
> We'll spill their bloods until they all die …
> We'll stop their annual processions in the streets
> As their poems hurl insults at us[1]

The threat from Iran and the threat from within

The second of our case studies takes place in the aftermath of the Arab Uprisings on the island of Bahrain, home to a Shi'a majority ruled by a Sunni minority. Situated in the Persian Gulf between Saudi Arabia and Iran, Bahrain is seen by many to be the epicentre of the Middle East's sectarian competition. In the years after the Arab Uprisings it has been a site of competition between a range of different actors seeking to shape the future of Bahrain, seemingly along sectarian lines yet with clear political agendas.

On February 14th, protests began in Bahrain, as huge numbers of people took to the streets protesting against the Al Khalifa run political system. Comprised of a range of different groups and members of different sects, in possession of multifarious desired outcomes, the protests gained international attention. Shortly after, Saudi-led forces under the auspices of the GCC crossed the King Fahd causeway and entered Bahrain to ensure the survival of the ruling Al Khalifa regime. Between April and October 2011, more than 500 people were convicted of crimes against the state and prominent members of leading opposition parties were also arrested (Sarah 2012). Amidst this unrest and the spate of arrests were regular allegations at Iranian involvement in orchestrating the protests.

Politics – defined broadly – in Bahrain is shaped by the interaction of *asabiyyah* (kinship) and *al-din* (religious principles) (Khaldûn 1967) and its location results in a strong history of trade driven immigration (Fuccaro 2009). Such conditions have created a vibrant and multifarious society, with a range of different identities playing out in civil society. This melange of identity groups – with their own set of complex histories with state structures (Khuri 1980) – has created the perception of external involvement in driving particular agendas, best seen in the case of the Shi'a, who are seen by many as an Iranian 5th column, a term initially coined by King Abdullah of Jordan reflecting concerns about Iran's capacity to influence Shi'a groups across the Middle East (NBC 2008; 06RIYADH3312 2006).

Facilitating conditions

In the aftermath of the Arab Uprisings the Al Khalifa regime attempted to frame the protest movements as part of an Iranian strategy to create uncertainty across the region. Despite the BICI finding no evidence of Iranian involvement, the regime line was to stress Iranian manipulation of Shi'a populations. Shi'a experiences in Bahrain are multifarious, shaped by a range of other factors, including class, gender, and ethnicity (Gengler 2013). As a consequence of decades of political, social, and economic repression by the Sunni minority, the Islamic Front for the Liberation of Bahrain was created in Bahrain, with support from Iranian agents. The group would attempt a *coup d'etat* against the Al Khalifa regime in 1981, having been trained and funded by the Iranian Revolutionary Guards Corps (Alhasan 2011). Although unsuccessful, the coup created a legacy of external – Iranian – interference in the domestic affairs of Bahrain and as such, any unrest within Shi'a groups was immediately framed as a consequence of Iranian manipulation.

A former US ambassador to Bahrain would describe the situation thus:

> For the government and ruling family, the existential threat is Iran and its historical claims to Bahrain. Iran's increased aggressiveness under President Ahmadinejad, coupled with perceived Iranian inroads in Iraq, have only heightened Bahraini concerns. The government is only too happy to have us focus on potential threats from Iran and their alleged Shia allies in Bahrain. In contrast, Sunnis, even Sunni extremists, form the base of support against a potential Shia/Iranian threat. The government fully understands that any kind of terror attack by Sunni extremists in Bahrain – against U.S. or Bahraini interests – would be a disaster for the country and its economy, and it is ready to cooperate with us fully to make sure that doesn't happen. But our future cooperation will continue to be affected by two factors: Bahraini confidence that, in this small island country, the authorities can stay one step ahead of and deal with any extremists planning a local operation; and Bahraini reluctance to move against or alienate the Sunni Islamist community at a time of heightened concern about Iran and rising Shia influence in the region. (07MANAMA669_a 2007)

Such comments stress the severity of the threat posed by Iran. When placed within broader regional dynamics, the changing nature of regional security and fragile demographic balance in Bahrain become increasingly intertwined.

Iranian press outlets would further such concerns, as newspapers such as *Kayhan* would suggest that

> Bahrain is a special case among GCC countries in the Persian Gulf because Bahrain is part of the Iranian territories and had been separated from Iran in light of an illegal settlement between the executed Shah an the governments of the United States and Britain. And the main demand for the Bahrain people is to return its province – which was separated from Iran – to the motherland which is Islamic Iran. It is self-evident that Iran and the people of this separated province must not give up this ultimate right. (07MANAMA650_a)

These remarks would fuel suspicion of Iranian manipulation, providing additional scope to speak to three different audiences.

Shi'a experiences in Bahrain are largely intersectional, shaped by political dynamics across the archipelago, but also as a consequence of regional dynamics, stemming from shared religious experiences across the region. An unpublished report for the Gulf Centre for Democratic Development noted how

> the marginalization of Sunnīs and the lessening of their role in Bahrain is part of a larger regional problem, whereas [our] sons of the Sunnī sect in Iraq face the same problem, meaning there is a direct correlation between [the Iraqi situation and] the marginalization of the Sunna in the Gulf countries, and their marginalization in Bahrain in particular. Thus there is a dangerous challenge facing Bahraini society in the increased role of the Shī'a [and] the retreat of the role of the Sunna in the Bahraini political system; namely, the problem concerns the country's [Bahrain's] national security, and the likelihood of political regime change in the long term by means of the current relationships between Bahrain's Shī'a and all the Shī'a in Iran, Iraq, Saudi Arabia's eastern region, and Kuwait. (Gengler 2013)

The fusion of political and religious identities became increasingly prominent and amidst changing regional dynamics, became framed as a security threat.

As Justin Gengler argues, the Al Khalifa strategy had three dimensions: The first was to exclude the Shi'a from prominent ministries and security services; the second was to dilute demographic influence of Shi'a citizens; while the third was to mobilize Sunni against Shi'a to ensure the vitality of the support basis (Gengler 2013). There is, however, a fourth aspect that is explored later, notably with regard to securing the support of external audiences.

Throughout this process, the King was vocal in expressing his suspicion about Iranian action and intent, alongside the potential for Tehran to incite unrest among Shi'a communities in Bahrain. In conversation with the US ambassador, King Hamad argued that 'as long as Khamenei has the title of Commander-in-Chief, Bahrain must worry about the loyalty of Shia who maintain ties and allegiance to Iran' (06MANAMA409_a). Fawaz bin Mohammed Al Khalifa, the Bahraini ambassador to the UK, argued that the Iranian threat was greater than that posed by Da'ish. Moreover, he also condemned the 'expansionist ambitions of the Persian Shia establishment', who he blamed for unrest in Bahrain, Lebanon, Kuwait and Yemen (Al Khalifa 2016).

Audiences and success

Once again, we can see that the Al Khalifa's securitization efforts involved speaking to audiences at different levels, with different goals in mind. At a domestic level, the Al Khalifa sought to divide protest groups along sectarian lines and, in doing so, to defuse demands for political reform. By framing the protests as a consequence of Iranian manipulation, the regime hoped to ensure the loyalty of Sunni Arabs, who had a long history of suspicion directed at their Persian Gulf neighbours. Allegations at Iranian involvement in the unrest in Bahrain were not limited to Bahraini officials; rather, the British ambassador was also keen to stress Iranian involvement, along with embassy officials, who also suggested Iranian complicity in the development of a bomb-making factory in 2013.[2]

The main target of these securitization efforts is twofold. First, to domestic audiences, where separating Sunni and Shi'a protestors while limiting Shi'a influence archipelago was paramount. Second, the Al Khalifa also sought to ensure the continued support of Saudi Arabia, regional allies, and ultimately the US. At this time, Saudi Arabia had continued a process of securitization, publishing opinion pieces in Western news outlets. Al Jubeir, the Saudi Foreign Minister stressed that Iran was to blame for regional unrest, and that Tehran attempted to 'obscure its dangerous sectarian and expansionist policies, as well as its support for terrorism, by leveling unsubstantiated charges against the Kingdom of Saudi Arabia' (Al-Jubeir and Ahmed 2016). For Al Jubeir, 'the single-most-belligerent-actor in the region, and its actions display both a commitment to regional hegemony and a deeply held view that conciliatory gestures signal weakness either on Iran's part or on the part of its adversaries' (Al-Jubeir and Ahmed 2016). By supporting this narrative, Bahrain was ensuring the continued support of Saudi Arabia, placing it at the vanguard of the struggle against Iranian expansionism. Manama was also seeking to erode US and Western criticism at its handling of the Arab Uprisings in 2011. The aftermath of the uprisings continued amidst seemingly endemic structural violence aimed at Shi'a groups and the removal of political agency.

The process was also aimed at Western audiences, whose presence in Bahrain drew unwanted attention to the repressive nature of the post-uprisings landscape. In support of this, a number of PR companies were hired by the Al Khalifa to improve this image (Bahrain Watch, Azizi 2012) while celebrities were also paid to tweet about their visits to the island (Kardashian 2012).

In spite of this, a number of people were not convinced. For US President Barack Obama,

> The only way forward is for the government and opposition to engage in a dialogue, and you can't have a real dialogue when parts of the peaceful opposition are in jail. The government must create the conditions for dialogue, and the opposition must participate to forge a just future for all Bahrainis. (Reuters 2011)

Obama later called on the government and the main opposition groups 'to pursue a meaningful dialogue that brings peaceful change that is responsive to the people.' (White House 2011) Shortly after, British Prime Minister David Cameron stressed that 'whenever and wherever violence is used against peaceful demonstrators, we must not hesitate to condemn it' (Cameron 2011). A year later, US comments on the political unrest in Bahrain was relegated to a two-paragraph statement from the Press Secretary (White House 2012) and normative aspects of the Bahraini case became largely ignored.

The suspension of normal politics in this instance demonstrates the complexity of normal politics, stressing how such a concept is concept specific. While there is a clear structure within the context, we must also provide more specific detail as to what 'normal politics' means. For many, at the heart of US foreign policy is the support for democracy, human rights and the role of law. As we can see, in the early stages of the uprisings in Bahrain, Western leaders were critical of the handling of the protests, yet very quickly, this narrative changed to support for the Al Khalifa. Such a move can easily be understood as the suspension of normal politics.

Lessons for securitization in the non-West

From the emergence of Saudi Arabia as a leading figure in the post uprisings Middle East, it was hardly surprising that the alignment of regimes across the region would take place along sectarian lines. While formerly reliant upon the US as a guarantor, Saudi Arabia has occupied this role, providing financial muscle to support monarchical allies across the region.

What we see from our two case studies is that regimes in Riyadh and Manama have carefully sought to frame political uncertainty and human security issues within the bigger context of traditional conceptions of security. In doing this, the more unconventional issues that are revealed by the Copenhagen School and securitization processes are pushed into the background, sacrificed in an attempt to remove the threat posed from more traditional sources, but also in an effort to maintain regime security and national identity.

It also becomes apparent that the processes of securitization are not linear. That the moves made by ruling elites to ensure their security take place within broader networks of securitizing moves, building upon political and normative environments that have begun to characterize the region. As a consequence, there is undeniable 'spillover', where securitization moves have unintended consequences across the region – and sometimes beyond – as speech acts find traction within a number of different contexts. Moreover, both cases of securitization show how the process is fluid and cyclical, wherein process builds upon process, impacting upon the construction of normal politics, which in itself becomes constructed. While normal politics is typically understood as the politics of a liberal democracy, we can see how rules and structures – both formal and informal – can shape behaviour, but also how such behaviour can change rules and structures. While we consider particular instances of securitization, in many cases in the Middle East we must also locate them within broader normative environments and, potentially, within other processes of securitization.

While securitization deals with concepts of sovereignty, the liberal ontology inherent in the term is challenged in a number of different ways. The first is that the legacy of state building and the establishment of political organization across the Middle East has meant that securitization moves within one state speak to audiences in others, either intentionally or unintentionally. This serves to locate securitization processes within broader regional security dynamics, fusing levels of analysis. Moreover, there is scope for unintentional consequences to emerge from securitization processes, with audiences spread across a region. This emerges as a consequence of the spread of normative values across the region – stemming from shared ethnic and religious ties – but also as a consequence of shared histories, particularly with regard to perceptions of Iranian manipulation

We also see securitization efforts aimed at actors at different levels of analysis. In the first case study, Saudi Arabia urged the US to suspend normal politics towards Iran. In the second case study, the Bahraini ruling elite attempted to locate the uprisings in the context of a broader regional struggle between Saudi Arabia and Iran. While in both cases one can make the argument that securitization processes failed, we must consider alternative readings of success, and the implications for political dynamics across the region.

In our first case, Saudi Arabia attempted to securitize the threat from Iran to the US, calling for a suspension of normal politics, while in the second, the Al Khalifa attempted to securitize Shi'a protesters to ensure their survival. The failure of the first strategy, despite many in Washington sharing Riyadh's concerns, would drive a wedge between Saudi Arabia and the US, causing Riyadh to re-calculate its security strategies. The second case also demonstrates how a state in the Gulf called for the suspension of normal politics, yet in this case, we can see how that may be perceived as a success. The success of the second process of securitization demonstrates how shared normative environments can have different outcomes at different levels.

In this case, we must consider what constitutes normal politics in the Middle East and indeed, within the Gulf. Tensions between Saudi Arabia and Iran were furthered with the emergence of Da'ish in the summer of 2014. While both perceived the group to be a serious threat – as did Tehran – differences arose with regard to strategy in Syria, with Saudi Arabia focussing on toppling Assad while the US was focussed upon Da'ish targets. This divergence on strategy reflects Riyadh's perception that Assad – and indeed Shi'a organizations generally – posed the greatest threat to regional security across the Middle East.

Obama's comments reflect the shortcomings of Saudi Arabia's efforts to call for an end to 'normal politics', particularly so if we view this in light of King Abdullah's claims to 'cut off the head of the snake'. Instead, Obama stated that

> The competition between the Saudis and the Iranians – which has helped to feed proxy wars and chaos in Syria and Iraq and Yemen – requires us to say to our friends as well as to the Iranians that they need to find an effective way to share the neighborhood and institute some sort of cold peace. (Goldberg 2016)

Of course, political dynamics would change with the election of Donald Trump in late 2016. Shortly after taking office in January 2017, Trump tweeted 'Iran is playing with fire – they don't appreciate how "kind" President Obama was to them. Not me!' (Donald J. Trump, Feb 3, 2017). In the coming months, this rhetoric would continue, building upon an environment created not only by previous Saudi securitization efforts but also Israeli efforts.

Conclusions

As this article has argued, processes of securitization can be applied to the Middle East and that although the general framework of securitization works, there are different logics at play. The construction of the Middle East system and regional security complex provides a different set of logics to populate the framework of securitization, particularly with regard to different audiences and the power of normative values across state borders. The role of religion within the fabric of states in the region should not be understated, as this provides fertile ground for securitization moves to take place, not only at the state level but also at the regional and international levels.

As such, to truly understand the nature of politics and security, we must explore a much bigger picture, drawing upon history, politics and religion, placing the subjects of our study within broader regional and international environments. The penetration of the region by hegemonic powers, in this case the US, requires greater exploration of how securitization works at different levels of analysis; moreover, we must ascertain how these moves are made. What is all too clear is that once securitization processes have been begun, the ramifications are felt region wide. Moreover, once they begin, history means that they are increasingly difficult to stop.

Notes

1. Prose written by Khalid bin Ahmad Al Khalifa in 1995. Cited in Gengler (2013).
2. Interviews with British and American officials, Manama and London, 2013.

Disclosure statement

No potential conflict of interest was reported by the author.

References

"Any Differences?" *Khamenei.IR*, January 02, 2016. http://english.khamenei.ir/news/3018/Any-differences

"Final Communiqué of the Extraordinary Meeting of the Council of Foreign Ministers of the Organization of Islamic Cooperation on Aggressions on the Embassy of the Kingdom of Saudi Arabia in Tehran and Its Consulate General in Mashhad." *Organisation of Islamic Cooperation*, January 22, 2016. http://www.oic-oci.org/oicv2/topic/?t_id=10837&t_ref=4262&lan=en

"Key Quotes from Obama's Middle East Speech." *Reuters*, May 19, 2011. http://uk.reuters.com/article/us-obama-mideast-quotes-idUKTRE74I63A20110519

"Excerpts from Khomeini's Speeches." *New York Times*, August 04, 1987. http://www.nytimes.com/1987/08/04/world/excerpts-from-khomeini-speeches.html?pagewanted=all&src=pm

"Hardball with Chris Matthews: King Abdullah II of Jordan." *NBC News*, December 7 2008. Event occurs at 02:06.

06MANAMA409_a. 2006. "Luncheon with King Hamad." March 15. Accessed 16 December 2015. https://wikileaks.org/plusd/cables/06MANAMA409_a.html

06RIYADH3312. 2006. "The Saudi Shi'a: Where Do Their Loyalties Lie?" May 02. Accessed 10 June 2015. https://wikileaks.org/plusd/cables/06RIYADH3312_a.html

06RIYADH9175_a. 2006. "Saudi Moi Head Says if U.S. Leaves Iraq, Saudi Arabia Will Stand with Sunnis." December 26. https://wikileaks.org/plusd/cables/06RIYADH9175_a.html

07MANAMA650_a. 2007. "Bahrain Reacts Angrily to Iranian Territorial Claim on Bahrain." July 12. https://wikileaks.org/plusd/cables/07MANAMA650_a.html

07MANAMA669_a. 2007. "Future of Bahrain: Ambassador's Parting Thoughts." July 19. https://wikileaks.org/plusd/cables/07MANAMA669_a.html

08BAGHDAD239_a. 2008. ""The Street Is Stronger than Parliament:" Sadrist Vows Opposition to Ltsr." January 27. https://wikileaks.org/plusd/cables/08BAGHDAD239_a.html

08RIYADH649_a. 2008. "Saudi King Abdullah and Senior Princes on Saudi Policy Towards Iraq." April 20. https://wikileaks.org/plusd/cables/08RIYADH649_a.html

09RIYADH447_a. 2014. "Counterterrorism Adviser Brennan's Meeting with Saudi King Abdullah." March 22. prepared by the *Gulf Center for Democratic Development* Accessed September 2006. https://wikileaks.org/plusd/cables/09RIYADH447_a.html

Al Khalifa, F. B. M. 2016. "The Gulf States are Stuck between Isil and Iran." *The Telegraph*, January 21. http://www.telegraph.co.uk/news/worldnews/middleeast/bahrain/12113355/The-Gulf-states-are-stuck-between-Isil-and-Iran.html

Alhasan, H. T. 2011. "The Role of Iran in the Failed Coup of 1981: The IFLB In Bahrain." *The Middle East Journal* 65 (4): 603–617, p603. doi:10.3751/65.4.15.

Al-Jubeir, A., and B. Ahmed. 2016. "Can Iran Change?" *The New York Times*, January 19. Accessed 20 January 2016 http://www.nytimes.com/2016/01/19/opinion/saudi-arabia-can-iran-change.html?_r=2

Al-Rasheed, M. 2012. "The Saudi Response to the 'Arab Spring': Containment and Co-Option." *Open Democracy*, January 10. http://www.opendemocracy.net/5050/madawi-al-rasheed/saudi-response-to-%E2%80%98arab-spring%E2%80%99-containment-and-co- option

Azizi, S. 2012. "US PR Firm Spends $9,150 on Fb Ads to Promote Bahrain Government". *Blottr*, 13 June. http://www.blottr.com/world/breaking-news/us-pr-firm-spent-9150-facebook-ads-promote-bahrain-govt

Balzacq, T., S. Léonard, and J. Ruzicka. 2016. "'Securitization' Revisited: Theory and Cases." *International Relations* 30 (4): 494–531. doi: 10.1177/0047117815596590.

Buzan, B., O. Wæver, and J. de Wilde. 1998. *Security: A New Framework for Analysis*. Boulder, CO: Lynne Rienner.

Cameron, D. 2011. *Speech to the National Assembly, Full Transcript*. Kuwait. Accessed on 22 February 2011. https://www.newstatesman.com/middle-east/2011/02/kuwait-british-arab-security

Chubin, S., and C. Tripp. 1996. *Iran-Saudi Arabia Relations and Regional Order*. London: OUP for IISS.

Darwich, M., and T. Fakhoury. 2016. "Casting the Other as an Existential Threat: The Securitisation of Sectarianism in the International Relations of the Syria Crisis." *Global Discourse* 6 (4): 712–732.

El-Husseini, R. 2010. "Hezbollah and the Axis of Refusal: Hamas, Iran and Syria." *Third World Quarterly* 31 (5): 803–815. doi:10.1080/01436597.2010.502695.

Fathollah-Nejad, A. 2016. "Iran and Saudi Arabia: The Impending Storm." *Qantara.de*, January 06. https://en.qantara.de/content/iran-and-saudi-arabia-the-impending-storm

Fisher, M. 2016. "How Saudi Arabia Captured Washington." *Vox*, March 21. http://www.vox.com/2016/3/21/11275354/saudi-arabia-gulf-washington

Fuccaro, N. 2009. *Histories of City and State in the Persian Gulf: Manama since 1800*. Cambridge: Cambridge University Press.

Fürtig, H. 2006. *Iran's Rivalry with Saudi Arabia between the Gulf Wars*. Reading, UK: Ithica Press.

Gengler, J. J. 2013. "Royal Factionalism, the Khawalid, and the Securitization of 'The Shi'a Problem' in Bahrain." *Journal of Arabian Studies* 3: 1. doi:10.1080/21534764.2013.802944.

Goldberg, J. 2016. "The Obama Doctrine." *The Atlantic*, http://www.theatlantic.com/magazine/archive/2016/04/the-obama-doctrine/471525/#5

Goldberg, J. 1987. "The Saudi Arabian Kingdom." In: *Middle East Contemporary Survey Volume XI: 1987*, edited by R. Itovar. and S. Haim., 589. Boulder: Westview Press.

Haddad, F. 2013. "Sectarian Relations in Arab Iraq: Contextualising the Civil War of 2006-2007." *British Journal of Middle Eastern Studies* 40 (2): 118. doi:10.1080/13530194.2013.790289.

Kardashian, K. 2012. "Twitter." https://twitter.com/KimKardashian/status/274950396861095937

Keynoush, B. 2016. *Saudi Arabia and Iran: Friends or Foes?* London: Palgrave.

Khaldûn, I. 1967. *The Muqaddimah: An Introduction to History*. Translated by F. Rosenthal. Princeton, NJ: Princeton University Press.

Khuri, F. I. 1980. *Tribe and State in Bahrain*. Chicago: Chicago University Press.

Lynch, M. 2016. *The New Arab Wars: Uprisings and Anarchy in the Middle East*. New York: Public Affairs.

Mabon, S. 2012. "Kingdom in Crisis: The Arab Spring and Instability in Saudi Arabia." *Contemporary Security Policy* 33: 3. doi:10.1080/13523260.2012.727683.

Mabon, S. 2013. *Saudi Arabia and Iran: Soft Power Rivalry in the Middle East*. London: I.B. Tauris.

Mabon, S. 2016. "Sovereignty, Arab Uprisings and Bare Life." *Third World Quarterly* 38 (8): 1782–1799.

Mabon, S. 2017. "Muting the Trumpets of Sabotage: Saudi Arabia, the US and the Quest to Securitize Iran." *British Journal of Middle Eastern Studies*. doi: 10.1080/13530194.2017.1343123.

Mabon, S., and S. Royle. 2017. *The Origins of Isis: The Collapse of Nations and Revolution in the Middle East*. London: I.B. Tauris.

Mason, R. 2014. *Foreign Policy in Iran and Saudi Arabia: Economics and Diplomacy in the Middle East*. London: I.B. Tauris.

Matthiesen, T. 2010. "Hizbullah al-Hijaz: A History of the Most Radical Saudi Shi'a Opposition Group." *The Middle East Journal* 64 (2): 179–197.

Matthiessen, T. 2013. *Sectarian Gulf: Bahrain, Saudi Arabia and the Arab Spring that Wasn't*. Stanford: Stanford University Press.

Nasr, V. 2007. *The Shia Revival: How Conflicts within Islam Will Shape the Future*. New York: W.W. Norton.

Rubin, L. 2014. *Islam in the Balance: Ideational Threats in Arab Politics*. Stanford: Stanford Security Studies.

The White House. 2011. "Remarks by President Obama in Address to the United Nations General Assembly." September 21. https://obamawhitehouse.archives.gov/the-press-office/2011/09/21/remarks-president-obama-address-united-nations-general-assembly

The White House. 2012. "Statement by the Press Secretary on the Situation in Bahrain." April 11. https://obamawhitehouse.archives.gov/the-press-office/2012/04/11/statement-press-secretary-situation-bahrain

Tripp, C. 2007. *A History of Iraq*. Cambridge: Cambridge University Press.

Wilkinson, C. 2007. "The Copenhagen School on Tour in Kyrgyzstan: Is Securitization Theory Useable outside Europe?" *Security Dialogue* 38 (1): 5–25. doi:10.1177/0967010607075964.

Whitson, S. L. 2012. "No Justice In Bahrain." *Human Rights Watch*, February 28.

Review of 'Existential threats and regulating life: securitization in the contemporary Middle East', by Simon Mabon

John Gledhill

This is a reply to:

Mabon, Simon. 2018. "Existential threats and regulating life: securitization in the contemporary Middle East." *Global Discourse* 8 (1): 42–58. https://doi.org/10.1080/23269995.2017.1410001.

This timely article makes a valuable contribution to debate about the extent to which the Copenhagen School's ideas can be applied outside the West, emphasizing throughout that the original formulations embodied a 'hegemonic Liberal ontology'. Mabon argues that in the postcolonial non-western world, we cannot treat post-Westphalian western understandings of politics, sovereignty and the relationship between state and society as universals, which obliges us to ask deeper questions about the substance of the 'normal politics' that is suspended by the securitization process's declaration of a state of exception. Furthermore, since the power to decide on the exception is definitional of sovereignty in the Carl Schmitt-inspired account of what securitization *does* offered by Ole Wæver, we need to ask what happens when, as in the Middle East, 'securitization moves take place across sovereign boundaries, drawing upon collective histories and experiences to provide justification'. Wæver (2011), 478 insisted that he did not want to replicate Schmitt's concept of the exception being decided 'by a singular will', rather than by 'people in a political situation'. But Mabon extends his analysis of the logic of securitization to the diversity of 'audiences' to which securitization speech acts are being addressed within a regional environment transcending the boundaries of a single nation state and a context in which regional actors seek to engage the government of the United States and other non-Arab powers including Israel. This enables him to explore political situations in which securitization moves have unintended consequences and different 'normative environments' came into play, as historically rooted religious differences were politicized not only for geopolitical ends but also in short-term strategies of regime survival, post-Arab Spring, that prejudiced long-term stability, exacerbated state fragmentation and generated sectarian conflicts. As Islam took on an increasing existential importance for regimes, the paper shows that sectarian differences became central to expression of the growing antagonism between Iran and Saudi Arabia as competing regional hegemons following the US overthrow of the Ba'athist regime in Iraq and for shaping the patterns of interstate alliances and external interference in the affairs of states undergoing fragmentation. But sectarianism was also instrumentalized as a tool for dividing the protest groups that challenged the political status quo from 2011 onwards.

The analysis employs two case studies, selected for what they tell us about underlying similarities in regional logics of securitization. The first focuses on the framing of Iran as a security threat to the region by Saudi Arabia and the Gulf states in terms of its support for the 'crescent' of Shi'a populations, now painted as a 'fifth column', distributed across territories controlled by Sunni regimes. Using the evidence of diplomatic cables released by Wikileaks, Mabon explores how the Saudis sought to give this securitization narrative traction in the United States and brought Israel onside in this endeavour, reinforcing diplomatic efforts by sponsoring support from think tanks and universities in the United States. At the same time, they directed the narrative domestically, drawing on anti-Shi'a sentiment to placate the Wahhabist clergy at home and reach out to other nervous Sunni regimes. The sectarian framing of uprisings helped to deflect attention from democratic, social and economic reform. This seems helpful for understanding cases such as Yemen, where religious differences were previously less salient than provincial discontent with the corruption associated with 40 years of inept central government, but Saudi intervention pushed rebels from the Shi'a minority back into alliance with the very forces they had formerly opposed. In the second case study, Bahrain, a Shi'a majority is governed by a Sunni minority. Although citizens from both religious communities participated in political protests against the Al Khalifa regime, the Iran threat narrative, which could be grounded in past history, not only did its work of division when addressed to a domestic audience but found a receptive audience in the British Embassy as well as Saudi Arabia and the United States. Yet although the regime made a considerable propaganda investment to mute criticisms from the West of the violence rained down on the Shi'a population, both the Obama and Cameron administrations initially found the repression of peaceful protest unacceptable, only to fall silent a year later. Mabon suggests that in this case, securitization succeeded in suspending 'normal politics' as understood in the West (support for democracy, human rights and the rule of law).

Many people subjected to the colonial and post-colonial regimes of western power, including immigrants in the United Kingdom, might dispute whether this 'normal' has ever really applied to them. But Mabon argues that the 'success' of a securitization strategy that gravitated towards 'traditional' notions of national and regional security despite its 'unconventional' elements was limited by the sticking points of northern liberalism and provoked non-trivial changes in established relations, particularly apparent in Saudi focus on undermining Assad rather than prioritizing Da'ish, even if the mentally unstable racist currently occupying the White House is more amenable to the Iranian threat narrative. The human suffering that this narrative (along with western economic interests, including arms sales) is still producing in the Middle East confirms the importance of recognizing the force of securitization logics but also the kinds of contradictions that Mabon highlights. Searching for similarities while recognizing local and regional contexts advances understanding in important ways. Interregional comparisons are also important. For example, Yemen replicates a more global pattern in which armed conflict provides business opportunities for military actors and local leaderships at the same time as it condemns others to humanitarian catastrophe, making a return to peace and restoration of central government more difficult (Salisbury 2017). Yet a deoccidentialized securitization theory attentive to non-linear logics, different scales of analysis and unintended consequences clearly advance a more critical discussion of what constitutes 'normal politics' and 'success'.

Disclosure statement

No potential conflict of interest was reported by the authors.

References

Salisbury, P. 2017. "Yemen and the Business of War." Accessed 30 July 2017. https://www.chatham house.org/system/files/publications/twt/Yemen%20and%20the%20business%20of%20war% 20Salisbury.pdf.
Wæver, O. 2011. "Politics, Security, Theory." *Security Dialogue* 42 (4–5): 465–480. doi:10.1177/ 0967010611418718.

From Copenhagen to Uri and across the Line of Control: India's 'surgical strikes' as a case of securitisation in two acts

Saloni Kapur

ABSTRACT

This article sets out to critique India's security discourse surrounding the 'surgical strikes' of September 2016, using the theoretical framework provided by securitisation. It aims to answer two central questions: First, can securitisation theory provide fresh empirical insights on India's conflict with Pakistan over Jammu and Kashmir that have been overlooked by more traditional approaches to security studies? Secondly, in what way can this case further our understanding of securitisation and thus contribute to the development of the theory? In this article, I have argued that, much like a two-act play, India's securitisation of the Pakistani threat occurred in two distinct (speech) acts. The first illocutionary move preceded the extraordinary measure of Indian troops crossing the Line of Control separating Indian- and Pakistani-administered Jammu and Kashmir. The second speech act followed this action and occurred when the Indian state uttered the words 'surgical strikes.' This defies securitisation theory's chronological structure, which posits that the speech act always precedes the implementation of an exceptional measure. Secondly, I suggest that the Copenhagen School's emphasis on the subjective nature of security and on the normative preferability of de-securitisation offers valuable insights on the empirical stalemate that is the Kashmir conflict.

Introduction

Following a September 2016 militant attack on an army base in the town of Uri in Indian-administered Jammu and Kashmir (J&K), Indian officials made a series of statements that directly and implicitly blamed groups operating out of Pakistan, as well as the Pakistani state itself (Ahmad, Phillips, and Berlinger 2016; Nation 2016; Times of India 2016). Later the same month, India's director general of military operations (DGMO), Lt. Gen. Ranbir Singh, announced to the press that 'the Indian Army [had] conducted surgical strikes' in Pakistani-administered J&K '[b]ased on receiving specific and credible inputs that some terrorist teams had positioned themselves at launch pads along [the] Line of Control to carry out infiltration and conduct terrorist strikes.' Ranbir Singh declared that the operation had caused 'significant casualties … to the terrorists and those providing support to them' (*Indian Express* 2016b).

This article sets out to critique India's security discourse surrounding the 'surgical strikes,' using the theoretical framework provided by securitisation. It aims to answer two central questions: First, can securitisation theory provide fresh empirical insights on India's conflict with Pakistan over J&K that have been overlooked by more traditional approaches to security studies? Secondly, in what way can this case further our under-standing of securitisation and thus contribute to the development of the theory?

In this article, I have argued that, much like a two-act play, India's securitisation of the Pakistani threat occurred in two distinct (speech) acts. The first illocutionary move preceded the extraordinary measure of Indian troops crossing the Line of Control (LOC) separating Indian- and Pakistani-administered J&K, which the two countries agreed not to breach in the Simla Agreement of 1972 (Indian Ministry of External Affairs 1972). The second speech act followed this action and occurred when the Indian state uttered the words 'surgical strikes.' This defies securitisation theory's chron-ological structure, which posits that the speech act always precedes the implementation of an exceptional measure. It is remarkable that these two distinct speech acts were used to justify a *single* extraordinary action of crossing the LOC to conduct 'surgical strikes.' There is little reason to believe this is a phenomenon that is limited to non-Western contexts, and in that sense the article does not claim to contribute to this special issue's theoretical agenda of widening the theory to better explain phenomena in the non-West. However, it does claim to have uncovered an interesting case of securitisation that does not fit the theory's linear pattern, through its application of the theory to an empirical case in the non-Western world. In this sense, the article widens securitisation theory by arguing for the possibility of a double speech act that both precedes and follows the extraordinary action – whether in the West or non-West.

Secondly, I suggest that the Copenhagen School's emphasis on the subjective nature of security and on the normative preferability of de-securitisation offers important insights on the empirical stalemate that is the Kashmir conflict. Securitisation theory reveals the subjective nature of India's perception that Pakistan's claim to J&K is an existential threat to India's survival as a state and a nation. In praxeological terms, de-securitisation shows Indian policymakers that they could choose not to securitise the issue and to deal with it through political means instead. The insight about security being subjective is not limited to the securitisation approach; it is, rather, a more general understanding of security within critical security studies. However, securitisation theory takes this point further by arguing that if an issue can be *securitised* through discourse, it can, equally, be *de-securitised* through a shift in discourse. There is a general dearth of critical studies of security in South Asia – analyses of security dynamics in the region tend to be informed by realist approaches. This article contributes to the literature on South Asian security by applying a critical approach such as securitisation to the long-standing India-Pakistan conflict, and more specifically, by highlighting the value of securitisation theory's emphasis on *de-securitisation* for policymaking on the Indian subcontinent.

The remainder of this article is organised into five sections. The first section outlines the contours of securitisation theory and the challenges scholars have encountered in attempting to apply the theory to cases outside the Western world. In the second section, I critically analyse the statements Indian government representatives made in the aftermath of the Uri attack, demonstrating how these speech acts represented securitising moves that sought to construct a threat emanating from Pakistan. The third section considers the Indian operation in Pakistani-administered J&K, and reflects on whether the widespread use of the ambiguous term 'surgical strikes' constituted a second speech act. In the fourth section, I argue that the Copenhagen School's normative preference for de-securitisation offers valuable empirical insights on the seemingly intractable conflict over J&K. Finally, a concluding section pulls together the key findings of the article.

Securitisation theory, democratic bias, and the world's largest democracy

Buzan, Wæver, and de Wilde (1998, 1) justify their development of the concept of securitisation based on the widening of security studies by critical scholars to include non-military threats. Although they are in basic agreement with this widening move, they postulate that there are 'intellectual and political dangers in simply tacking the word *security* onto an ever wider range of issues.'

To address this problem, Buzan, Wæver, and de Wilde (1998, 23–24) reconceptualise 'security' as 'the move that takes politics beyond the established rules of the game and frames the issue either as a special kind of politics or as above politics.' They posit that for something to count as a security issue, it has 'to be staged as [an] existential threat[] to a referent object by a securitizing actor who thereby generates endorsement of emergency measures beyond rules that would otherwise bind' (Buzan, Wæver, and de Wilde 1998, 5). This process is what the Copenhagen School refers to as securitisation.

Thus, securitisation theory contains six key concepts:

> the securitizing actor (i.e. the agent who presents an issue as a threat through a securitizing move), the referent subject (i.e. the entity that is threatening), the referent object (i.e. the entity that is threatened), the audience (the agreement of which is necessary to confer an intersubjective status to the threat), the context and the adoption of distinctive policies ('exceptional' or not) (Balzacq, Léonard, and Ruzicka 2016, 495).

Buzan, Wæver, and de Wilde (1998, 22–23) put forward five sectors in which securitisation may take place. These include the military, the political, the economic, the societal and the environmental. They suggest that in the international context, 'security is about survival,' and securitisation occurs 'when an issue is presented as posing an existential threat to a designated referent object (traditionally, but not necessarily, the state, incorporating government, territory, and society)' (Buzan, Wæver, and de Wilde 1998, 21). Thus, at the international level of analysis, securitisation 'means to present an issue as urgent and existential, as so important that it should not be exposed to the normal haggling of politics but should be dealt with decisively by top leaders prior to other issues' (Buzan, Wæver, and de Wilde 1998, 29).

Several scholars have argued that securitisation theory contains a European bias (Balzacq, Léonard, and Ruzicka 2016, 507; Vuori 2008, 65–66). Wilkinson (2007), for instance, contends that the theory assumes 'that European understandings of society and the state are universal.' Greenwood and Wæver (2013, 485–500) expand the concern about Eurocentrism to one of West-centrism; they apply the theory to Egypt in the context of the Arab Spring and find that the theory assumes a basic level of stability for there to be such a thing as normal politics. In Egypt during the Arab Spring, the whole situation was exceptional, leaving no room for normal politics. This, for Greenwood and Wæver (2013, 501), suggested a Western bias in the theory, because, in their words, 'Western societies no longer confront (nor de facto run their politics on real expectations of) this kind of ultra-political moment.'

Similarly, Holbraad and Pederson (2012, 193) take exception to securitisation theory's distinction between 'ordinary and special politics,' which, they argue, assumes a rule-based order and reveals the theory's liberal ontological underpinnings. Holbraad and Pederson (2012, 168–94) clarify that their point is not that securitisation theory 'applies best to liberal democracies (although this may be the case), but that it involves certain political ontological premises associated with liberalist thought,' which is problematic when studying non-Western contexts where the form of governance is non-liberal, such as their case study of Cuba.

Vuori's (2008, 69) perspective contrasts with that of Holbraad and Pederson (2012), in that he points out 'that all societies have "rules," [which] are products of historical and social contingencies.' He also differs from Holbraad and Pederson in his clear articulation of the democratic bias within securitisation theory, arguing that scholars have understood securitisation to be a way 'of moving certain issues beyond the democratic process of government' (Vuori 2008, 66). Vuori's (2008, 66–68) point is that securitisation *does* take place in non-democratic settings, because all governments – democratic or non-democratic – require some amount of political legitimacy to survive.

The question of securitisation theory's success in explaining events in non-democratic contexts is also addressed by Wilkinson (2007, 20), who postulates that there may be limits to free speech in such contexts, 'especially for non-state actors,' which renders securitisation theory's linear construction and emphasis on the speech act problematic. Wilkinson (2007, 12) highlights the possibility that securitisation may take place through mediums other than speech, such as 'words, images and actions.' In addition, she suggests that,

> Contrary to the linear dynamic described by securitization, starting with a securitizing actor who then constructs a referent object and threat narrative to be accepted or rejected, the process may in practice start at any point, with the component parts developing simultaneously and contributing to each other's construction (Wilkinson 2007, 20).

For Wilkinson (2007, 22), in fact, '"sufficient action" may replace or supplement the speech-act as the driving logic in the process of securitization.'

In the context of these conversations about securitisation theory's European – and, more broadly, Western – assumptions, and whether the theory can unproblematically explain events in non-Western, non-liberal and non-democratic countries, India presents an interesting case. As shown above, scholars who have questioned the Western assumptions of securitisation theory have tended to focus on what happens when the theory is applied to non-democratic or non-liberal settings in the non-West. India, however, constitutes a case of a non-Western democratic state. According to Mishra (2012, 33), India is a non-liberal democracy, while Mitra (2013, 227) proposes that India has combined 'western liberal democratic forms and non-western cultures.' Thus, India provides an intriguing case for studying securitisation. In the next section, I will employ securitisation theory to explore how political and military actors in India securitised the threat emanating from Pakistan in the aftermath of the September 2016 attack in Uri.

Act one: the Uri attack

As noted above, the process of securitisation requires six elements: a securitising actor, a referent subject, a referent object, an audience, a context, and the legitimisation of 'emergency measures or other steps that would not have been possible had the discourse not taken the form of existential threats, point of no return, and necessity' (Buzan, Wæver, and de Wilde 1998, 25). When the securitising actor frames the referent subject as an existential threat, this constitutes a *securitising move*. However, for this securitising move to turn into a successful securitisation, it needs to be accepted by the audience (Buzan, Wæver, and de Wilde 1998, 25).

In the military sector, the most common referent object is the state and, more implicitly, the nation (Buzan, Wæver, and de Wilde 1998, 36). When the state is the referent object, the securitising actor is often also the state speaking 'through its authorized representatives' (Buzan, Wæver, and de Wilde 1998, 42). In this section I will show how the Indian state, through government officials, sought to frame Pakistan and Pakistan-based militants – the referent subject – as an existential threat to the Indian state and nation by appealing to an audience consisting of the citizens of India. I do so by referring to official statements made after the attack in Uri, relying on the Indian news media, the Twitter accounts of government officials, and an Indian defence journal as primary sources. Following Jackson (2005, 7), I use bold typeface to emphasise significant words in the discourse of the Indian state. Additionally, I discuss how the securitising move took place in the context of a surge in violent unrest against Indian rule in the Kashmir valley, as well as exploring the role of the national audience in accepting the securitising move. The emergency measures that were legitimised through this process of securitisation are dealt with in the subsequent section.

Analysing the Indian discourse on Uri

The attack on the military base in Uri took place on the morning of 18 September; nineteen soldiers and all four militants were killed (Al Jazeera 2016; Safi 2016; *Scroll.in* 2016b). The same day, President Pranab Mukherjee tweeted, 'India will not be cowed down by such attacks, **we will thwart the evil designs of terrorists and their backers**' (Twitter post, 18 September 2016 [3:55 a.m.], accessed 22 May 2017, https://twitter.com/ RashtrapatiBhvn/status/777461121137582080). Prime Minister Narendra Modi also took to Twitter to 'strongly condemn the cowardly terror attack in Uri' and 'assure the **nation** that **those behind this despicable attack will not go unpunished**' (Twitter post, 18 September 2016 [1:01 a.m.], accessed 22 May 2017, https://twitter.com/narendra modi/status/777417302912430080?lang=en).

Rajnath Singh, the minister for home affairs, tweeted: '**Pakistan is a terrorist state** and it should be identified and isolated as such' (Twitter post, 18 September 2016 [1:54 a.m.], accessed 22 May 2017, https://twitter.com/rajnathsingh/status/ 777430703726211072?lang=en). In a subsequent tweet, he added, 'I am deeply disap-pointed with **Pakistan's continued and direct support to terrorism and terrorist** groups' (Twitter post, 18 September 2016 [1:56 a.m.], accessed 22 May 2017, https://twitter.com/rajnathsingh/status/777431140474818562?lang=en). Meanwhile, Finance Minister Arun Jaitley promised that the '[p]erpetrators of Uri terror attack **shall be punished**' (Twitter post, 18 September 2016 [5:45 a.m.], accessed 22 May 2017, https://twitter.com/arunjaitley/status/777488820195332096). Media reports also quoted Jaitley as declaring, 'It is clear that **our neighbour is using terror** to create menace in our country' (*Scroll.in* 2016c).

Also on 18 September, Ranbir Singh told the media that '[i]nitial reports indicate[d] that the slain terrorists belong[ed] to **Jaish-e-Mohammed** tanzeem,' adding that 'the terrorists had some items with **Pakistani markings**.' He said he had 'spoken to Pakistan DGMO and conveyed our serious concerns' (Indian Defence Review 2016).

Then, on 26 September, External Affairs Minister Sushma Swaraj used her speech at the United Nations General Assembly (UNGA) as an opportunity 'to ask – **who is behind this and who benefits from it**? Terrorists do not own banks or weapons factories, so let us ask the real question: **who finances these terrorists, who arms them and provides sanctuaries**?' More directly, Swaraj declared:

> In our midst, **there are nations that still speak the language of terrorism, that nurture it, peddle it, and export it**. To shelter terrorists has become their calling card. **We must identify these nations and hold them to account. These nations**, in which UN declared terrorists roam freely, lead processions and deliver their poisonous sermons of hate with impunity, **are as culpable as the very terrorists they harbour**. Such countries should have no place in the comity of nations.

To alleviate any doubts as to which nation she was referring to, Swaraj went on to complain that Pakistan had responded to India's friendly overtures with 'Pathankot, Bahadur Ali, and Uri,' and spoke about '**Pakistan's complicity in cross-border terror**' aimed at 'obtain[ing] the territory it covets ... Jammu and Kashmir' (*Indian Express* 2016c).

Thus, representatives of the executive and military branches of the Indian government used a combination of speech and words to frame Pakistan-based militant groups and, by extension, the Pakistani state as a threat to the Indian state. The securitising actor was, thus, the Indian state, speaking through its authorised representatives. Mukherjee's assertion that '**India** w[ould] not be cowed down by such attacks,' and Jaitley's reference to the 'menace in **our country**' suggest that the Indian state was also the referent object. Mukherjee referred to 'the evil designs of **terrorists**,' and Ranbir Singh to '**Jaish-e-Mohammed** tanzeem,' indicating that the Pakistan-based Jaish-e-Mohammed (JEM) militant group was being framed as the referent subject. However, the discourse extended the referent subject to the Pakistani state, as is evident in Mukherjee's tweet about 'terrorists and **their backers**,' Rajnath Singh's comments about '**Pakistan** [being] a **terrorist state**' and '**Pakistan's** continued and direct support to terrorism and terrorist groups,' Jaitley's remark about '**our neighbour**,' and Ranbir Singh's mention of '**Pakistani** markings.' Swaraj's rhetoric at the UNGA more systematically constructed Pakistan as the referent subject, as demonstrated by her utterances about '**nations** that still speak the language of terrorism, that nurture it, peddle it, and export it,' '**nations** in which UN declared terrorists roam freely, lead processions and deliver their poisonous sermons of hate with impunity,' and '**Pakistan's** complicity in cross-border terror.'

Swaraj also drew a link between the attack in Uri and the dispute between Pakistan and India over J&K. Her statements about J&K allude to the violence in the Indian-administered Kashmir valley amidst which the 18 September militant attack took place. Amnesty International (2016) wrote on 12 September that at least seventy-eight people had been killed in Indian-administered J&K in violent protests since the security forces on 8 July killed Burhan Wani of the Hizbul Mujahideen militant separatist group. The human-rights organisation observed that the '[s]ecurity forces [we]re using arbitrary and excessive force in response to protests in Jammu and Kashmir, violating international standards and worsening the human rights crisis in the state.'

As Buzan, Wæver, and de Wilde (1998, 29) note, securitisation 'is always a political choice.' By choosing to securitise the Uri attack in the manner in which they did, Indian state representatives swept the Kashmiri context within which the incident occurred under the carpet. Furthermore, by making the mental leap from blaming the JEM to blaming Pakistan, the Indian state officials denied agency to Kashmir-focused militant groups, which, according to Stern (2003, 108), have access to other sources of funding, and 'are no longer beholden to a single sponsor[, which] has emboldened them to the degree that they are prepared publicly to threaten Pakistan's leadership.'

(De)constructing an existential threat

While the previous subsection established that the Indian state as a securitising actor constructed a threat to itself emanating from Pakistan and militant groups operating from its territory, it is not clear that an *existential* threat was being portrayed. To comprehend the existential nature of the perceived threat, it is necessary to dig a little deeper, and to refer to Buzan, Wæver, and de Wilde's (1998, 36) assertion that '[f]or a state, survival is about sovereignty, and for a nation it is about identity.'

By assuming that it was another state, and not a non-state actor, that was the 'real' perpetrator of the attack, the incident was framed as a violation of India's sovereignty over Indian-administered J&K. Furthermore, as Bose (2003, 9) explains, the Indian nationalist discourse considers Kashmir to be 'India's *atoot ang* (integral part),' which signals that holding on to Kashmir has become a part of India's national identity. At her UNGA speech, Swaraj repeated the Indian refrain 'that Jammu and Kashmir is an **integral part** of India and will always remain so' (*Indian Express* 2016c). Additionally, Snedden (2013, 221) points out that the Kashmir dispute is partly about 'competing and irreconcilable ideas of nationhood, respectively based around the predominance of secularism or religion.' His argument demonstrates why it is so important for India to maintain control of the Muslim-majority Kashmir region of J&K, which is where disgruntlement over the status quo is centred. Keeping Kashmir has something to do with India's identity as a secular state, and its ideological competition with the two-nation theory that is Pakistan's foundational doctrine, which insists that Muslims and Hindus comprise distinct nations (Ganguly 2015).

In this way, the subtext of the Indian narrative following the Uri assault was that India's sovereignty and identity were being threatened. This implied threat to the survival of the Indian state and nation in their current form was understood by the intended audience of the Indian state's speech act: the Indian people. It is to this audience that the next subsection turns.

The role of the audience

Although Swaraj addressed her UNGA speech to the member states of the United Nations (UN), that is, to the international society of states, the primary audience for India's speech act was the citizens of India. This adheres to a common pattern observed by Vuori (2008, 72), who notes that in most of the literature on securitisation, it is 'the citizens of a state' who are considered the audience for a securitising move.

The framework of securitisation theory predicates successful securitisation upon audience acceptance (Balzacq 2005, 173; Balzacq, Léonard, and Ruzicka 2016, 499; Buzan, Wæver, and de Wilde 1998, 25; Côté 2016, 542; Vuori 2008, 70). In this sense, securitisation is conceived of as an inter-subjective process negotiated between the securitising actor and the audience (Balzacq, Léonard, and Ruzicka 2016, 499; Buzan, Wæver, and de Wilde 1998, 26; Côté 2016, 541). However, several authors have discerned a tension between the Copenhagen School's conceptualisation of securitisation on the one hand as a speech act, or a self-referential practice by the securitising actor, and on the other hand as an inter-subjective process involving both the securitising actor and the audience (Balzacq 2005, 177; Balzacq, Léonard, and Ruzicka 2016, 501; Côté 2016, 542). It has been argued that although the Copenhagen School claims that the audience is essential to securitisation, the concept of the audience has been under-developed, the audience has effectively been ignored in the securitisation framework, and the theory consequently leans towards an understanding of securitisation as a self-referential practice in which the illocutionary act is sufficient to produce securitisation (Balzacq 2005, 177; Côté 2016, 542).

The identification of this problem leads to a distinction between active and passive audiences. Côté (2016, 551) argues that while the theoretical literature on securitisation characterises 'the audience as a passive receiver of security arguments,' in fact, 'audiences are active participants in securitization processes with the potential to undertake independent actions that can produce tangible security effects.' Vuori (2008, 70) introduces the idea of 'active passivity' on the part of the audience, suggesting that while elections are one way of determining the audience's support for a securitising move, a lack of support can be demonstrated through protests, riots, revolts, coups, or non-participation. Audience inaction, on the other hand, indicates its acceptance of a securitisation. Balzacq (2005, 185) suggests that formal audience legitimation can be obtained through a vote in the national parliament or the UN Security Council, for example – although this contradicts the notion that securitisation conveys an urgency that allows 'the normal bargaining processes of' politics to be transcended (Buzan, Wæver, and de Wilde 1998, 4).

In the case of the Indian state's securitisation of the threat from Pakistan, no parliamentary vote was held, but at the same time, there were no signs of dissent from the populace, even after the army announced its 'surgical strikes.' Balzacq (2005,

186) points to the importance of 'collective memory and the *Zeitgeist* condition' in determining 'how a given community perceives and symbolizes urgency,' while Buzan, Wæver, and de Wilde (1998, 60) contend that 'the existence of a bitter history and memories of previous wars facilitate the process of securitization.' Seen in this light, the bitter history of the India-Pakistan relationship and the emotional charge of the issue for the Indian public is likely to have supported the audience's acquiescence in the state's securitisation of the Uri attack. Indeed, the ruling Bharatiya Janata Party (BJP) swept state-level elections held in February-March 2017 in Uttar Pradesh, India's most populous state, in the lead-up to which BJP politicians flaunted the 'surgical strikes' (*Firstpost* 2016; *Hindu* 2016a; Shukla 2016; Vivek 2017). This provides an indication of the Indian state's success in obtaining the national audience's acceptance of its securitising move, despite the difficulty of measuring audience legitimisation.

Act two: the surgical strikes

Following the Indian state's speech acts of 18–26 September, which occurred in the context of the 18 September Uri attack and the general volatility of the Kashmir valley since July, the Indian DGMO announced on 29 September that,

> Based on receiving specific and credible inputs that some terrorist teams had positioned themselves at **launch pads** along Line of Control to carryout infiltration and conduct **terrorist strikes** inside Jammu and Kashmir and in various **metros in other states**, the Indian Army conducted **surgical strikes** at several of these launch pads to pre-empt **infiltration by terrorists** (*Indian Express* 2016b).

In this section, I argue that this reference to terrorist 'launch pads,' imminent 'terrorist strikes' and the Indian army's 'surgical strikes' constituted a second speech act that *followed* the extraordinary action of Indian troops crossing the LOC. First, though, it is important to establish what is normal in the context of India, Pakistan and the LOC.

Pending the resolution of the dispute over J&K, the LOC, which runs through the state, serves as the de-facto border between Pakistan and India in J&K. Exchanges of fire between Pakistani and Indian soldiers stationed along the LOC occur regularly, and can be considered normal in this context. India also routinely accuses Pakistan of permitting militants to infiltrate into Indian-administered territory via the LOC. However, it is not normal for the national army of either side to breach the LOC, which both sides agreed to respect in the 1972 Simla Agreement, and a violation of which effectively constitutes an act of war (Indian Ministry of External Affairs 1972). Hence, the Indian army's claim of having conducted 'surgical strikes' across the LOC, inside Pakistani-administered J&K, qualifies as an extraordinary measure that deviates from the normal politics of the subcontinent.

Ranbir Singh's statement on the 'surgical strikes' announced that the Indian army had 'recovered various stores including GPS and items that clearly indicate their origins in **Pakistan**.' The DGMO also stated that 'captured terrorists hailing from **Pakistan** or Pakistan Occupied Kashmir have confessed to their training and arming in **Pakistan or territory under its control**' (*Indian Express* 2016b), although the Indian National Investigative Agency (NIA) eventually in February 2017 dropped charges against two schoolchildren from Pakistani-administered J&K who were arrested on 21 September on suspicion of having acted as guides for the four militants. The NIA concluded that the children had run away from home after arguing with their parents about schoolwork and accidentally crossed the LOC, although the authorities had previously said that the children had confessed to working for the JEM. The confession was brought into question when the Pakistan-based Lashkar-e-Taiba (LET) militant group claimed responsibility for the attack, and the NIA decided that it was, indeed, the LET, and not the JEM, that was the perpetrator (*Scroll.in* 2016a; Swami 2017).

The second speech act, then, involved the same securitising actor – the Indian state speaking through its representative – and referent subject – Pakistan. The mention of a threat not only to 'Jammu and Kashmir,' but also to 'various metros in other states,' suggested that the referent object encompassed *all* the states of India, or the totality of the Indian state. That Ranbir Singh's statement was addressed to the Indian press indicates that the audience, too, was still the Indian people.

This second speech act was notable for two reasons. First, it *followed* the action, whereas securitisation theory assumes a linear progression from speech act to action. Secondly, the use of the phrase 'surgical strikes' produced a special kind of speech act, as I will show below.

'What is a surgical strike?'

In a fascinating article about the US administration's securitisation of Iraq in 2002–2003 through the assertion that the Iraqi regime possessed 'weapons of mass destruction,' Oren and Solomon (2015, 313) 'seek to reinvigorate' the illocutionary aspect of securitisation theory by arguing that 'the utterances of securitising actors [consist] not in arguments so much as in repetitive spouting of ambiguous phrases (WMD, rogue states, ethnic cleansing).' Oren and Solomon (2015, 313) 'further propose that audience acceptance consists not in persuasion so much as in joining the securitising actors in a ritualised chanting of the securitising phrase.'

The ambiguity of the phrase 'surgical strikes' was highlighted by the response of Pakistan's Inter Services Public Relations (ISPR) to the Indian claim. In a press release on 29 September, the ISPR declared:

> There has been no surgical strike by India, instead there had been cross LOC fire initiated and conducted by India which is existential phenomenon. The notion of surgical strike linked to alleged terrorist bases is an illusion being deliberately generated by Indian to create false effects. This quest by Indian establishment to create media hype by rebranding cross border fire as surgical strike is fabrication of truth (Inter Services Public Relations 2016).

Meanwhile, Indian and Pakistani news outlets mulled over the meaning of the term (*Aaj Tak* 2016; Guruswamy 2016; *InKhabar* 2016; Rehman 2016; Roy 2016), revealing it to be what Oren and Solomon (2015, 322) refer to as 'a securitising phrase (with ultimately contestable meaning).' Oren and Solomon (2015, 332) point out that many Americans had no idea what a weapon of mass destruction was before 2002 and 'had barely heard the term.' Additionally, even a concerted effort to pin down its meaning would prove to be a challenge. As Oren and Solomon (2015, 324) put it, 'Audience members cannot quite check the accuracy of the securitising phrases they hear because … these phrases are typically ambiguous (what exactly is a "rogue state"? a "weapon of mass destruction"?) and new to most people (how many people were familiar with "ethnic cleansing" before it became a stock phrase in the 1990s?).'

Despite its ambiguity, Guruswamy (2016) observed that 'the term "surgical strikes" has dominated prime-time debates, social media chatter and dinner-table conversations.' Unwittingly, Guruswamy was echoing Oren and Solomon (2015, 324), who posit that

> [s]ecuritisation succeeds when the 'mantras' repeated by securitising actors in speeches and news releases jump to the pages of the print media, skip into the wording of frequently-asked and widely-reported opinion poll questions, reverberate through talk shows, news broadcasts, and other electronic media programming, echo throughout the blogosphere, and, increasingly in recent years, flood the social media. Mediated by these media forms, the securitising phrase infiltrates and even infects everyday talk, including, for example, dinner party conversations, chatter around water coolers, and discussions in school and college classrooms.

The fact that India is a multilingual country where a multitude of languages are spoken could have potentially impeded the securitising effect of the English phrase 'surgical strikes.' However, it is common for Indians to speak more than one language and to creatively combine languages in everyday parlance, and a scan through Hindi news sources suggests that the local-language news media adopted the English terminology of the 'surgical strikes' (*Aaj Tak* 2016; *InKhabar* 2016; Ranjan 2017).

Thus, to paraphrase Oren and Solomon (2015, 316), the collective incantation of the phrase 'surgical strikes' by the Indian administration, media and public as a ritualistic choral chant served to securitise the Pakistani state *after* the exceptional measure of breaching the LOC had taken place. The Indian army's depiction of terrorists at their 'launch pads' on the verge of crossing over into Indian territory constructed a threat that retroactively justified the 'surgical strikes,' even as the Pakistani state denied they had ever taken place. This leads to the question – *did they really take place?* The next subsection attempts to solve what Hussain (2017) refers to as the '[m]ystery of the "surgical strike."'

The 'mystery of the "surgical strike"'

Buzan, Wæver and de Wilde (1998, 25) opine that securitisation does not require the implementation of an emergency measure – the legitimisation of such measures or other exceptional steps through discourse is sufficient. Even so, this article's argument that the Indian state's securitisation of Pakistan occurred in two steps – a speech act before as well as after the exceptional action – is based on the assumption that such an action actually occurred. Pakistan's official denial of the surgical strikes, however, raises a doubt as to what really happened. This subsection is an attempt at solving the mystery, even if it is impossible to conclusively establish what occurred on the morning of 29 September.

I refer to three key news reports. The first is an *India Today* article that claims 'exclusive details of the inside story behind the surgical strikes.' The article reports that twenty-five Indian commandos crossed the LOC in Dhruv Advanced Light Helicopters and dropped into 'enemy territory.' The commandos reportedly crawled three kilometres into Pakistani-administered J&K, heading for seven terrorist 'launch pads' in the 'Bhimbar, Kel, Tattapani and Leepa areas.' The article goes on to describe how the Indian soldiers 'completely destroyed' three of their targets, killing 'at least 50 terrorists' as well as two Pakistani soldiers (Negi 2016).

In the second article, a *New York Times* journalist recounts how the Pakistani military flew a group of reporters into Bhimber district in Pakistani-administered J&K to verify whether any 'surgical strikes' had taken place. The *New York Times* reporter spoke to a villager called Malik Rustom from Mandhole village, near which one of the militant bases the Indian army claims to have targeted is supposed to have been located. Rustom reportedly said that the Indian troops had not left their posts and crossed the LOC, while '[a] group of villagers standing nearby nodded in agreement' (Masood 2016).

The third report is by Ilyas Khan (2016), a *BBC* reporter who visited the LOC and spoke to local people and police officers in Pakistani-administered J&K. Ilyas Khan's investigation suggested that what had occurred was a ground assault that targeted posts of the Pakistani military, with Indian soldiers crossing about a kilometre into Pakistani-administered territory. Although no commandos were airdropped, Indian troops reportedly destroyed a Pakistani army post in the Madarpur-Titrinot area of Poonch. They also blew up an army post and mosque near Mundakali village in the Leepa valley, as well as two more military bases further up the mountains. In addition, Ilyas Khan was told that the Indians had entered the Dudhnial area in the Neelum valley. While two Pakistani soldiers were killed, Ilyas Khan was unable to find much evidence of militant bases having been hit. He found that militant camps in Bhimber, Leepa and Neelum appeared intact, although 'one or two damaged structures' in Dudhnial might possibly have been militant bases that were struck on 29 September.

These divergent accounts suggest that, as Ilyas Khan (2016) puts it, 'There is no conclusive evidence to prove either side's claims – the truth probably lies somewhere in the middle.' However, Ilyas Khan's account seems the most convincing, not least because Negi's (2016) 'inside story' is likely to have been obtained from sources within the Indian establishment, while Masood (2016) appears to have been flown into Bhimber in a Pakistani military helicopter, which suggests he may have been exposed to a selective rendering of the story. Ilyas Khan's account also seems to tread the middle ground between Negi and Masood's versions.

De-securitising the India-Pakistan conflict over Kashmir

For Buzan, Wæver, and de Wilde (1998, 4–29), de-securitisation – 'the shifting of issues out of emergency mode and into the normal bargaining processes of the political sphere' – is the ideal in the long run. Securitisation theory, with its understanding that security is subjectively determined by actors, and that securitising an issue or accepting a securitisation is a political choice, opens up the possibility for such a transformation from securitisation to normal politics (Buzan, Wæver, and de Wilde 1998, 29–31).

In the case of the India-Pakistan conflict over J&K, a shift from security politics to normal politics would involve engaging in a political dialogue over the issue with the aim of resolving it through 'the normal bargaining processes of the political sphere'

(Buzan, Wæver, and de Wilde 1998, 4). The Pakistani foreign secretary in August 2016 invited his Indian counterpart to talks on J&K, to which Indian Foreign Secretary S. Jaishankar responded that J&K was 'an integral part of India where Pakistan has no locus standi,' but that India was open to discussing 'aspects related to cross-border terrorism [that] are central to the current situation in J&K' (Haidar and Bhattacharjee 2016; *Hindu* 2016b; *Indian Express* 2016a).

In April 2017, in the context of continuing violent protests in the Kashmir valley since the July 2016 killing of Wani, Kashmiri politician Farooq Abdullah told an Indian journalist:

> The situation is quite bad, and don't tell me Pakistan is not a party to this problem. Whether you like it or not, you have to talk to Pakistan. If you want to beat the threat of the terrorists, then you better start talking now… . You are losing Kashmir. You better wake up, and start thinking on not a military solution, but a political way (Udayakumar 2017).

Later the same month, the Indian Supreme Court advised the central government to engage in a dialogue with the Kashmiri demonstrators; the administration replied that it 'would come to the negotiation table only if the legally recognised stakeholders parti-cipate in the dialogue and not with the separatist elements who rake up the issue of accession or Azadi in Kashmir' (*Indian Express* 2017; Mahapatra 2017; *NDTV* 2017).

As discussed in a previous section, Pakistan's claim to J&K is perceived by India as an existential threat to its sovereignty as a state and its identity as a nation. However, if an 'issue becomes a security issue [not] necessarily because a real existential threat exists but because the issue is presented as such a threat,' then policymakers have the choice of presenting the issue differently, and thereby transforming the situation (Buzan, Wæver, and de Wilde 1998, 24). If India were to negotiate a settlement of the Kashmir conflict through talks with Pakistan and Kashmiris,[1] even if this involved losing some territory, it would probably *enhance* India's sense of security by radically defusing tensions in the subcontinent.

Despite the seemingly obvious advantages of actively pursuing peace, the key actors in the conflict continue to neurotically reproduce patterns of destructive behaviour. This substantiates Buzan, Wæver, and de Wilde's (1998, 70) claim that historical, geographical and political factors can combine to create a mutually reinforcing pattern of securitisa-tion that is difficult to dislodge.

Browning and Joenniemi (2017) link the challenge posed by entrenched cases of securitisation to the concepts of self, identity and ontological security. They explain that most of the literature on ontological security assumes that international actors 'prefer stability and certitude to change, [and] are therefore liable to reassert established patterns of behaviour, routines and identities, rather than embrace change precisely because of the perceived need and value of maintaining stable self-concepts' (Browning and Joenniemi 2017, 31–32). Thus, states may prefer that a conflictual relationship continue, 'because the enduring conflict reaffirms a sense of certainty about the identity of both oneself and the other' (Browning and Joenniemi 2017, 34).

While this explanation seems to encapsulate the unending Pakistan-India conflict, Browning and Joenniemi (2017, 35) are clear that an actor needs to be able to some-times deal with change and to adapt its identity, rather than neurotically holding on to a conflictual but stable situation. The literature Browning and Joenniemi (2017, 37) critique suggests that with long-running conflicts (such as Kashmir), the possibility of arriving at a rational resolution becomes diluted by the fact that the conflict has 'come to frame the identities of the parties,' while '[r]esolution would ... require identity transformation.' For conflict resolution, what is needed is 'flexibility, a willingness to rethink both the identity of the self and the other,' which causes anxiety 'about whether identities can remain stable, and therefore about what the future world will look like, what our identity will be in the absence of the enemy, what will we do, will we any longer be who we think we are.'

However, these arguments are problematic for Browning and Joenniemi (2017, 38) because they naturalise securitisation. Like Buzan, Wæver, and de Wilde (1998), Browning and Joenniemi (2017, 38) insist that there are always options other than securitisation. They suggest that securitisation can cause as much anxiety as de-securitisation, because the initial process of securitisation marks a shift 'from a former situation when identity was not securitized and was more open.' Securitisation 'entails a movement of rigidifying, closing down and bordering,' while 'desecuritizations may actually suggest the existence of a self possessing the reflexive ability to step back, employ alternative channels of articulation and opt for some other identity – abilities ... that are actually precisely at the heart of ontological security' (Browning and Joenniemi 2017, 39).

In South Asian philosophical terms, Indian Sufi sheikh Hazrat Azad Rasool (2002, 35) points to the potential for positively transforming the self when he writes, 'When one has transformed the lower self (an-nafs an-ammārah), the beauty one perceives and the love one feels is comprehensive, energizing, and spiritually fulfilling.' Singers such as Pakistan's Nusrat Fateh Ali Khan (1989; 1992) and Abida Parveen and Rahat Fateh Ali Khan (2014), have beautifully rendered Indian Sufi poet Amir Khusro's 'Chaap Tilak,' which celebrates the joyous possibilities in surrendering one's identity. These examples demonstrate that the intellectual foundations for the conceptualisation of a self who possesses the ability to consciously choose a different identity already exist in the shared philosophical, cultural and spiritual traditions of India and Pakistan.

Conclusion

This article makes two main contributions. On the theoretical side, it has shown that securitisation can sometimes occur through not one, but two speech acts. This was demonstrated by arguing that the Indian state securitised its traditional enemy, Pakistan, through a securitising discourse that preceded the implementation of the extraordinary measure of Indian soldiers crossing the LOC. This was then followed by a second speech act that both described and justified the exceptional action by once again constructing an existential threat.

At the empirical level of analysis, I have argued that if India's perception of an existential threat emanating from Pakistan's claim to J&K is understood as subjective, then Indian policymakers have the political choice of opting to pursue a path of de-securitisation. I have suggested that moving the issue from the realm of security to the political negotiating table would enhance rather than detract from India's (and Pakistan's) sense of security.

In addition to these two central claims, the article makes several observations that contribute to the literature on securitisation as well as the Pakistan-India conflict over Kashmir. First, it notes that Indian officials used a combination of speech and words (in the form of Twitter posts) to convey their securitising narrative to their audience, supporting Wilkinson's (2007) point about the Copenhagen School's overemphasis on speech. Secondly, it draws on Oren and Solomon (2015) to show that the words 'surgical strikes,' through their vagueness, themselves constituted a speech act that involved the securitising actor and audience joining in the ritualistic chanting of the ambiguous phrase. By applying Oren and Solomon's idea to a multilingual context, the article demonstrates that catchy phrases can be effectively deployed by securitising actors even in linguistically diverse non-Western contexts. Thirdly, the article suggests that the resistance of the Kashmir conflict to resolution is a result of the identities of the Indian and Pakistani states becoming dependent upon their conflictual relationship. Even so, I have argued, Browning and Joenniemi (2017) are right to highlight the potential actors possess to flexibly adapt their identities, and this is not a new idea for Indians and Pakistanis, as I have revealed through my references to Sufi literature from the subcontinent.

Note

1. As Snedden (2013, 220) points out, the Kashmir valley is the only region of J&K where dissatisfaction with the status quo of being administered by India runs deep. In contrast, Jammu and Ladakh appear content to be a part of India, while Poonch and Gilgit-Baltistan appear satisfied with being with Pakistan.

Acknowledgements

I am grateful to the participants of the workshop on Securitisation in the Non-West held at Lancaster University in March 2017 for their encouraging feedback on an initial draft of this article. I am further thankful to Dr. Simon Mabon for his thoughtful and detailed comments on a previous draft, and to Mona Kanwal Sheikh for reviewing a successive version of the paper.

Disclosure statement

No potential conflict of interest was reported by the author.

References

Aaj Tak. 2016. "Sena ne kiya PoK par surgical strike, janein kya hai ye?" October 2. Accessed May 24 2017. http://aajtak.intoday.in/education/story/what-is-surgical-strike-indian-army-military-attack-pok-after-uri-attack-1-890248.html.

Ahmad, M., R. Phillips, and J. Berlinger. 2016. "Soldiers Killed in Army Base Attack in Indian-Administered Kashmir." *CNN*, September 19. Accessed May 2 2017. http://edition.cnn.com/2016/09/18/asia/india-kashmir-attack/.

Al Jazeera. 2016. "More than 20 Dead in Attack on Army Base in Kashmir." September 18. Accessed May 8 2017. http://www.aljazeera.com/news/2016/09/20-dead-attack-army-base-kashmir-160918055803596.html.

Amnesty International. 2016. *Global Standards on Police Use of Force Violated in Kashmir*. New Delhi: Amnesty International India. Accessed May 23 2017. https://www.amnesty.org.in/show/news/global-standards-on-police-use-of-force-violated-in-kashmir/.

Balzacq, T. 2005. "The Three Faces of Securitization: Political Agency, Audience and Context." *European Journal of International Relations* 11 (2): 171–201. doi:10.1177/1354066105052960.

Balzacq, T., S. Léonard, and J. Ruzicka. 2016. "'Securitization' Revisited: Theory and Cases." *International Relations* 30 (4): 494–531. doi:10.1177/0047117815596590.

Bose, S. 2003. *Kashmir: Roots of Conflict, Paths to Peace*. Cambridge, MA: Harvard University Press.

Browning, C. S., and P. Joenniemi. 2017. "Ontological Security, Self-Articulation and the Securitization of Identity." *Cooperation and Conflict* 52 (1): 31–47. doi:10.1177/0010836716653161.

Buzan, B., O. Wæver, and J. de Wilde. 1998. *Security: A New Framework for Analysis*. Boulder, CO: Lynne Rienner.

Côté, A. 2016. "Agents without Agency: Assessing the Role of the Audience in Securitization Theory." *Security Dialogue* 47 (6): 541–558. doi:10.1177/0967010616672150.

Firstpost. 2016. "Posters in UP Lauding BJP for Surgical Strikes Show Everyone Is Politicising the Issue." October 6. Accessed May 12 2017. http://www.firstpost.com/politics/posters-in-up-lauding-bjp-for-surgical-strikes-show-oppn-isnt-alone-in-politicising-issue-3037152.html.

Ganguly, S. 2015. "Affirming the Two-Nation Theory." *Deccan Chronicle*, January 3. Accessed May 12 2017. http://www.deccanchronicle.com/150103/commentary-columnists/article/affirming-two-nation-theory.

Greenwood, M. T., O. Wæver, J. P. Burgess, and C. M. Constantinou. 2013. "Copenhagen-Cairo on A Roundtrip: A Security Theory Meets the Revolution." *Security Dialogue* 44 (5–6): 485–506. Accessed December 23 2016. http://journals.sagepub.com.ezproxy.lancs.ac.uk/doi/pdf/10.1177/0967010613502573. doi:10.1177/0967010613502573.

Guruswamy, M. 2016. "What a Surgical Strike Really Is (And Why the Army Action across the LOC May Not Qualify as One." *Scroll.in*, October 7. Accessed May 24 2017. https://scroll.in/article/818398/what-a-surgical-strike-really-is-and-why-the-army-action-across-the-loc-may-not-qualify-as-one.

Haidar, S., and K. Bhattacharjee. 2016. "India Willing to Talk to Pakistan on Terror, Not Kashmir." *Hindu*, August 17. Accessed May 25 2017. http://www.thehindu.com/news/national/India-willing-to-talk-to-Pakistan-on-terror-not-Kashmir/article14574585.ece.

Hindu. 2016a. "BJP Banners across UP Laud 'Surgical Strikes.'" October 5. Accessed May 12 2017. http://www.thehindu.com/news/national/other-states/BJP-banners-across-U.P.-laud-%E2%80%98surgical-strikes%E2%80%99/article15425612.ece.

Hindu. 2016b. "Pakistan Invites India for Talks on Kashmir." August 15. Accessed May 25 2017. http://www.thehindu.com/news/national/Pakistan-invites-India-for-talks-on-Kashmir/article14571296.ece.

Holbraad, M., and M. A. Pederson. 2012. "Revolutionary Securitization: An Anthropological Extension of Securitization Theory." *International Theory* 4 (2): 165–197. Accessed January 6 2017. https://www-cambridge-org.ezproxy.lancs.ac.uk/core/services/aop-cambridge-core/content/view/4BEEBFDBD34816889510C13C5EF736F9/S1752971912000061a.pdf/div-class-title-revolutionary-securitization-an-anthropological-extension-of-securitization-theory-div.pdf. doi:10.1017/S1752971912000061.

Hussain, Z. 2017. "Mystery of the 'Surgical Strike.'" *Dawn*, January 13. Accessed May 24 2017. https://www.dawn.com/news/1288083.

Indian Defence Review. 2016. "Uri Terror Attack: Statement by DGMO to Media." September 18. Accessed May 22 2017. http://www.indiandefencereview.com/news/uri-terror-attack-statement-by-dgmo-to-media/.

Indian Express. 2016a. "India Rejects Pakistan's Invitation for Talks, Says Ready to Discuss Cross-Border Terrorism Not Kashmir." August 17. Accessed May 25 2017. http://indianexpress.com/article/india/india-news-india/jammu-and-kashmir-india-pakistan-foreign-secretary-level-talks-2980895/.

Indian Express. 2016b. "Surgical Strikes: Full Text of Indian Army DGMO Lt Gen Ranbir Singh's Press Conference." September 29. Accessed May 21 2017. http://indianexpress.com/article/india/

india-news-india/pakistan-infiltration-attempts-indian-army-surgical-strikes-line-of-control-jammu-and-kashmir-uri-poonch-pok-3055874/.

Indian Express. 2016c. "Sushma Swaraj's UNGA Speech: Here Is the Full Text." September 27. Accessed May 22 2017. http://indianexpress.com/article/india/india-news-india/sushma-swaraj-unga-speech-full-text-3051409/.

Indian Express. 2017. "April 29, 9 am News Update: SC Tells Govt, Kashmir Protesters to Initiate Talks, Priyanka Gandhi Land Deal, North Korea Fires Ballistic Missile and Other Top Stories." April 29. Accessed May 25 2017. http://indianexpress.com/article/india/april-29-9-am-news-update-sc-tells-govt-kashmir-protesters-to-initiate-talks-priyanka-gandhi-land-deal-north-korea-fires-ballistic-missile-and-other-top-stories-4632697/.

Indian Ministry of External Affairs. 1972. Simla Agreement. India-Pakistan. July 2. Accessed May 12 2017. http://mea.gov.in/in-focus-article.htm?19005/Simla+Agreement+July+2+1972.

InKhabar. 2016. "Kya hai surgical strike, kaise diya jata hai anjaam?" September 29. Accessed May 24 2017. http://www.inkhabar.com/national/25351-know-what-surgical-strike.

Inter Services Public Relations. 2016. *Press Release*. PR-334/2016-ISPR, September 29. Accessed May 24 2017. https://www.ispr.gov.pk/front/main.asp?o=t-press_release&id=3483&search=1 (Pakistan).

Jackson, R. 2005. *Writing the War on Terrorism: Language, Politics and Counter-Terrorism*. Manchester: Manchester University Press.

Khan, M. I. 2016. "India's Surgical Strikes in Kashmir: Truth or Illusion?" *BBC*, October 23. Accessed May 25 2017. http://www.bbc.com/news/world-asia-india-37702790.

Khan, N. F. A. 1989/1992. "Main Jagi Piya Ke Sangh," by Hazrat Amir Khusrau. *Traditional Sufi Qawwalis Vol. 2*. Recorded December 1989 and September 1992. Sony Music, 1996. CD.

Mahapatra, D. 2017. "Won't Talk with Separatists Who Demand 'Azaadi': Centre to SC about Dialogue on Kashmir Unrest." *Times of India*, April 28. Accessed May 25, 2017. http://timesofindia.indiatimes.com/india/wont-talk-with-separatists-who-demand-azaadi-centre-to-sc-about-dialogue-on-kashmir-unrest/articleshow/58414980.cms.

Masood, S. 2016. "In Kashmir, Pakistan Questions India's 'Surgical Strikes' on Militants." *New York Times*, October 1. Accessed May 25 2017. https://www.nytimes.com/2016/10/02/world/asia/kashmir-pakistan-india.html?_r=0.

Mishra, A. 2012. "India's Non-Liberal Democracy and the Discourse of Democracy Promotion." *South Asian Survey* 19 (1): 33–59. doi:10.1177/0971523114539584.

Mitra, S. K. 2013. "How Exceptional Is India's Democracy? Path Dependence, Political Capital, and Context in South Asia." *India Review* 12 (4) (November): 227–244. doi:10.1080/14736489.2013.846783.

Nation. 2016. "Rajnath Calls Pakistan 'Terrorist State' in Scathing Attack." September 18. Accessed May 2 2017. http://nation.com.pk/international/18-Sep-2016/rajnath-calls-pakistan-terrorist-state-in-scathing-attack.

NDTV. 2017. "No Talks with Separatists in Jammu and Kashmir, Centre Tells Supreme Court." April 29. Accessed May 25 2017. http://www.ndtv.com/india-news/no-talks-with-separatists-in-jammu-and-kashmir-centre-tells-supreme-court-1687394.

Negi, M. S. 2016. "Surgical Strikes in PoK: How Indian Para Commandos Killed 50 Terrorists, Hit 7 Camps." *India Today*, September 29. Accessed May 25 2017. http://indiatoday.intoday.in/story/uri-avenged-inside-story-indian-army-surgical-strikes-pok/1/776433.html.

Oren, I., and T. Solomon. 2015. "WMD, WMD, WMD: Securitisation through Ritualised Incantation of Ambiguous Phrases." *Review of International Studies* 41: 313–336. doi: 10.1017/S0260210514000205.

Parveen, A., and R. F. A. Khan. 2014. "Chaap Tilak," by Hazrat Amir Khusrau. Coke Studio Season 7 Episode 6. Streaming Audio. Accessed August 20 2017. http://www.cokestudio.com.pk/season7/episode6.html?WT.cl=1&WT.mn=Episode%20Six.

Ranjan, R. 2017. "Surgical Strike ke baavjood Pak mein ab bhi sakriya hain aatankiyon ke kareeb 50 Training Camp." *NDTV India*, May 3. Accessed May 24 2017. https://khabar.ndtv.com/news/india/terror-camps-in-pakistan-still-active-1689230.

Rasool, S. A.-T. H. A. 2002. *Turning toward the Heart: Awakening to the Sufi Way*. Louisville, KY: Fons Vitae.

Rehman, A. 2016. "What Is a 'Surgical Strike'?" *Dawn*, September 29. Accessed May 24 2017. https://www.dawn.com/news/1286893.

Roy, D. D. 2016. "What Is a Surgical Strike? Military Experts Explain." *NDTV*, September 29. Accessed May 24 2017. http://www.ndtv.com/india-news/what-is-a-surgical-strike-1468025.

Safi, M. 2016. "Seventeen Indian Soldiers and Four Militants Killed in Kashmir Attack." *Guardian*, September 18. Accessed May 8 2017. https://www.theguardian.com/world/2016/sep/18/nine-indian-soldiers-and-four-militants-killed-in-kashmir-attack.

Scroll.in. 2016a. "Lashkar-e-Taiba Claims Responsibility for Uri Attack through Poster on Social Media." October 25. Accessed May 8 2017. https://scroll.in/article/print/819920.

Scroll.in. 2016b. "Uri: Another Soldier Succumbs to Injuries, Toll from Militant Attack Rises to 19." September 30. Accessed May 8 2017. https://scroll.in/article/print/817848.

Scroll.in. 2016c. "Uri Attack: Initial Reports Indicate JeM Involvement, Says Military Operations Chief." September 18. Accessed May 22 2017. https://scroll.in/article/print/816848.

Shukla, A. 2016. "Army Mute as BJP Election Posters Feature Soldier, Surgical Strikes." *Wire*, October 9. Accessed May 12 2017. https://thewire.in/71973/army-silent-surgical-strikes-bjp-election-posters/.

Snedden, C. 2013. *Kashmir: The Unwritten History*. Noida, India: HarperCollins.

Stern, J. 2003. *Terror in the Name of God: Why Religious Militants Kill*. New York: HarperCollins.

Swami, P. 2017. "Pakistani Teens Wrongly Accused of Being Uri Terror Guides Finally Home." *Indian Express*, March 10. Accessed November 19 2017. http://indianexpress.com/article/india/pakistani-teens-wrongly-accused-of-being-uri-terror-guides-finally-home-4563355/.

Times of India. 2016. "Uri Terror Attack: 17 Soldiers Killed, 19 Injured in Strike on Army Camp." September 30. Accessed May 2 2017. http://timesofindia.indiatimes.com/india/Uri-terror-attack-Indian-Army-camp-attacked-in-Jammu-and-Kashmir-17-killed-19-injured/articleshow/54389451.cms.

Udayakumar, G. K. R. 2017. "Farooq Abdullah: Wake up India, Talk to Pakistan or Lose Kashmir." *India Today*, April 11. Accessed May 25 2017. http://indiatoday.intoday.in/story/farooq-abdullah-srinagar-bypoll-kashmir-pakistan-national-conference/1/925802.html.

Vivek, T. R. 2017. "With Yogi Adityanath as CM of India's Largest State, the BJP Has Launched Project Polarisation 2.0." *Scroll.in*, March 20. Accessed May 12 2017. http://scroll.in/article/832222/with-yogi-adityanath-as-cm-of-indias-largest-state-the-bjp-has-launched-project-polarisation-2-0.

Vuori, J. A. 2008. "Illocutionary Logic and Strands of Securitization: Applying the Theory of Securitization to the Study of Non-Democratic Political Orders." *European Journal of International Relations* 14 (1): 65–99. doi:10.1177/1354066107087767.

Wilkinson, C. 2007. "The Copenhagen School on Tour in Kyrgyzstan: Is Securitization Theory Useable outside Europe?" *Security Dialogue* 38 (1): 5–25. Accessed December 16 2016. http://journals.sagepub.com.ezproxy.lancs.ac.uk/doi/pdf/10.1177/0967010607075964.   doi:10.1177/0967010607075964.

REPLY

Securitization analysis beyond its power-critique

Mona Kanwal Sheikh

This is a reply to:

Kapur, S. 2018. "From Copenhagen to Uri and across the Line of Control: India's 'surgical strikes' as a case of securitisation in two acts", *Global Discourse* 8 (1): 62–79. https://doi.org/10.1080/23269995.2017.1406633.

Saloni Kapur's article applies securitization theory to explain, and raise a critique of, India's official security narratives that justified the Indian launch of surgical strikes into Pakistan in September 2016. Kapur's application of the securitization framework to study state-sanctioned extraordinary measures is a classical way of conducting securitization analysis, which underlines its critical potential, but also its popular utility in state-centered analyses. She analyzes the statements of Indian government representatives and the military, demonstrating how these speech acts represent securitizing moves that construct a threat emanating from Pakistan, ultimately arguing that the security claims made by India are not based on objective observations but have a 'subjective nature'.

Kapur contributes to the bulk of literature that applies securitization theory in similar ways: to reveal problematic power-practices and the constructed-ness of security claims that justify acts of war (e.g. Wilhelmsen 2017, Geri 2017; Olesker 2013; Vultee 2010). This criticism of power-practices is relevant as an add-on to other critical studies that reiterate the main ideas of securitization theory: that 'more security' is not an unambiguous good, threats are not objective observations, but rather they are narratives about an existential life threat that enable extraordinary action. While such points are indeed interesting in a context, where the country is known to be the largest democracy in the world, there must be more we can derive from applying securitization theory to the non-western case of India.

Kapur's article does not provide any direct answers to whether the particular case of India displays potential limitations of securitization theory, or how it might teach us something about India beyond the critique. Kapur's contribution points more in the direction of confirming that there is a universal securitization dynamics, which is somehow stronger than the contextual specifics that matters according to other authors (e.g. Holbraad and Pedersen 2012; Greenwood and Wæver 2013; Wilkinson 2007; Bilgin 2011). But the case of India might, qua its non-western-ness, have much more to add to the debate that this special issue takes up, than if it was any other case, particularly since Kapur hints at the fact that India is a hybrid between 'western liberal democratic forms and non-western cultures' (Mitra 2013, 227).

One of the entries to understand the specificity of India is the audience. Securitization has an underdeveloped potential that lies in its original claim that security is *intersubjective* rather than subjective (Buzan, Waever, and de Wilde 1997), which places the audience in a quite central position. This gives rise to the question of whether and how the specificity of the audience or the political culture matter for the securitization process and the criteria for success. Kapur mentions the multi-lingual context, which is specific for the case of India, and perhaps the multi-lingual context opens up for diverse interpretations of the same words with more or less securitizing potentials that would be interesting to explore.

One of Kapur's main findings is that the securitizing speech act is not necessarily something that comes before the extraordinary action, but also something that can follow the implementation of an exceptional measure. This might not, as Kapur also writes, be a point that is only valid for the case of India, but for the dynamics of the securitization process as such. However, for future research this is something that needs follow-up: Is the action-before-speech act dynamics only prevalent in contexts where there are certain flaws in the democratic culture, or can we observe similar patterns in for example a Scandinavian country, where levels of corruptions are low, and the demands about accountability are high?

Securitization theory has from the beginning pointed at the audience as the filter between the speech act and the emergency action, which is perhaps also one of its most 'western' characteristics reflecting the strong accountability demands in the political culture of Western Europe. In a recent article (2016), Rita Floyd has argued that securitization theory should skip the idea of a sanctioning audience and instead measure success by whether the securitization move is followed by concrete action by the securitizing actor. She puts forward that the theory suffers from a constructivist deficit because the criterion for the 'success' of securitization is typically set by scholars, whereas a more 'radically constructivist [theory] regarding security' would require practitioners to be in charge of defining the 'success' of securitization. Kapur seems to be on the same page, since she do not grant the nature of the audience any specific analytic attention, but instead analyzes the events and actions that unfold before and after the speech acts.

Skipping an in-depth analysis of the audience and their sentiments might allow for an easier travelling to contexts, which are less democratic than the western European one where securitization theory was invented. But it would also then become a conform analytical model producing conform conclusions, inclined to focus on the official power holders, while the power of 'the people' and their potential sanctioning potential, as the Arab Spring revolutions for instance displayed, would be given less attention.

Securitization theory has long been criticized for an under-developed concept of the audience, and for being too silent about the cultural context in which the audience is situated, instead attributing too much power to the speech-act of security. According to Balzacq (2005), effective securitization remains audience-dependent and successful securitization only occurs when the securitizing agent and the audience reach a common, structured perception or interpretation of the referent object being threatened (177, 181). This implies that the analysts must take into consideration the psycho-cultural disposition of the audience and the power that both the speaker and listener bring to the interaction (172), in addition to the discourse of the securitizing actor. The ability of securitizing actors to identify with the audience's feelings, needs and interests or to capture the Zeitgeist based on collective memory, social views, trends and ideological and political attitudes is thus important as they constitute the cultural context in which the audience is situated (Balzacq 2005, 186).

This is also valid when thinking about de-securitization. Kapur refers to de-securitization as a simple call for applying political means to solve tensions. Nevertheless, it would be fruitful to ask what de-securitization of the Kashmir issue means in this specific context: Does it just mean to talk the tensions down? What particular challenges do the historical tensions between Pakistan and India, and the religion-layer of the conflict constellation, pose to de-securitization attempts?

Most work on securitization theory and the application of it ends with boosting its central claims by showing that securitization theory captures some real dynamics out there. However, its critical potential should not just stop there. The global travel of the theory bears a promise of a broader applicability of the theory, which do not only draw from its power-critical potential, but also from its potential to say something substantial about the context it is taken to: its culture, its sentiments, the larger frames of inter-pretation of political events, including the role of religious imagery.

Disclosure statement

No potential conflict of interest was reported by the author.

References

Balzacq, T. 2005. "The Three Faces of Securitization: Political Agency, Audience and Context." *European Journal of International Relations* 11 (2): 171–201. doi:10.1177/1354066105052960.

Bilgin, P. 2011. "The Politics of Studying Securitization? the Copenhagen School in Turkey." *Security Dialogue* 42 (4–5): 399–412. doi:10.1177/0967010611418711.

Buzan, B., O. Waever, and J. H. De Wilde. 1997. *Security: A New Framework of Analysis.* Boulder, CO: Lynne Rienner.

Floyd, R. 2016. "Extraordinary or Ordinary Emergency Measures: What, and Who, Defines the 'Success' of Securitization?" *Cambridge Review of International Affairs* 29: 677–694. doi:10.1080/09557571.2015.1077651.

Geri, M. 2017. "The Securitization of the Kurdish Minority in Turkey: Ontological Insecurity and Elite's Power Struggle as Reasons of the Recent Re-Securitization." *Domes* 26: 187–202. doi:10.1111/dome.2017.26.issue-1.

Greenwood, M. T., and O. Wæver. 2013. "Copenhagen–Cairo on A Roundtrip: A Security Theory Meets the Revolution." *Security Dialogue* 44 (5–6): 485–506. doi:10.1177/0967010613502573.

Holbraad, M., and M. Pedersen. 2012. "Revolutionary Securitization: An Anthropological Extension of Securitization Theory." *International Theory* 4 (2): 165–197. doi:10.1017/S1752971912000061.

Kapur, S. 2018. "From Copenhagen to Uri and across the Line of Control: India's 'Surgical Strikes' as a Case of Securitisation in Two Acts." *Global Discourse* 8 (1).

Mitra, S. K. 2013. "How Exceptional Is India's Democracy? Path Dependence, Political Capital, and Context in South Asia." *India Review* 12 (4, November): 227–244. doi:10.1080/14736489.2013.846783.

Olesker, R. 2013. "National Identity and Securitization in Israel." *Ethnicities* 14 (3): 371–391. doi:10.1177/1468796813504093.

Vultee, F. 2010. "Securitization." *Journalism Practice* 4: 1, 33–47. doi:10.1080/17512780903172049.

Wilhelmsen, J. 2017. *Russia's Securitization of Chechnya: How War Became Acceptable.* New York, NY: Routledge.

Wilkinson, C. 2007. "The Copenhagen School on Tour in Kyrgyzstan: Is Securitization Theory Useable outside Europe?" *Security Dialogue* 38 (1): 5–25. doi:10.1177/0967010607075964.

Securitization outside of the West: conceptualizing the securitization–neo-patrimonialism nexus in Africa

Edwin Ezeokafor ⓘⓓ and Christian Kaunert

ABSTRACT

Securitization is arguably the most successful theoretical framework to analyse security beyond the military confines with the nation state as the dominant actor within the international system. Amongst the critical voices, securitization has become the gold standard for analysing emerging challenges, such as migration, terrorism, human security, intra-state and cross-border issues, as well as environmental challenges. Yet, despite its broadening agenda, the framework has also been accused of a Western bias with a Western political context and democratic governance structure at its heart. This article aims to re-conceptualize the framework in a way that suits a non-Western context better, notably by re-conceptualizing the securitization–neo-patrimonialism nexus in Africa, which gives us significant new insights into non-Western political contexts. It analyses the securitization processes among the political elites in a neo-patrimonial statehood. It further stretches the conceptualization of securitization into African statehood, characterized by a blurred line between the leader and the state.

Introduction

The most popular concepts in the discipline of international relations (IR) and the debates thereof are deeply rooted in Western (especially Europe and North America) historical and political epistemology. As the domain and scope of the discipline influences not much of other social science disciplines, rather it is constantly being influenced, it also lacks contextual dynamism. In other words, the IR discipline focuses more on European and North American political terrain without significantly accommodating sociocultural variations of other societies. This has therefore wrongly (we argue that it is overstated) earned the discipline of IR serious bashing as a failed intellectual project (Buzan and Little 2001). The authors of that statement made a provocative and interesting statement which some people may perceive as going a little bit too far. Another reason for this unfriendly tagging of IR also arose from what has been explained as its Westphalian straitjacket; 'the strong tendency to assume that the model established in seventeenth century Europe should define what the international system is for all times and places' (Buzan and Little 2001, 25).

The sub-discipline of security studies is not an exception in this intellectual parochialism – the Westphalian and Eurocentric bias in understanding security. From the realists (Morgenthau 1965), to neo-realists (Waltz 1979) and the neo-liberals (Keohane and Nye 1977), the focus of security debate remained on the place of state (a Westphalian contraption) in explaining the international security dynamics. The discussions coming from these various corners were anchored on certain historical or founding problematique created by the First World War, Second World Wars and the Cold War which were mainly European and Northern American creations. The intellectual world was fed with a realist perspective of security along the state-military-power line. While the neo-liberals differed a little, they still leaned towards the primacy of state as major actor and referent object in the security debate. The problem with this lies with the Westphalian understanding of state which does not appreciate other societies from other cultures at various stages of sociopolitical development. This narrow way of viewing global politics meant that even security studies were seen as strictly addressing issues of military power, national/state security paying little or no attention to emerging challenges such as migration, ethnic minorities, intra-state and cross-border security issues, human security challenges, environmental challenges and terrorism.

Shifting the goal post of security studies from that traditional standpoint eventually became 'something of a cottage industry' as observed by David Baldwin (1997, 5). There are now the critical security studies, emancipatory security and Human security (Krause and Williams 1997; Booth 1991; Kaldor 2007) creating cacophony of voices over the same subject. It is apparent that one of the most popular and successful of these efforts has been the securitization theory of the Copenhagen School (Waever 1995; Buzan, de Wilde and Waever 1998; Buzan and Waever 2003), which has generated a lot of commentaries and footnotes (Booth 1991, 37). However, while Buzan and Little accused the discipline of IR of Westphalian straitjacket, he and his other colleagues in the securitization project can be argued to have become guilty of the same bias (c.f., Waever 1995; Buzan, de Wilde and Waever 1998; Buzan and Waever 2003). The idea of securitization was developed and applied consciously or unconsciously aimed at established political contexts and democracies of Europe. Even later works and commentaries on the subject of securitization were to considerable extent not significantly different (Huysmans 1998, 2000; Balzacq 2011; Karyotis 2010; Leonard 2010). To this effect, Claire Wilkinson (2007) questioned if securitization theory can be useful outside European security and political environment.

Can the securitization framework be rid of its Eurocentric parochialism in order to accommodate other security contexts and political structures? If we accept the general logic of securitization – that there is an existential threat, a securitizing actor and an emergency action based on a specific rhetorical process and acquiescence by a given audience – how do we unpack and demarcate their boundaries in non-Western security environment and political culture? The Copenhagen School rule is that 'a discourse that takes the form of presenting something as an existential threat to a referent object does not by itself create securitization; that is the securitizing move, but the issue is securitized only if and when the audience accepts is as such' (Buzan, de Wilde and Waever 1998, 25). This is about the only discussion on audience in the framework – an important element of the securitization process. To this effect, Leonard and Kaunert (2011) have made the argument that the idea of audience has been under-theorized. Vuori (2008) also argued that even in military regimes outside the usual established democracies, military leaders require and do have audiences to carry out the process of securitizing threats. The challenge therefore is on how to identify the formal and informal audiences especially in non-Western political cultures.

Very significantly, Wilkinson (2007) also advocated for some contextualization of the security environment or the region in order to appreciate the region's security dynamics. In line with this, Balzacq (2005) goes further to point out the oversimplification, generalization and universal application of the speech act in securitization especially with regard to the idea of an audience disregarding differences in security environments; 'including the context, the psycho-cultural disposition of the audience, and the power that both speaker and listener bring to the interaction' (Balzacq 2005, 172). Applying the concept of securitization in non-Western societies such as Africa will factor in the difference in political development before identifying the audiences. The issue of context is very important and in the context of Africa, the attention is focused on the neo-patrimonial statehood – patronage politics. Here, neo-patrimonialism is explained as the hybrid system of leadership in which the formal legal bureaucratic model of authority mixes with the informal political ties in a power relations mainly characterized by patron–client favour for support exchange.

This article conceptualizes an interface between the concept of securitization; the process of construction of security threats and the interface with neo-patrimonialism. It analyses the securitization processes among the political elites in neo-patrimonial statehood. It further stretches the conceptualization of securitization beyond the original European security environment into other regions; for example, African statehood characterized by a blurred line between leader and state. The political elite for clarification stand for group of individuals who wield so much power and wealth at the corridors of political power. They can come from military, media, religious, corporate and bureaucratic background. They are intricately connected and control the decision making of the state.

This article builds on the classical literature on securitization and neo-patrimonialism, as well as subsequent works which focused on various elements of these concepts. It examines a few cases in West Africa in order to explain the securitization–neo-patrimonialism dynamics. The article seeks to make vital contributions to the literature in two major areas by suggesting (a) there is an absence of an institutionalized and non-personalized securitization framework in neo-patrimonial statehood, (b) what is defined as a security threat is a function of the narrow threat perception of the neo-patrimonial states' leaders at national and subregional levels and (c) the Copenhagen School application of securitization ignores contextual differences in security environments and levels of statehood. Thus, theoretically, the article introduces a new securitization–neo-patrimonialism framework for security analysis outside Europe and the West, a framework based on a synthesis of the concepts of securitization and neo-patrimonialism.

Following a background overview of the development of securitization theory – considering critiques and application of its core ideas especially audience and context – the discussion will proceed to the political culture of neo-patrimonialism before synthesizing elements of the two. There will be an empirical discussion of the application of securitization in the West African context. Specifically, the article will be empirically anchored on the intervention of the Economic Community of West African States (ECOWAS) in the crises that engulfed the two states of Liberia and Sierra Leone at the end of the Cold War in the 1990s. Considering that the ECOWAS was not *ab initio* a security arrangement but rather an economic organization, it is important to find out what led to transformation, the creation of ECOWAS Monitoring Group (ECOMOG) and eventual intervention in the conflict areas; the power play among the leaders. What was the securitization process? Who was the audience in that context? And what role did neo-patrimonial political culture play in the process?

Theory of securitization: managing audience and context problematique

Securitization has been defined as a speech-act process 'through which an inter-subjective understanding is constructed within a political community to treat something as an existential threat to a valued referent object and to enable a call for urgent and exceptional measures to deal with the threat' (Buzan, de Wilde and Waever 1998, 30; Buzan and Waever 2003, 491). But the threat only becomes securitized 'only if and when the audience accepts it as such' (Buzan, de Wilde and Waever 1998, 25). Through the speech-act process, an issue is tagged a security threat by a securitizing actor and through some rhetorical speech or persuasion an audience finds some resonance with the speech or argument and the issue is treated as a security threat requiring an emergency action to be contained. In other words, no issue is objectively a security issue but securitizing actor places recognition on it according to security perception. According to Williams (2003, 513), 'in securitization theory, "security" is treated not as an objective condition but as the outcome of a specific social process: the social construc-tion of security issues'. The identity of the securitizing actor(s) is made clear – 'political leaders, bureaucracies, governments, lobbyists, and pressure groups' (Buzan, de Wilde and Waever 1998, 40). It is easier to locate the actor and the audience in an established democracy or political order. The identity and roles of the audience are clearly known. But it is more complicated in non-democratic settings. This is because of the blurry line in the power relations among the political elite, the actors and their client followers and audiences. It is therefore important to unpack the audience and context. But before doing that, it is import to bring out few criticisms against the theory of securitization.

Since Barry Buzan and his colleagues introduced an innovation into security studies through the concept of 'securitization' (Buzzan 1993; Waever 1995; Buzan, de Wilde and Waever 1998), it has attracted both positive and negative comments. The project nurtured in Copenhagen, Denmark, which McSweeny (1996) 'christened' the 'Copenhagen School' has become famous for its paradigm shift on security studies. It shifted security discourse from the traditional realist state-military-power perspective to other referent objects. The Copenhagen project has brought into focus several security threats and aided in security analysis of various regions of the world, especially Europe. Much as the contribution of the 'securitization concept' to security studies is appre-ciated, it is riddled with loopholes. The focus here will be more on those issues that this article seeks to address especially in the context of non-Western security environment, particularly neo-patrimonial statehood in Africa.

In the first instance, there is serious issue with the idea of audience in the securitiza-tion process. In the same manner, the idea of audience as articulated by the

Copenhagen School has been criticized as being under-theorized (see Leonard and Kaunert 2011, 57–70). The point is that for a security actor to declare any threat, a serious issue meriting a measure outside normal politics – exceptional and emergency approaches – the actor should be able to convince (perlocutionary effect) the public or an audience who will permit the speaker or accede to his argument. Balzacq (2011, 9) proposed that 'to persuade the audience (e.g. the public) that is, to achieve a perlocutionary effect, the speaker has to tune his/her language to the audience's experience'. On the surface, this is very easy but when one considers the complexity of publics and differences in political orders, securitization in its simplistic form becomes harder to apply, especially in Africa. Williams (2003, 7) posited that 'this raises questions about who counts as a "significant audience" and how this idea should be applied to states or organizations that do not boast a functioning public sphere' or an established democratic decision process (Vuori 2008, 68).

Concerned about this ambiguity as to who constitutes an audience and how to assess its security threat argument, Leonard and Kaunert (2011) made a profound contribution in re-conceptualizing this aspect of securitization concept. Whilst significantly advancing the debate, it is simultaneously restricted to well-established liberal democracies. This article agrees with Vuori (2008), who applied securitization to non-democratic orders, but it shifts its focus to Africa which is inundated with neo-patrimonial, authoritarian statehood and regimes. This, according to Vuori (2008, 66), is very important in order to appreciate the idea of securitization; 'If Securitization Studies is to be an encompassing research programme, it should take into account security speech and politics in all types of political systems'.

The Copenhagen School of Security Studies ascribed a special position or role to the 'audience' in the securitization process. Buzan, de Wilde and Waever (1998, 30, 31) argued that 'securitization, like politicization, has to be understood as an essentially intersubjective process … securitization is intersubjective and socially constructed'. The emphasis is on the intersubjective character of the process of securitization. If it is intersubjective, it therefore requires a dialogue or a consensus for effectiveness. At one end of the spectrum is a securitizing actor and at the other end is an audience who accedes to the reasoning of the securitizing actor. Buzan, de Wilde and Waever (1998, 25) again argued that 'a discourse that takes the form of presenting something as an existential threat to referent object does not by itself create securitization – this is *securitizing move* but the issue is securitized only if and when the audience accepts it as such'. Other considerations of the audience can also be found in Buzan, de Wilde and Waever (1998, 34). Granted that securitization is accepted as speech-act process, they argued that 'the speech-act approach says only that it is the actor who by securitizing an issue – and the audience by accepting the claim – makes it a security issue'. In order to further strengthen the argument, Buzan, de Wilde and Waever. (1998, 31) stated that 'successful securitization is not decided by the securitizer but by the audience of the security speech act'. It is not argued that the idea of an audience in the securitization process is not accepted, but as other analysts have argued (see for instance Balzacq 2005, 173; McDonald 2008; Vuori 2008), clarity is demanded in order to benefit security analysis of especially undemocratic regimes and uninformed public.

Buzan, de Wilde and Waever (1998, 40) submit that 'a *securitizing actor* is someone, or a group, who performs the security speech act. Common players in this role are political leaders, bureaucracies, governments, lobbyists, and pressure groups' (at least in advanced democracies). One would expect that such attempt would apply to clarify who an audience is within the securitization framework. Leonard and Kaunert (2011) stepped in to clear the conceptual fog around the idea of audience in securitization analysis. According to Leonard and Kaunert (2011, 50),

> The role of the audience in securitization processes remains significantly under-theorised in the Copenhagen School's formulation of securitization theory. Although Buzan, Waever and de Wilde emphasise that securitization is an *intersubjective* process, in which the audience seemingly plays a crucial role, this concept remains rather vague and under-specified. How it could be operationalised in empirical studies is also far from clear.

Leonard and Kaunert (2011) built their re-conceptualization of the audience on a key suggestions by Balzacq (2005, 172–3) that securitization should not be interpreted wholly as a speech act but rather as a strategic practice amalgamating several 'circumstances including the context, the psycho-cultural disposition of the audience, and the power that both speaker and listener bring to the interaction'. The speech-act model presents securitization as a sustained strategic actions aimed at convincing a target audience to accept *based on what it knows about the world*. But Balzacq (2005, 172) proposes to recast this speech act model by elevating 'securitization above its normative setting and in so doing ensconces it in the social context, a field of power struggles in which securitizing actors align on a security issue to swing the audience's support toward a policy or course of action'. The idea here is that the actor has to find a platform or line of argument that will effectively resonate with or swing the audience in full of support of the intended line of action. Segregating these issues will make the securitization approach empirically more operational especially in West Africa.

Other suggestion came in form of Vuori's (2008) proposition of possibility of multiple audiences depending on specific contexts and 'specific socio-historical situations' (Leonard and Kaunert 2011, 61). This is very significant in the African context where there is the possibility of diverse allegiances, ethnic cleavages and interests. The audience during an interethnic war in West Africa certainly will be different from the audience when issues of cross-border crimes, illicit drugs and illegal weapons for instances are being securitized by national governments or subregional body. Vuori (2008) therefore submits that 'audiences depend on the function the securitization act is intended to serve'. It may also be difficult in societies where issues of religion and politics are intricately interwoven (Karyotis 2010, 13). The audience may not necessarily be the public. It could also be members of government institutions and representatives whose political support is very important. Such support has been classified as formal support whilst the one from the public as moral support, which frequently is not enough to move an issue to the realm of *securityness* (see Balzacq 2005, 185; Leonard and Kaunert 2011, 62; Roe 2008). Beyond European security environment and far away from institutionalized democracies are clusters of security structures hugely influenced by political culture characterized by dynamics of favour-for-support, big man–small man power relations. This seriously affects the workings of securitization processes and makes the theory unworkable in its original format. The next section unpacks the concept of neo-patrimonialism and how it works.

Patrimonialism–neo-patrimonialism continuum

In an interwoven labyrinth of 'big man–small man' networks of favour for support, the political elite in Africa have monopolized both the tangible and intangible resources of the state to maintain their hold on power and define the security pattern of their individual countries. The preceding section dissected the body of the securitization framework especially as it relates to the securitizing actor and the audience. Borrowing from Leonard and Kaunert (2011) contribution, the intention is to advance and stretch the frontier of the Eurocentric and under-theorized concept to benefit the discourse on African security in a setting of neo-patrimonial statehood: who frames the threats and to what extent the neo-patrimonial character of the state plays a role in securitization process in Africa, especially since the end of the Cold War? This section starts by discussing the idea of neo-patrimonialism and synthesizes it with securitization before moving on to operationalize the synergy.

There has been a significant effort on the part of the Africanists from the African divide to deny the influence neo-patrimonialism can have on the whole workings of the state (Mkandawire 2015, 106–136) and an overstatement or distortion of the dynamics of the patrimonial system (Bayart, Ellis, and Hibou 1999, 131). Nothing can better explain the trend or direction of a state's policy than its internal dynamics. Taylor (2010, 2) remarked that 'erroneous is the unwillingness to acknowledge that the state-society complex evident across many parts of sub-Saharan Africa has critical implications and a vital – possibly decisive – influence upon many aspects of the continent's international relations'. Falola and Heaton 2008, 18) argued that the 'nature of the patron-client system in a country is necessary to understand the behaviour and activities of members of the political class and warlords'. Part of the reason for this disagreement is probably because the issue of patrimonialism has been painted in a negative light. It should be understood as an integral part of the African society that has been bastardized and capitalized on for personal aggrandizement by the political class.

The aim here is to explore this system that has been variously dubbed the 'politics of the belly' (Bayart 1993, 228–259), the 'politics of belonging' (Chabal 2010, 43–64), the 'state–society complex' (Taylor 2010, 1–8) and the 'politics of regime survival' (Clapham 1996, 4). What is significant in these works is their total recognition of the agency of African states in their IRs or their political development whilst the extent to which it affects the construction of security threats in Africa remains largely uncharted.

Patrimonialism therefore is a system of 'personal leadership on the basis of loyalties that do not require any belief in the ruler's unique personal qualification, but are inextricably linked to material incentives and rewards' (Guenther 1968, 194–206). This is an adaptation of Max Weber's types of authority based on legal authority; traditional authority and charismatic authority (see Weber 1947 especially 304–350). Without going into much detail, it will just highlight the essential elements of Weber's (1947) thesis and show how the concepts of authority apply to African states.

According to Weber (1947), legal authority is where the person in authority exercises power not because of his person but based on a legal document and/or agreement – for instance, the constitution establishing the authority. The traditional authority on the other hand respects not any given agreement but is more representative of ancient traditions and is the custodian of the established culture. Obedience is not to the person but the traditions, precepts and the spirit of the ancestors. The third variant in the Weberian model of authority is charismatic which hinges on the natural charisma for leadership that the person in authority (usually the chief) seems to possess. 'The chief, as the embodiment of the living community, the point of contact with its ancestral past, and the trustee of its generational future is usually surrounded by highly elaborate rituals that emphasize all or any combination of these sacral roles' (Levine 1980, 659).

The patrimonial system of authority can accordingly be said to draw from a combination of the traditional and charismatic authority. The chief gains 'legitimacy' from his being a custodian of traditional ways of the people and a certain heroism he might have displayed in wars against the people's enemies. Instead of a bureaucratic staff, his staffs are drawn from his household members, slaves, personal retainers and also from his cronies who are beholden to him in a favour-for-support reciprocity. The precolonial patrimonial authority in Africa – whether headed by Shaka of Zulu kingdom, Osei Tutu of Ashanti confederation or other renowned rulers such as Othman dan Fodio and Samori – fits well into this 'big man–small man' arrangement. It must be recognized that the chief does not have the freedom to do as he pleases because he is bound under a certain unwritten constitutionalism that does not allow him to overstep his bound or else he would incur the wrath of the community and could be deposed. This description of authority under patrimonial system is significant because it illustrates that it is a system that has survived over the years. It was not a negative system per se and should not be mistaken for authoritarianism, exclusiveness or totalitarianism but part of the everyday life of the people. It has also evolved into different things for different people and has been equally bastardized (see Price 1974, 172–204; Lemarchand and Legg 1972, 149–178; Theobald 1972, 548–559; Kaufman 1974, 254–308).

It is equally noteworthy that patrimonialism is not restricted to Africa whether in its traditional precolonial form or in the postcolonial fashion. For example Weber (1947) identified the existence of such system in Japan, Middle East and even in feudal Europe. Roth (1968, 198) also suggested that behind the fabled charismatic appeal of president John F. Kennedy of America was actually a Kennedy 'clan', a clique kitchen cabinet, and his personal apparatus who were beholden to him in an intricate web of reciprocity. The same could also be said of post-Cold War Russia, the inheritor of much of the former Soviet politburo machinery which has survived to present day. In other words, every leadership of any government probably has a veneer of personal leadership arising from an old platform of patrimonialism whether in the advanced institutionalized bureaucracies or in the blurry potpourri system of developing democracies. The argument is that patrimonialism in Africa has been practiced in an extreme form, thereby undermining the benefits of the system. In summary, patrimonialism in its default form is not a negative system. Second, it is part and parcel of the workings of all traditional societies – Africa, America, Asia and Europe. In other words, it is not restricted to Africa. Finally, its bastardization in Africa especially came as a result of ethnic and class consciousness originating from their colonial experiences.

The evolution of patrimonialism with a 'neo' prefix started in the 1980s with the works of Medard (1982) and Clapham (1996). It came to be seen as the corrupt and bastardized form of patrimonialism which was regarded as a critical part of African society which the ruling elite latched on for personal benefits once they are in power. Ever since then, it has assumed a prominent place in the literature on African studies

(Clapham 1982; Bratton and Van de Walle 1997; Chabal and Daloz 1999; Van de Walle 2001; Williams 2003; Erdmann and Engel 2007; Chabal and Vidal 2008; De Grassi 2008; Pitcher, Moran, and Johnston 2009). While patrimonialism was seen in terms of social capital as a way of explaining political cohesion in Africa societies (Theobald 1972, 555), neo-patrimonialism is 'regarded as a functional threat to the peaceful political development of African states and the development of societies in general' (Erdmann and Engel 2007, 97).

The salient feature of the neo-patrimonial system of authority is that the Weberian rational–legal bureaucracy is inconsequential. In other words, even though there are institutions and bureaucracies, they are personal tools in the hands of the ruler to wield his authority over the people. It is neo-patrimonial because it is a medley of tradition and modernity in which the prince-leader controls the whole modern state apparatuses including the security sector in the same way the chief in the traditional authority in precolonial days would do. Any semblance of dichotomy between the public and private is a mere charade as 'these rulers bear the national synonym of sovereign statehood in the manner of "l" Etat, c'est moi' (Bøås 2001, 699). Kamuzu Banda was Malawi personified as Nkrumah was the embodiment of Ghana. Zaire (The Democratic Republic of the Congo (DRC)) was the personal property of General Mobutu as Houphet Boigny was seen as 'father' of the people of Ivory Coast. The African variant of the Machiavellian prince will not tolerate any opposition to the seat of state power as he uses the state's resources to securitize any semblance of opposition, control the military, the police, the judiciary and in some cases the media are seriously circumscribed and gagged while the constitution is severely manipulated, all in the bid to ensure the survival of the 'big man' in the state house (see Clapham 1996, 3; Cammack 2007, 604–5).

What lubricates the tool of neo-patrimonialism and keeps it functioning is the oil of resources, in the form of wealth accruing from the abundant natural resources in many of the postcolonial states in Africa under the control of individual rulers. Where a state is lacking in natural resources or the price slumps, the 'hand-out' – aid, loans and grants from foreign donor patrons – become a 'pull factor' towards a competition to control the state power in order to be in control of such funds. In both cases, the contracts, the mining licenses, oil blocks and choice appointments are handed out to the patron's faithful 'servants', 'friends' (local and foreign), family members or people from his ethnic group (see McFerson 2010, 342–344) and for Chabal and Daloz (1999, 81–87) that is the way Africa works. For Richards (1996, xviii), the Sierra Leone war as well as the ones in Liberia, Guinea Bissau, Congo DR, Côte d'Ivoire and the restiveness in the Niger Delta region of Nigeria are all 'a product of this protracted, post-colonial crisis of patrimonialism'. Let it be quickly reiterated that like traditional patrimonialism, the 'neo' version is not in any way restricted to postcolonial states of Africa. Taylor (2010, 3) and McFerson (2010, 343) have noted that it can also be identified in other places such as Ukraine, North Korea, Kazakhstan, Turkmenistan, Myanmar, Indonesia, Russia and various Latin American nations (see also Clapham 1982).

The impetus for the intricacies and dynamics of neo-patrimonialism in Africa lies in what Chabal (2010, 43–64) termed the 'politics of belonging', in which the kinship affiliation is very strong and the people always want to identify with where they come from. The abuse of this by political elite becomes an extreme manifestation of neo-patrimonialism. This can be evidenced from the cases of 'indigene and stranger', 'insider and outsider' politics in Africa and of course the ethnic favouritism pervading the political landscape of Africa. It can be safe to suggest that neo-patrimonialism in Africa is as a result of a struggle by a continent stuck between a need to find its route back to its identity and a need to benefit from the modernization and the wave of democratization especially after the end of the Cold War politics. Empirical cases will aid us in understanding the dynamics of neo-patrimonialism and securitization in Africa. The two interventions in West Africa (Liberia and Sierra Leone) by the ECOWAS community at the end of the Cold War in the 1990s are used here to bring out the relationship. It is demonstrated that unlike the way securitization works in European security environment, the concept will have to be re-conceptualized to fit neo-patrimonial statehood in Africa. The question of who the audience is in such context has to be defined. It is to be seen that the character of the audience also differs according to the context.

Empirical application: Liberia and Sierra Leone

It was not a surprise when in 1990 ECOWAS, under the Nigerian leadership, created the ECOMOG to intervene in Liberia in the early days of the wars in that country. There were arguments and criticisms against such a military move. Blaise Compaoré of Burkina Faso argued for instance that 'ECOMOG did not conform to the constitutional legal requirement of ECOWS' (Adebajo 2002, 64–65; see also Wippman 1993, 157–203). From earlier information about his relationships, it is not difficult to fathom where he was coming from. Given that there was no authorization anywhere in the protocols for such action in Liberia, why did the member states intervene? There were yes and no votes from the member states. The point is that the military action (securitization) was more political than based in law – and the politics is based on the interrelationships among the leaders in West Africa with biased interests. For instance, Compaoré (see above) had equally become a 'special one' in the subregion. Adebajo (2002, 64) again revealed that Compaoré had a client–patron ties with Eyadéma, President of Togo, who had supported him when he gained power in Burkina Faso. Compaoré reciprocated by mediating in Togo's internal crisis and sending troops to monitor Togolese elections in 1993. Mali and Niger had benefited from Compaoré's 'good gesture' when he helped in resolving Tuareg challenges in the two countries. Remember the special relationship that Compaoré and Boigny of Côte d'Ivoire shared – a relationship based on matrimonial ties. The support was extended to Charles Taylor and his National Patriotic Front of Liberia (see Obi 2009; Adeleke 1995; Adibe 1997).

The regional security thinking and securitization processes drifted from the interests of the population of the community to those of individual leaders. According to Adibe (1997, 482),

> In this regard, in West Africa and much of Africa, diplomacy has really been about the politics of personality. In the case of Liberia, a complex web of personal ties and 'friendship' involving the principal actors in the conflict – Samuel Doe, Charles Taylor, Ibrahim Babangida, Blaise Compaore and Jerry Rawlings, among others posed enormous challenges to the presumption of impartiality by ECOWAS.

The clauses in the ECOWAS Treaty or the protocols could either be circumvented or abused to achieve those personal interests of the leaders. When Samuel Doe asked for assistance from President Babangida of Nigeria at the point when former's regime was caving in, he did so believing first in the strength of their relationship. The intervention of ECOWAS could be argued to largely be a fall-out of this intersection of interpersonal conviviality and interests of individual states according to the security perceptions of the 'big men' at the top. This intricate and complex diplomacy neutralizes the common good agenda in the securitization of West African security issues. Accordingly Brown (1999, 11) suggested that

> Looking at the players involved and the final score card, it appears that ECOWAS states overcame their differences in support of a common cause. In reality, preservation of the unique self-interests of the West African states propelled them to work together to resolve the Liberian crisis.

Consider these instances: Mali became involved in ECOWAS's effort in Liberia by sending troops. This was seen as a diversionary strategy by the President Alpha Omar Konaré. Having succeeded the former leader Moussa Traore, Konaré decided to send troops comprising those that were loyal to the Traore administration. In other words, it was a way of keeping them busy abroad instead of staying at home to cause trouble for Konaré's regime (see Keita 1998, 22–23). Second, it was another attempt by a French-speaking state at balancing Nigeria's (English speaking) hegemony in the subregion. So, Konaré essentially was using his domestic security perception to approach the securitization of regional security crisis. Like Mali, Ibrahim Bare of Niger in 1996 came to power through a bloodless coup. Sending troops to Liberia was a ploy to keep the troops busy. There was relative equanimity in the north of the country following the settling of the Tuareg insurgency. There was nothing to keep the military busy. Considering that not all members of the Armed Forces supported Bare, it would be a security miscalculation to keep them at home (Brown 1999, 15–16). There was a need to enhance the international image of the regime, having been criticized for violent overthrow of former regime.

It is interesting how regimes that came to power through illegal and unpopular means sent military help to places where the same thing was happening. According to Ofuatey-Kodjoe (1994, 295), 'the notion that a group of states headed by military dictatorships have the right to intervene in another state in order to establish a democratic regime is grotesque'. Apart from sending help to rescue a friend in Liberia, Nigeria's Babangida was concerned about the effect of the crisis in the subregion in terms of encouraging soldiers to do the same in other countries. Sierra Leone and Guinea had a significant number of men involved in the war in Liberia and there were also many Liberians living as refuges in these two countries and beyond including Ghana and Côte d'Ivoire. So, it is argued that the countries and their leaders could only be concerned about how that would affect their regime security and not necessarily because of the securitization of subregional security issues. Furthermore, it has implications for the audience in the securitization process in that it is not the public that is the audience as would be expected in a democratic order. The audience instead are the fellow West African leaders and other political actors who need to be persuaded of every securitization move or extra political measure.

The successes recorded by ECOMOG in Liberia encouraged the subregional leaders to try the same approach in Sierra Leone. The end of Cold War and its implications on global geopolitics helped to localize the security politics in the subregion of West Africa. Starting from Liberia and extending to Sierra Leone, the subregional leaders faced a lack of adequate support from external patrons and thus articulated their security actions to manage the emerging security challenges by themselves. ECOWAS did not have any prior security mechanism to address security issues in Sierra Leone; the same way it did not have any before intervening in Liberia. It is argued that the processes of securitizing the issues that emerged in Sierra Leone and the subsequent securitization processes put in place for future security threats were influenced by the neo-patrimonial disposition and dynamics in the subregion, rather than the larger security interest of the subregion. It is important to bear in mind that the close-knit nature of the states in the subregion means that what affects one state has spillover effect on the other state. It is strategically wrong to ignore security development in one neighbouring state because they will definitely cause ripples (Bah 2005, 1).

A brief overview of the events leading to the ECOWAS intervention in Sierra Leone will suffice here. A group of Revolutionary United Front (RUF) rebels sponsored by Charles Taylor in Liberia tried to overthrow the government of Joseph Momoh in Sierra Leone in March 1991 but did not succeed because of the assistance of external hands including Nigeria and a pro-government militia, the Kamajors. The government was eventually overthrown by Captain Valentine Strasser who eventually became president in 1992. Brig-General Bio overthrew Valentine in 1996 and organized an election that brought in Ahmad Tejan Kabah as president. However, on 25 May 1997, Kabah himself was forced to flee to Guinea in a coup by Armed Forces Revolutionary Council led by Major Johnny Paul Koroma and supported by Sankoh and his RUF (McGregor 1999; Berman and Sams 2000; Bah 2005; Gberie 2005; Rashid 2013). It was at this point that Nigeria intervened to rescue the situation. The Sierra Leonean crises definitely were serious security problems in the Mano River Basin and beyond. But how these were securitized and perceived by different individual regimes in the subregion was interesting. Let us consider that ECOWAS member states put in place some protocols such as the protocol on conflict prevention, management and resolution; moratorium on small arms; protocol on democracy and good governance. There is also a protocol on free movement of persons in the subregion.

The ambition of the framers of these protocols and many more on other salient security issues was to transform ECOWAS from a security complex to security community. These protocols may sound noble but they did not command unanimity of opinions and actions from the leaders of individual member countries in implementing them. It is from this angle that we will view the intervention of ECOWAS in Sierra Leone. The intervention was fraught with much controversy as the ideals and interests of leaders clashed. First of all, the intervention spearheaded by Nigeria was a move by Nigerian leader General Sani Abacha to reinstate his friend President Kabbah who had been forced to flee to neighbouring Guinea (Gberie 2005, 112). Sierra Leone and Nigeria had concluded a bilateral defence agreement in 1997 which would provide training to the Sierra Leonean Army and presidential guard. About 900 Nigerian troops, a military training team and a battalion attached to ECOMOG were present before the coup that removed Kabbah (Berman and Sams 2000, 112–113). Nigeria did not have any legality or authorization to intervene in Sierra Leone. The subregion was just coming out from the Liberia crises and therefore had no institutionalized framework for action in Sierra Leone. Nigeria simply pursued another ad hoc securitization measure; acting first before asking for ECOWAS approval; reminiscent of a dimension of securitization processes being ad hoc. Also, it is suggested within securitization concept that

> if by means of an argument about the priority and urgency of an existential threat the securitizing actor (in this context Nigerian leader) has managed to break free of procedures or rules he or she would otherwise be bound by, we are witnessing a case of securitization. (Buzan, de Wilde and Waever 1998, 25)

It could only be interpersonal neo-patrimonial interests that guided the action. In order to get ECOWAS approve the military action, there were some subregional dynamics underpinning the for-and-against argument.

The approval for intervention to reinstate Kabba did not come until about 3 months after Nigeria has already intervened and there were a lot of troubling issues. Experience in Liberia made Ghana and Côte d'Ivoire wary of another costly encounter in Sierra Leone. Also, considering that Liberia's Charles Taylor and Burkina Faso were arming the RUF rebels, other ECOWAS members were doubtful of their commitment to the ECOWAS threat securitization moves. What is also a very important issue is that the Anglophone–Francophone divide and suspicion was pulling the fabrics of the security mechanism in the subregion apart. Though the old man of Côte d'Ivoire politics, Houphouët-Boigny, was dead at the time of the crisis, the colonial hangover was still an issue to the ECOWAS members. There was palpable fear of Nigerian domination expressed by the members.

Of much more interest to the subregion and even international community is the concern over the altruism of Nigerian leader in the intervention in Sierra Leone. Commentators (Olonisakin 1998; McGregor 1999; Berman and Sams 2000; Rashid 2013; Fawole 2001; Fawole 2003) have queried the genuineness of the intention of Nigerian leader General Sani Abacha. This is worth interrogating, considering that Nigerian state was groaning under his military jackboot while he was making efforts to reinstate an overthrown democratically elected Tejan Kabbah of Sierra Leone. Nigeria was a pariah nation at that point and so Abacha's strategy could be argued to be a way of seeking legitimacy and approval from the West. It cannot be dismissed that Abacha while trying to reinstate his friend to power was also using that as a strategy to distract the military at home and engage them abroad to avoid the military trying copy the situation in Sierra Leone. Furthermore, it is also suggested that Abacha did have some commercial interests in Sierra Leonean mineral resources. Berman and Sams (2000, 117) noted that 'when Kabbah had first come to power, Abacha had reportedly approached the Sierra Leonean authorities for mineral concessions'. In this context, the securitizing actors were the neo-patrimonial leaders in West Africa. The threat was the issue that was disturbing one of their fellow leaders led by Nigerian Abacha. But the issue was perceived differently according to their personal interests. The audience was the member leaders that needed to be carried along before any military action could take place. It was not the citizens at home that demonstrated the narrowness and failure in the securitization politics.

There is no doubt that West African leaders have made some efforts to transform the subregion into a security community. The experience in the Sierra Leonean and Liberian interventions however revealed the narrowness in their threat perception. There is certainly a lot of securitization processes going on but it is argued that they are heavily clogged by neo-patrimonial sentiments and calculations by the leaders. The processes of securitization are at best personal, dependent on the interests of the patron leaders and at worst do not consider the security interests of larger West African populace. The security architecture or processes of securitization are not independent of individual countries or leaders.

Conclusion

The article properly brought out the logic of securitization process – there was an issue, a securitizing actor, an emergency extra political measure and an audience to be persuaded. It demonstrated the dynamics of power play among the political elite in a neo-patrimonial setting. It was an effort aimed at taking securitization outside the security borders of Europe or advanced democracies – a construction of a nexus between securitization and neo-patrimonialism.

Considering that ECOWAS was not initially a security outfit, it is interesting to see how it managed the crises that threatened the subregion of West Africa in the 1990s. The argument and counter argument among the leaders in West Africa clearly showed the difference in their threat perception and displayed the neo-patrimonial power relations at the forefront of their consideration before the interventions in Liberia and Sierra Leone.

Whereas securitization theory in its original format failed to clearly identify audiences and contextual differences in the security environment, the article has provided new insights. The emergency measures in the intervention went through the rhetorical process by the Nigerian Head of State convincing an audience composed of his fellow leaders in West Africa and not necessarily the general public. Finally, the argument was developed that (1) issues in neo-patrimonial settings are securitized according to the threat perception of a narrow circle of elites and (2) thus, for securitization theory to benefit non-West security environments, differences in contexts must be taken into consideration.

Disclosure statement

No potential conflict of interest was reported by the authors.

ORCID

Edwin Ezeokafor http://orcid.org/0000-0002-6457-3452

References

Adebajo, A. 2002. *Liberia's Civil War: Nigeria, ECOMOG, and Regional Security in West Africa.* Colorado: Lynne Rienner.
Adeleke, A. 1995. "The Politics and Diplomacy of peacekeeping in West Africa: The Ecowas operation in Liberia." *The Journal of Modern African Studies* 33 (4): 569-593. doi:10.1017/S0022278X00021443.

Adibe, C. E. 1997. "The Liberian Conflict and the ECOWAS-UN Partnership." *Third World Quarterly* 18 (3): 471–488. doi:10.1080/01436599714821.

Bah, M. S. 2005. "West Africa: From a Security Complex to a Security Community." *African Security Review* 14 (2): 77–83. doi:10.1080/10246029.2005.9627357.

Baldwin, D. 1997. "The Concept of Security'." *Review of International Studies* 25: 5–26. doi:10.1017/S0260210597000053.

Balzacq, T. 2005. "Three Faces of Securitization: Political Agency, Audience and Context." *European Journal of International Relations* 11 (2): 171–201. doi:10.1177/1354066105052960.

Balzacq, T. ed. 2011. "A Theory of Securitization: Origin, Core Assumptions and Variants." In *Securitization Theory: How Security Problems Emerge and Dissolve*, 1–30. London: Routledge.

Bayart, J. F. 1993. *State in Africa: The Politics of the Belly*. London: Longman.

Bayart, J. F., S. Ellis, and B. Hibou. 1999. *Criminalization of the State in Africa*. Oxford: James Currey.

Berman, C. G., and K. E. Sams. 2000. *Peacekeeping in Africa - Capabilities and Culpabilities*. Geneva, Switzerland: United Nations Publications, UNIDR.

Bøås, M. 2001. "Liberia and Sierra leone—dead Ringers? The Logic of neopatrimonial Rule." *Third World Quarterly* 22 (5): 697–723. doi:10.1080/01436590120084566.

Booth, K. 1991. "Security and Emancipation." *Review of International Studies* 17 (4): 313–326. doi:10.1017/S0260210500112033.

Bratton, M., and N. Van de Walle. 1997. *Democratic Experiments in Africa*. Cambridge: Cambridge University Press.

Brown, N. 1999. "ECOWAS and the Liberian Experience: Peacekeeping and Self Preservation." Paper prepared for the US Department of State.

Buzan, B., and O. Waever. 2003. *Regions and Powers: The Structure of International Security*. Cambridge, UK: Cambridge University Press.

Buzan, B., and R. Little. 2001. "Why International Relations Has Failed as an Intellectual Project and What to Do about It." *Millennium Journal of International Studies* 30 (1): 19–39. doi:10.1177/03058298010300010401.

Buzan, B., J. de Wilde, and O. Waever. 1998. *Security: A New Framework for Analysis*. London: Lynne Rienner Pub.

Buzan, B. 1993. *People, States and Fear: An Agenda for International Studies in the Post Cold War Era*. United Kingdom: ECPR Press.

Cammack, D. 2007. "The Logic of African Neopatrimonialism: What Role for Donors." *Development Policy Review* 25 (5): 599–614. doi:10.1111/j.1467-7679.2007.00387.x.

Chabal, P. 2010. *Africa: The Politics of Suffering and Smiling*. London: Zed Books.

Chabal, P., and J. P. Daloz, ed. 1999. *Africa Works: Disorder as Political Instrument*. London: James Currey.

Chabal, P., and N. Vidal, eds. 2008. *Angola: The Weight of History*. New York, NY: Columbia University Press.

Clapham, C, ed. 1982. *Private and Public Power: Political Clientelism in Modern States*. London, UK: Pinter

Clapham, C. 1996. *Africa and the International System: The Politics of State Survival*. Cambridge, UK: Cambridge University Press.

De Grassi, A. 2008. "'Neopatrimonialism' and Agricultural Development in Africa: Contributions and Limitations of a Contested Concept." *African Studies Review* 51 (3): 107–133. doi:10.1353/arw.0.0087.

Erdmann, G., and U. Engel. 2007. "Neo-Patrimonialsim Reconsidered: Critical Review and Elaboration of an Elusive Concept." *Commonwealth Comparative Politics* 45 (1): 95-119. doi:10.1080/14662040601135813.

Falola, T., and M. M. Heaton. 2008. *A History of Nigeria*. Cambridge: Cambridge University Press.

Fawole, W. A. 2001. *Military Power and Third Party Conflict Mediation in West Africa: The Liberia and Sierra Leone*. Ile-Ife, Nigeria: Obafemi Awolowo University Press.

Fawole, W. A. 2003. *Nigeria's External Relations and Foreign Policy under Military Rule, 1966–1999*. Ile-Ife, Nigeria: Obafemi Awolowo University Press.

Gberie, L. 2005. *A Dirty War in West Africa: The RUF and the Destruction of Sierra Leone*. London: Hurst and Company.

Guenther, R. 1968. "Personal Rulership, Patrimonialism and Empire-Building in the New States." *World Politics* 20 (2, January): 194–206. doi:10.2307/2009795.

Huysmans, J. 1998. "Security! What Do You Mean? From Concept to Thick Signifier." *European Journal of International Law* 4 (2): 226–255.

Huysmans, J. 2000. "The European Union and the Securitization of Migration." *Journal of Common Market Studies* 38 (5): 751–777. doi:10.1111/jcms.2000.38.issue-5.

Kaldor, M. 2007. *Human Security: Reflections on Globalization and Intervention*. Cambridge, UK: Polity Press.

Keita, K. 1998. *Conflict and Conflict Resolution in the Sahel: The Tuareg Insurgency in Mali*. USA: Strategic Studies Institute.

Karyotis, G. 2010. "Religion, Securitization and Anti-Immigration Attitudes: The Case of Greece." *Journal of Peace Research* 47 (1): 43–57. doi:10.1177/0022343309350021.

Kaufman, R. 1974. "The Patron Client Concept and Marco-Politics: Prospects and Problem." *Comparative Studies in Society and History* 16 (3, June): 254–308. doi:10.1017/S0010417500012457.

Krause, K., and M. Williams. eds. 1997. Critical Security Studies: Concepts and Cases. London: Routledge.

Keohane, R., and J. Nye. 1977. *Power and Interdependence*. 4th ed. USA: Longman.

Lemarchand, R., and K. Legg. 1972. "Political Clientelism and Development." *Comparative Politics* 4 (2): 149–178. doi:10.2307/421508.

Leonard, S. 2010. "EU Border Security and Migration into the European Union: FRONTEX and Securtization through Practice." *European Security* 19 (2): 231–254. doi:10.1080/09662839.2010.526937.

Leonard, S., and C. Kaunert. 2011. "Reconceptualising the Audience in Securitization Theory." In *How Security Problems Emerge and Dissolve*, edited by T. Balzacq, 56–73. London: Routledge.

Levine, V. T. 1980. "African Patrimonial Regimes in Comparative Perspective." *Journal of Modern African Studies* 18 (4): 657-673. doi: 10.1017/S0022278X00014786.

McDonald, M. 2008. "Securitization and the Construction of Security." *European Journal of International Relations* 14 (4): 563-587. doi:10.1177/1354066108097553.

McFerson, H. 2010. "Extractive Industries and African Democracy: Can the Resource Curse Be Exorcised." *International Studies Perspective* 11 (4, November): 335–353. doi:10.1111/j.1528-3585.2010.00410.x.

McGregor, A. 1999. "Quagmire in West Africa: Nigerian Peacekeeping in Sierra Leone (1997-1998)." *Canadian Journal of Global Policy Analysis* 54 (3): 482-501. doi:10.1177/002070209905400309.

McSweeney, B. 1996. "Identity and Security: Buzan and the Copenhagen School." *Review of International Studies* 22 (1): 81–93. doi:10.1017/S0260210500118467.

Medard, J. F. 1982. "The Underdeveloped State in Tropical Africa: Political Clientelismor Neo-patrimonialism". In *Private Patronage and Public Power: Political Clientelism in the Modern Stat*, edited by Christopher Clapham, London: Frances Pinter.

Mkandawire, T. 2015. "Neopatrimonialism and the Political Economy of Economic Perfomance in Africa: Critical Reflections." *World Politics* 67 (3): 563–612. doi:10.1017/S004388711500009X.

Morgenthau, H. 1965. *Politics among Nations: The Struggle for Power and Peace*. 6th ed. USA: McGraw Companies.

Obi, I. C. 2009. "Economic Community of West African States on the Ground: Comparing Peacekeeping in Liberia, Sierra Leone, Guinea Bissau and Cote d'Ivoire." *African Security* 2 (2–3): 119–135. doi:10.1080/19362200903361945.

Ofuatey-Kodjoe, W. 1994. "Regional Organizations and the Resolution of Internal Conflicts: The ECOWAS Intervention in Liberia." *International Peacekeeping* 1 (3): 261–302. doi:10.1080/13533319408413509.

Olonisakin, F. 1998. "Nigeria and the Peacekeeping in Sierra Leone" Jane's Intelligence Review, July.

Pitcher, A., M. H. Moran, and M. Johnston. 2009. "Rethinking Patrimonialism and neopatrimonial-ism in Africa." *African Studies Review* 52 (1): 125-156. doi:10.1353/arw.0.0163.

Price, R. 1974. "Politics and Culture in Contemporary Ghana: The Big-Man, Small-Boy Syndrome." *Journal of African Studies* 1 (2): 172–204.

Rashid, I. 2013. "The Sierra Leone Civil War and the Making of ECOWAS." *Research in Sierra Leone Studies (RISLS)* 1 (1): 1–21.

Richards, P. 1996. *Fighting for the Rain Forest: War, Youth and Resources in Sierra Leone.* Oxford, UK: James Currey.

Roe, P. 2008. "Actor, Audience(S) and Emergency Measures: Securitization and the UK's Decision to Invade Iraq." *Security Dialogue* 39 (6): 615–665. doi:10.1177/0967010608098212.

Roth, G. 1968. "Personal Rulership, Patrimonialism, and Empire-Building in the New States." *World Politics* 20 (2): 194–206. doi:10.2307/2009795.

Taylor, I. 2010. *The International Relations of Sub-Saharan Africa.* New York, NY: Continuum Books.

Theobald, R. 1972. "Patrimonialism." *World Politics* 4 (2): 149–178.

Van de Walle, N. 2001. *African Economies and the Politics of Permanent Crisis, 1979-1999.* Cambridge, UK: Cambridge University Press.

Vuori, J. A. 2008. "Illocutionary Logic and Strands of Securitization: Applying the Theory of Securitization to the Study of Non-Democratic Political Orders." *European Journal of International Relations* 14 (1): 65–99. doi:10.1177/1354066107087767.

Waever, O. 1995. *In Ronnie Lipschutz: On Security.* New York: Columbia University Press.

Waltz, K. 1979. *Theory of International Politics.* USA: Waveland Press.

Weber, M. 1947. "The Theory of Social and Economic Orgnaization." In Translated and Edited by Talcott Persons. New York, NY: Oxford University Press.

Wilkinson, C. 2007. "The Copenhagen School on Tour in Kyrgyzstan: Is Securitization Theory Useable outside Europe." *Security Dialogue* 38 (1): 5–25. doi:10.1177/0967010607075964.

Williams, M. 2003. "Words, Images, Enemies: Securitization and International Politics." *International Studies Quarterly* 47: 511–531. doi:10.1046/j.0020-8833.2003.00277.x.

Wippman, D. 1993. *Enforcing the Peace: Ecowas and the Liberian War.* New York, NY: Council on Foreign Relations.

Securitization and the global politics of cybersecurity

Mark Lacy and Daniel Prince

ABSTRACT

In 'Digital disaster, cyber security, and the Copenhagen school', published in 2009, Lene Hansen and Helen Nissenbaum suggest ways in which securitization theory can help understand the politics of cybersecurity and cyberwar. What was significant about Hansen and Nissenbaum's article was the way it attempted to add new approaches and questions to a topic that tended to occupy a space in an often highly technical discourse of security, technology and strategy, a discourse that extended in to all aspects of life in a digitizing society. This article asks: What should international relations scholars be doing in addition to the challenge and task – to become more interdisciplinary in order to be able to engage with the potential technification and hypersecuritizations of cybersecurity policy and discourse – that was set out in Hansen and Nissenbaum's article?

Introduction

In 'Digital disaster, cyber security, and the Copenhagen school', published in 2009, Lene Hansen and Helen Nissenbaum suggest ways in which securitization theory can help us understand the politics of cybersecurity and cyberwar, a complex terrain that brings together a variety of technical and policy challenges that range from individual cybersecurity problems (cybercrime) through to issues of national and economic cybersecurity (anxieties about attacks on 'critical infrastructure') (Hansen and Nissenbaum 2009). Some of the threats point to futuristic 'black swan' disasters that result from our high-speed networked society; some of the challenges are traditional problems – abuse and harassment, grooming and recruitment, identity theft and fraud – carried out with new technologies. The cyber-terrain is one where there is an anxiety that an individual can become a national security problem in new and dangerous ways – and where cyber techniques and technologies of national security can play out at the level of the individual in new and unprecedented ways, with innovations in the surveillance and monitoring of everyday life: the security state becomes – to use the fashionable management term – increasingly *granular*. This article returns to Hansen and Nissenbaum's article, an article that introduced new complexities, questions and nuances to the study of cybersecurity in security studies and international relations (IR), to think about the changing terrain of cybersecurity in the second decade of the twenty-first century – and the importance (and problems) of thinking about the 'non-West' in research on (cyber)securitization.

Hansen and Nissenbaum are interested in how the collective 'referent objects' of 'the state', 'society', 'the nation' and 'the economy' are presented as being threatened through three types of securitization that 'tie referent objects and securitizing actors together' (Ibid, 1163): hypersecuritization, everyday security practices and technifications. On this view, hypersecuritzation refers to the expansion of a security problem into a realm where there is the danger that threats can be exaggerated, resulting in excessive countermeasures: these hypersecuritizations, according to Hansen and Nissenbaum, always 'mobilize the spectre of the future' while also using 'the past as a legitimating reference'(Ibid, 1164). In the public threat horizon of future threats and dangers, proponents of cyber fears often use historical analogies of 'electronic pearl harbors' or 'cyber 9/11s' in speculations on new types of threats: for the securitization theorists, the 're-animation' of past events works to give a 'form' or credibility to future threats that have yet to occur – or are yet to be imagined.

What was significant about Hansen and Nissenbaum's article was the way it attempted to add new approaches and questions to a topic that tended to occupy a space in an often highly technical discourse of security, technology and strategy, a discourse that extended in to all aspects of life in a digitizing society. Indeed, 'everyday security practices' in their work refer to the ways that individuals and organizations are integrated into the practices of securitization as 'both a responsible partner in fighting insecurity' and also as a potential threat, allowing for responses that can permeate all aspects of everyday life (Ibid, 1165). This was a discourse of security that due to the technical complexity was presented as occupying the 'cutting edges' of security, a zone that few outside of computer science would be able to engage with. In this sense, 'technification' refers to the manner in which cybersecurity becomes a terrain that depends on the 'expert authority' of the computer scientist and policy expert for its legitimacy, a domain where 'the experts' are the securitizing actors in a manner that risks to detach the issues from critical scrutiny and dialogue. Using the case study of Estonia in April–May in 2007, the authors illustrate how securitization theory can bring conceptual clarity and complexity to a terrain that can either be reduced to simplifications using the past as a means of understanding – or taking the issues into a zone where it is beyond our means of critical understanding and comprehension, where we feel overpowered by our inability to engage critically with the issues, issues that can leave us with the feeling we are in the realm of *geopolitical science fictions*, a world that feels increasingly like the 'cyberpunk' novels of William Gibson or films such as *Ghost in the Shell*.

Hansen and Nissenbaum reach a conclusion that resonates with the broader objectives of securitization theory and 'critical security studies': to develop strategies to counter and interrogate the 'exceptional' status of security issues – where an issue might be presented as 'exceptional' due to the threat to the national interest and/or exceptional due to the technical knowledge needed to evaluate the threat:

Cyber securitizations are particularly powerful precisely because they involve a double move out of the political realm: from the politicized to the securitized, from the political to the technified, and it takes an inter-disciplinary effort to assess the implications of the move, and possibly to counter it ... cyber security stands at the intersection of multiple disciplines and it is important that both analysis and academic communication is brought to bear on it. The technical underpinnings of cyber security require, for instance, that IR scholars acquire some familiarity with the main technical methods and dilemmas, and vice versa that computer scientists become more cognizant of the politicized field in which they design and how their decisions might impact the (discursively constituted) trade-offs between security, access, trust, and privacy. (Ibid, 1172)

The implication of this argument is an important one: we should develop the tools that enable us to challenge the ethico-political dangers of hypersecuritization in this rapidly changing (cyber) space; to be able to see into this zone of expert knowledge and authority, the spaces where decisions are made on the policies and technologies that will shape all areas of war and security (see Balzacq 2011). But this article asks: What should IR scholars be doing in addition to the challenge and task – to become more interdisciplinary in order to be able to engage with the potential technification and hypersecuritizations of cybersecurity policy and discourse – that was set out in Hansen and Nissenbaum's article?

What we want to do in this article is suggest that in the time since the article was published, there may be problems and trends that have emerged that require some additional approaches to this issue of hypersecuritization and technification. Simply put, we need to think again about the problems of cybersecurity in the 'political realm' and we need to develop research on cybersecurity and 'political realms' in different places around the planet; to go beyond the often hypersecuritizing images of digital danger and 'otherness' emerging from the 'non-West' to explore the complexity of cybersecurity both from the perspective of new 'everyday security strategies' that individuals may confront and also in terms of the potential for 'digital disasters' that might emerge from specific technological, legal, political and security contexts.

Following on from Hansen and Nissenbaum, our position in the article begins from the view that interdisciplinary attempts to engage critically with hypersecuritization is the primary task of work in this space: to be able to counter hypersecuritizations where threats are 'hyped up' – or unspecified future cyber dangers are invoked – is the first move for scholars who want to think critically about the 'threat horizons' that we are presented with on the (not so) clear and present/future dangers. In the time since the article has been published (2009), much of the debate has centered around the hyper-securitization of the concern with all things digital and the implications for the future of security and war (most notably in Thomas Rid's book *Cyberwar Will Not Take Place*). At the same time, there have also been events that have pointed to the possibility of the types of future problems that we could confront – from events that fit with the type of warnings on digital disaster that many have been making since the issue emerged (the hacking of Ukrainian power grids, the Central Bank of Bangladesh bank heist) to the emergence of events that were not considered in previous speculations on digital disaster (Zetter 2016a; Zetter 2016b): attempts to shape the political direction of other states through a combination of disruptive 'gray zone' tactics that may involve hacking and new uses of social media (the debate over 'fake news' and social media, the US Presidential election in 2016). The problem now is not simply hypersecuritization but the problem of what Ulrich Beck describes as 'organized irresponsibility' where the 'state administration, politics, industrial management and research negotiate the criteria of what is "rational and safe"'. Discussing environmental risks, Beck asks 'do we live in the context of "organized irresponsibility"?' (1999, 6). We would suggest the same question needs to be asked in the context of the securitization of digital risks and insecurities.

What we suggest in the article is this: once we have established that the first move in this area is think critically about cyber securitizations and the potential problems of the move from the political to the technified, we can consider the concerns of those who we describe as the 'cyber catastrophists' – those who continue to be concerned about the digital disasters that could impact on all aspects of life. We suggest that in this realm of cybersecurity, we see three positions that shape the ideas that are contributing to vibrant debate and discussion of the future of cyberwar and cybersecurity: the cyber catastrophist, the digital realist and the techno-optimist. The article rests on the position that each perspective presents us with questions about cybersecuritizations that we need to constantly remain open to – given the fast-moving and disruptive pace of geopolitical and technological change. We suggest that the point in Hansen and Nissenbaum's article about the need to counter hypersecuritizations needs to be supplemented by more exploratory questions about whether we confront the issue of organized irresponsibility in this space. The problem of technification is not simply on how it might add legitimacy to hypersecuritization, in what it enables us to visualize in the imagination of digital disaster – it is what it fails to see or ignores, the construction and legitimation of what is rational and safe. In other words, we need to examine the politics – and the different positions that may shape policy – in the spaces where important 'expert' decisions are made: to examine, for example, how risk and unintended consequences are being integrated into planning. But the questions opened up by the 'deconstruction' of cybersecurity and cyberwar by Hansen and Nissenbaum also point to inquiry on the changing nature of 'everyday security practices' and here we suggest that is clearer now is the need for IR scholars to examine the specific contexts, controversies and challenges in diverse spaces beyond the often simplistic geographies of cyber-threat that often serve to fuel the hypersecuritized visions of geopolitical imaginaries.

One of the geopolitical anxieties that circulates in many of the key positions we discuss is a concern with the cyber insecurities that we confront from the non-West or that may result from poor cyber governance in the non-West. While this use of the term 'non-West' can be problematic and limiting, it does remind us to think beyond the simplistic geography of 'cyber' danger that is often central to the debates about cybersecurity, the geopolitical imaginary filled with devious Bond-villains from former Communist-countries, cunning-'Oriental' cyber criminals from a cyberpunk movie, totalitarian states experimenting with new technologies of *Minority Report*-like control and 'feral' digital environments in states outside the 'tame zones' of global politics. Securitization perspectives – along with work influenced by poststructuralist writers – are often a call to see beyond the simplistic representations of global politics that continue to imagine the future through the same geographies of otherness and difference that shaped the past (Hansen 2006). This article suggests that – in the spirit of Hansen and Nissenbaum's article – we need to keep searching for the questions that need to be asked about a terrain that more than ever needs to be examined in its fast-moving complexity and messiness: to examine the difference, complexity and messiness of new trends, practices and behaviours in environments that are often ignored or reduced to the 'same' in a supposedly homogenizing and universalizing global technological culture.

The cyber catastrophist, the digital realist and the techno-optimist

The cyber catastrophist

The cyber catastrophist suggests that digital disaster is on the threat horizon – and it is often *underplayed* in the discourses of geopolitical danger. Few catastrophists, however, would see digital disasters resulting in social, economic and infrastructural collapse similar to the violence made possible by weapons of mass destruction. But there are exceptions. In *Global Trends 2030: Alternative Worlds* – the fifth instalment of the National Intelligence Councils reports on the future of global security and economy – the report includes a list of 'Potential Black Swans That Would Cause the Greatest Disruptive Impact':

> Nuclear powers such as Russia and Pakistan and potential aspirants such as Iran and North Korea see nuclear weapons as compensation for other political and security weaknesses, heightening the risk of their use. The chance of nonstate actors conducting a cyber attack – or using WMD – also is increasing. (National Intelligence Council 2012, xi)

What is interesting here – in a measured report not prone to doom-mongering or panic – is the partnering of cyber with the more traditional threat of nuclear attack and weapons of mass destruction. Although the exact nature of the consequences are left vague and unspecified, what is interesting for us is this move to frame cybersecurity or cyberweapons on the same level as weapons of mass destruction, a potentially hyper-securitizing move that includes non-state actors as potential contributors to digital disaster.

This anxiety about the potential capabilities of 'non-traditional' actors with 'non-traditional' weapons circulates in many speculations on future insecurity. The US Third Offset Strategy sets out to explore the cutting edge of technology, to try to 'stay ahead' of the enemy in a terrain where non-state actors might become a threat in a traditional sense and where state actors might become a threat in a non-traditional sense, operating in the 'grey zone', using the evolving tactics of 'ambiguous war'. In the Third Offset Strategy, the 'pace of change' is seen as a fundamental element in the security landscape. As Undersecretary for Defence Bob Work says in a speech on the strategy:

> Unlike the previous offsets, the fielding of tactical nuclear weapons and precision-guided bombs and missiles, which deterred war and gave the American military in some cases four decades of advantages over adversaries, this new technology probably won't provide an edge that long. (Work 2015)

The anxiety is that all the 'traditional' hierarchies – the order that 'international society' upheld – are disrupted by the pace of change, a pace of change that provides dangerous opportunities for non-state actors and 'peer competitors'. According to Work, the potential to lose the competitive edge in technology stems *from* vulnerabilities in cyberspace: 'What's more, some of the potential competitors are letting us do the research and development, then they steal it from us through cyber theft and they go right to development, rather than spending their own resources on Research and Development (R&D)'(Ibid). On this view, the cyber threat becomes a danger through the way it impacts on traditional elements of defence and security.

Great powers/peer competitors play the biggest role in this vision of future insecurity. In 2013, a small independent 'b' movie (film and popular culture can play a role in legitimating hypersecuritization) was released that depicted a cyberattack orchestrated by China on the critical infrastructure on the US. The cyberattack was a reaction to the failure of the US to pay back its debt. The Chinese are able to shut down critical infrastructure and invade the US: the movie becomes a twenty-first-century version of the 1980s' Cold War movie *Red Dawn* that depicted young Americans resisting an occupying force from Russia. *Dragon Day* (directed by Jeffrey Travis 2013) built this scenario on the fear – a fear that we have seen circulate in real-world discussions of cybersecurity – that some products 'made in china' may contain malware that can be activated to control/shut down the everyday technologies, we use and the critical infrastructure that we depend upon.

While the movie might tap into and express broader fears about the rise of China, most commentators would see this type of cyberwar scenario as geopolitical science fiction. Most cyber catastrophists would agree with Thomas Rid that sabotage, espionage and subversion are the primary cyber tactics that states will develop and deploy (Rid 2013). But where the 'extrinsic catastrophist' – those who argue threat comes from the outside – might differ with Rid is on the question of scale and destructiveness of new types of sabotage, espionage and subversion. The counterargument to this catastrophist position is that a state will not launch such a cyber-event because they will face the same constraints and deterrents that would apply to more traditional weapons. But for the *extrinsic* catastrophist, the issue is that the actions of deterritorialized and networked non-state actors will not be shaped by the same anxieties about retaliation and laws of war that will shape the behaviour of states. In addition, there might be states that support non-state actors, enabling them to orchestrate the type of destructive events that previously only states could orchestrate: states that engage in such practices of 'ambiguous war' will be playing with fire. But for the extrinsic catastrophist, the problem is that non-state actors might obtain the capability to act like states. Or even more troubling: an individual might obtain the destructive capacity of a state or non-state actor. We heard one expert refer to the possibility of the single individual massively destructive.

For the cyber catastrophist, the state is a realm of organized irresponsibility. For former National Coordinator for Security, Infrastructure Protection and Counterterrorism, Richard Clarke, we have to face the reality of possible cyber 9/11s or Pearl Harbors. For Clarke and Knake, we are moving headfirst into a more vulnerable and insecure security environment.

> The speed at which thousands of targets can be hit, almost anywhere in the world, brings with it the prospect of highly volatile crises. The force that prevented nuclear war, deterrence, does not work well in cyber war. The entire phenomenon of cyber war is shrouded in such government secrecy that it makes the Cold War look like a time of openness and transparency. The biggest secret in the world about cyber war may be that at the very same time the U.S. prepares for offensive cyber war, it is continuing policies that make it impossible to defend the nation effectively from cyber attack. (Clarke and Knake 2010, xi)

At the same time, there are cyber catastrophists outside the realm of national security thinkers and experts. The influential French philosophers and social critics Jean Baudrillard and Paul Virilio wrote about technology and catastrophe since the 1960s from the perspective of 'intrinsic catastrophists': Virilio and Baudrillard are both concerned that progress *is* catastrophe in our accelerated times; catastrophe comes from the worlds we build. For Paul Virilio, the problem is the possibility of the integral accident (Virilio 2007). The integral accident is the possibility of the accident that is magnified due to the interconnected nature of the world we live in: an example might be a financial crisis or the possibility of cascading global impacts that result from human-generated climate change. Our complex, interconnected world generates the possibility of accidents and disasters that are not confined to a locality – the local accident can become global and the impact of the local event can extend through time. Virilio suggests we are too seduced by the possibilities of transforming society offered by new technologies, the promise of speed, efficiency and networked existence. For Virilio, the problem is that we are designing and creating a fragile technological infrastructure that will exceed our capacity to control it. Jean Baudrillard adds this suggestion on the future of insecurity: in modernity, we view history as a process that improves the human condition. But for Baudrillard, the pace of technological change now has the capacity to be too disruptive: the pace of change that we are witnessing in technology will lead to 'exponential instability' (Baudrillard 1994, 87). These are problems that reach beyond the problem of organized irresponsibility and failures of governance and regulation.

The cyber catastrophist suggests that while we need to be wary of inflated and unsupported threats, the primary task here is to take seriously the possibility of digital disasters and catastrophes – and to assess whether different organizations tasked with securing and protecting us are acting responsibly. While the digital disaster scenarios of movies like *Dragon Day* are geopolitical science fictions, we are seeing events that suggest that unprecedented cyber catastrophes could take place – but they would not look like anything we can currently imagine in a world of 'exponential instability'. The question the catastrophist leaves us with: where are the vulnerabilities and what are we failing to see?

The digital realist

For the digital realist of cybersecurity and cyberwar, *Dragon Day* would be an example of the most extreme panic and paranoia in debates about cybersecurity. The digital realist is positioned as a counterpoint to the cyber catastrophist, arguing against the 'hype' of the catastrophist in the hypersecuritization of digital disaster and catastrophe. Visions of future catastrophic events – such as the attacks on transportation networks in London depicted in the James Bond film *Skyfall* (orchestrated by a 'foreigner' with a grudge against the UK) – create very marketable products in popular culture. There will also be those who benefit economically from the political economy of cybersecurity created by new threats and insecurities. Indeed, one cybersecurity expert told us about how some organizations, businesses and parts of governments were becoming increasingly sceptical about some of the catastrophic scenarios that were used in the promotional material for the cyber solutions and tools that they wanted to sell. Like Hansen and Nissenbaum, the digital realist sees countering hypersecuritization as the primary task in this space, and this countering of hypersecuritization has become central to debates on cyberwar and cybersecurity.

Thomas Rid argues that it is highly problematic to talk about the possibility of cyber *war*. We are unlikely to be involved in conflict where a cyber instrument is the primary 'weapon'. War is the use of violence to achieve specific political or economic objectives through techniques that make the enemy defenceless. Even if it were possible to fight a war with cyberweapons, they are unlikely to have the violent capability of more traditional weapons. According to Rid, what we are likely to see are cyber instruments used for espionage, sabotage and subversion (see also Valeriano and Maness 2015). It might be the case that subversion results in events the far more extreme than anything we have been used to, where, for example, an attempt is made by an external actor to shape the election campaign of another state. But we will become more prepared to counter such threats.

The realist would most likely support this point in the *Global Agenda 2030* report on the 'game-changing' potential of cyber as a weapon of war:

> The degree to which cyber instruments will shape the future of warfare is unclear, however. Historians of war believe cyberpower may end up somewhat akin to early 20th century projections of the decisiveness of air power. Although air power played a significant role in 20th-century conflicts, it never achieved what its most ardent enthusiasts claimed it would: an independent war-winning capability. (National Intelligence Council 2012, 67)

But all this is not to say that cyber techniques of conflict, crime and disruption are not destructive to the national interest. But when we talk about the impact on the national interest and security, the consequences are generally not physical death and destruction. The key challenge for the military will be how to benefit from digitization in terms of speed, safety, efficiency and cost-effectiveness while not creating new types of vulnerability. But, at root, cyber is just another in a long list of problems that society confronts and much of the impact – the reason for it being a security threat – is the economic impact. In *Securing Britain in an Age of Uncertainty*, the data to support the argument that cyber had become a threat to national security is all economic (The Cabinet Office 2010).

All the problems associated with cyber are just nuisances in the lives of citizens, corporations and states. But they are nuisances that will often emerge from the territories in the non-West where governments are unable to govern – and maybe even encourage – criminal organizations able to exploit vulnerabilities in digital economies. A key 'villain' in reports of various cyber events – from the Sony hack to the Bangladesh Central Bank heist – is often North Korea, presented as a state that is so far out of the international system that it can use tactics that no one else would, willing to take risks no one else would. This representation of the geopolitics of cybersecurity might provide an 'easy target' through which to explain an emerging terrain that is far more diplomatically complex than can be revealed in the public sphere; a geopolitical terrain represented with a new generation of cyber 'villains', often with 'oriental' cyberpunks and hackers depicted causing clever types of digital disruption, experts in the new techniques of corporate/military espionage, a trope that we find in cult cyberpunk such as *Ghost in the Shell* through to mainstream movies such as Christopher Nolan's *Inception*.

But for the digital realist, cyber is a twenty-first-century *nuisance* – and a relatively minor one compared to the benefits that digital technologies provide in our lives and economies. Cyber will play a role in the security landscape we will be confronted with but we should not overstate the cyber element. Our virtual territories of data and intellectual property might be under attack but the type of scenario depicted by *Dragon Day* is not going to happen. Putting to one side the issue whether it would be even possible to shut down the US *remotely*, it is not going to happen for the same reason that great power conflict becomes less likely: the threat that traditional weapons of mass destruction will be used. There would have to be a severe degradation of the international 'scene' for traditional territorial war between great powers to return, and if the degradation of the terrain reached such a critical point, it is unlikely that cyberweapons would play a decisive role.

Of course, one of the arguments in this terrain is that in the coming century, non-state actors will be empowered in new ways. But, for the digital realist, it is unlikely to get to the point where they could do anything significant: critical infrastructures are too resilient (Calvety 2008, 139); states will retain the monopoly over violence and weapons of mass destruction (and the monopoly of cyber-offensive and cyber-defensive capability). Some might argue that the cyberweapons that states have deployed – such as Stuxnet – will be developed and used by non-state actors. But malware like Stuxnet are expensive to develop and require long-term planning and research, with a high level of access to information about the infrastructure that will be attacked (Singer and Friedman 2013). Malware like Stuxnet are state-of-the art projects by the most powerful actors in the international system, and even if non-state actors develop similar projects in coming decades, they will have to deal with the fact that there will be increased research and development in the protection of systems. Of course, there could be well-funded research facilities in shadow economies and failed states but there are less sophisticated ways of making money or making a political point. As Myriam Dunn Calvety suggests, '[t]hese doomsday scenarios are quite frightening. But it is good to know that they are about as likely to happen as a landing of alien spaceships' (2011).

The digital realist would argue that we should continue to focus on the development of offensive and defensive cybersecurity and cyberwar strategies. But we need to be careful not to equate cyberweapons with 'game changers' that will transform the future of war and create the possibility for destructive scenarios common in science fiction movies. On this view, there will always be technical fixes to secure critical infrastructures; non-state (and non-West) actors will lack the capability and states – even if they could – would lack the incentive to create a cyber-catastrophe that resulted in 'physical' violence.

We have to recognize that there are limits to what we can do: cyberspace is only partly controlled or controllable by governments. For the digital realist, it all comes back to the problem of resources. We do not want to over-react in our response to threats with costly measures and uncertain benefits, leaving government with less for middle to low impact but high-probability threats (Calvety 2008, 151). Like Hansen and Nissenbaum, the digital realist suggests that we need to counter hypersecuritizations, remaining alert to the possibility that the conditions of cyberwar may change – but for now are twenty-first-century nuisances with primarily social and economic consequences. The questions the digital realist leaves us with are: how can we avoid exaggerating the threat of cyberwar – and how (for the more 'strategically' minded) can we use these new techniques and technologies to 'improve' performance in our traditional militaries *without* creating new vulnerabilities?

The techno-optimist

Rejecting the pessimism of thinkers like Virilio and Baudrillard, the techno-optimist views History as a story of Progress. Improvement in the human condition is primarily driven by the emergence of liberal democracy – where despotic power is limited by the will of the people and where 'tribal' identities are overtaken by more expansive and potentially cosmopolitan ones – and by the emergence of new technologies that improve health, communication, economy and security. Societies are transformed by changing values, norms and institutions that move towards the inclusion of those who would previously been seen as inferior and through laws that protect human rights (Pinkers 2012). The techno-optimist believes that if societies develop the right type of institutions and political culture, we can continue the process of overcoming the catastrophes and dangers of the human condition. The liberal democratic world is not perfect: things go wrong, mistakes are made – but liberal societies have mechanisms of critique and reflection that enable learning and improvement. This is part of the resilience of liberal democracy.

Writing about what he terms 'protopia', Kevin Kelly (one of the leading 'thought leaders' on new technology and the impact on society) suggests that 'neither dystopia or utopia is our destination': 'Protopia is a state of becoming, rather than a destination. It is a process. In the protopian mode, things are better today than they were yesterday, although only a little better' (Kelly 2016, 13). The techno-optimism of this 'protopia' rests on the view that

> The problems of today were caused by yesterday's technological successes, and the technological solutions to today's problems will cause the problems of tomorrow. The circular expansion of both problems and solutions hides a steady accumulation of small net benefits over time. Ever since the Enlightenment and the invention of science we've managed to create a tiny bit more than we've destroyed each year. (Ibid, 13)

Kelly suggests that while there is clearly the potential for catastrophic events emerging from new technology, we should recognize that in the 'protopia' this 'circle of new good provoking new bad which provokes new good which spawns new bad is just spinning us in place, only faster and faster' (Ibid, 275).

For the techno-optimist (or protopian), there will be accidents and disasters but they will not have the impact of the worst-case scenarios of the hypersecuritizer, and in the 'protopia', we will build capacity in response to vulnerabilities and dangers; we will reduce the dangers in times when the digitization of all aspects of life will exceed anything we can imagine. For the techno-optimist, what we need to be doing is focusing on research and education; we need, for example, to be supporting research that will provide the technical fixes to fight the insecurities of the digital age: we need to be training the next generation of cybersecurity experts to help secure individuals, corporations, states and the military. Most cyber 'catastrophes' result from errors or sloppiness that will be easy to rectify: for example, an attempt to make fraudulent transfers totalling $951 million after cyber criminals hacked Bangladesh Bank in 2016 was possible due to the lack of a Firewall (and the bank used second hand $10 switches to connect to the SWIFT global payment network) (Quadir 2016). An international legal architecture will emerge to control and shape the behaviour of states and non-state actors in cyberspace; we might be experiencing a moment when our technology is leading us into unchartered and ambiguous terrain but we will be becoming better at making sure law and global governance keeps up with the pace of change.

In terms of cybersecurity and cyberwar, the techno-optimist is enthusiastic about the digital age. The risk of cyber catastrophes on the threat horizon will be eradicated by the technological solutions produced by artificial intelligence and better ways of spotting vulnerabilities, the 'glitches' in code that create unintended consequences (Vatamunu 2016). The primary fear is not about future cyberwar or cyber catastrophes but on the way that states will use new technology for surveillance and the control of populations. The techno-optimist is primarily concerned with the militarization or 'Balkanization' of the internet: the techno-optimist sees the global community that exists on the internet as one of the most important and positive aspects of digital culture. But one of the problems for the techno-optimist is how liberal, progressive ideas can spread in the territories that cultivate authoritarian political structures. The ideal scenario for the techno-optimist is for political change to emerge peacefully from the 'bottom-up': the techno-optimist is concerned that – after some initial post-Cold War optimism about the future of liberal democracy – we live in a world where authoritarian regimes seem to be in good health, balancing dynamic economies with authoritarian political cultures. The anxiety here is that the hypersecuritizing obsessions of the state turns inwards, using new innovations to monitor and police populations, and in the debates on security in the 'non-West', there is a concern about the *Minority Report*-like futures that will be possible in a way that is unlikely to materialize in a West anxious about privacy and civil liberties (although this could change – and perhaps is already changing – driven by hypersecuritized anxieties).

The possibilities of positive cultural and political change are even weaker if the internet is militarized or Balkanized: the possibility of grassroots communication, education and mobilization becomes limited. For example, in July 2014, the Russian Parliament passed a bill requiring all technology companies to store the personal data of all their users in the country; coming into effect in September 2016, the policy was justified in terms of national security. It was the first serious step to assert national control over segments of the web in the light of the revelations about the surveillance by the US National Security Agency; Russia's internet regulator had complained about the lack of cooperation from tech companies like Google, Facebook and Twitter in blocking content deemed illegal by the state (Hills 2014). A fragmented internet moves from being a potential space of freedom to a tightly controlled 'shopping mall' developing new and improved techniques to sell 'stuff' and monitor populations. There will be those who can bypass these controls. But these numbers will be small; the possibility for popular resistance will be limited. For the techno-optimist, the global politics of cybersecurity should be focused on protecting the cybersecurity of the citizen against a hypersecuritized threat horizon shaped by states and their new everyday security practices.

The digital realist would most likely remain cautious about the faith in new technology to transform war into something more humane: the techno-optimist will see positive 'protopian' developments in the waging of war. On this view, military technology is moving in a direction that reduces the risks faced by the soldiers of liberal democracy – and the precision of weapons creates less collateral damage on civilians close to the targets. This trend towards more humane forms of war will increase and the evolution of malware like Stuxnet will create a new generation of digital weapons (Coker 2001). States will be able to use 'information bombs' that will destroy the technological infrastructure of city or town without killing human beings – but forcing change in the behaviour of opponents. Of course, there are those (the catastrophists) who argue that we are entering an age where far from making war more humane and controlled technology is creating a type of war that will be fought be machines and artificial intelligence that will have the power to decide who lives and dies. But the techno-optimist will reply that liberal democracies will continue to impose limits on what is permissible. Our culture of human rights means that there is a great deal that is possible in terms of military technology that simply will not be realized – at least by liberal democracies (what China and other states build is another matter) – and we will always place legal constraints on what is permissible in war. The trend in military technology is not towards automated killing machines but towards smart cyberweapons that *enable destruction without destruction*, 'novel munitions', non-lethal weapons and *incapacitators* that will create 'bloodless' war.

For the techno-realist, the task is to counter – in particular – the securitization of everyday life, the invocation of threats – domestic or foreign – to justify new measures to regulate people's digital lives and to justify the introduction of new tactics and technologies to regulate all aspects of everyday life. This is, in many ways, the concern Hansen and Nissenbaum articulate on how computer scientists might become 'more cognizant of the politicized field in which they design and how their decisions might impact the (discursively constituted) trade-offs between security, access, trust, and privacy'. The question the techno-optimist leaves is with is – how do we resist attempts to limit the freedom of our digital lives and where are the innovations that will transform conflict in the coming century?

Concluding remarks: granular security and the geographies of cybersecurity

Since the publication of the article by Hansen and Nissenbaum in 2009, attempts to counter the hypersecuritzation of cybersecurity and cyberwar have intensified – from a variety of perspectives and theoretical backgrounds (the most notable being Thomas Rids *Cyberwar Will Not Take Place* and Rid's debate with John Arquilla) (Arquilla 2012). What we outline in this article are what we see as the three key positions on cyberse-curity and cyberwar that are currently central to the debates circulating in this emerging terrain: the cyber-catastrophist, the digital realist and the techno-optimist. Here, we are trying to go beyond the framing of the cyber debate in terms of cyberwar will take place (and it might be as destructive as traditional war) and cyberwar will not happen (it will involve new tools for older techniques of statecraft). We are suggesting that while the debates that have been waged on the changing character of cyberwar have been vital in clarifying the issues at stake, we need to remain open to the possibilities revealed in each position. This openness needs to be maintained exactly because of the – to use some US military jargon – volatile, uncertain, complex and ambiguous (VUCA) nature of things at this point in time: the extremes of these positions might veer into geopolitical science fiction but the questions each position poses are important ones and questions that will grow in significance exactly because of the pace of geopolitical and technological change; we need to move between them, constantly re-examining the key questions and assumptions as the 'terrain' changes (and as new questions and positions undoubtedly emerge).

In particular, we are suggesting that – while the point that Hansen and Nissenbaum conclude with on the need to be able to counter hypersecuritization and technification remains the key issue here – we need also to examine what questions and concerns are sidelined *in* the zones of technification. What we have found talking to cybersecurity professionals working in a variety of organizations is that many would see an importance in the questions and concerns of each perspective; we heard one expert say that they felt like a catastrophist working in organization x and an optimist working in organization y. One cyber 'expert' from the military world remarked to us that 'in cyber the one eyed man is king'. In 2017, for example, it was reported that National Health Service Trusts were left vulnerable to Ransomware attacks in May of that year because cybersecurity recommendations were not followed (Cellan-Jones 2017). While these events may not be described as 'catastrophic' (6900 appointments were cancelled), the question is clearly about future catastrophic events and the organized irresponsibility that may neglect or ignore certain vulnerabilities: in the organizations that are shaping the future elements in the security and military apparatus, there may be failures of imagination on future threats or the digital disasters (or 'integral accidents') that may emerge from the environments that are being designed.

The problem of technification is not simply on how it might add legitimacy to hypersecuritization, in what it enables us to visualize in the imagination of digital disaster – it is what it fails to see or ignores. This risk might intensify in a time when a variety of actors are shaping the digital worlds we inhabit. Or put another way, we need to assess the possibility that there is a problem of 'desecuritization' in the zones of technification: we need to consider the possibility that organizations that play important roles in all areas and elements in security and war might fail to examine vulnerabilities in the race for efficiency, speed and cost-effectiveness. On this view, we need to examine how cyber securitizations move from the political into the technified but also how issues and concerns can be erased – or desecuritized – through the dominance of a particular group or mindset *inside* the zones of technification. These concerns may be overstated – maybe 'organized irresponsibility' is an ungrounded fear – but these are questions that require attention.

But another trend is clearer now than it perhaps was in 2009. Thinking about the various problems/levels of cybersecurity – from the everyday and individual, the critical infrastructures of national security, the corporate and economic – in the context of securitization and the 'non-West' raises a number of issues. Securitization theory – and poststructuralist work in global politics – is interested in how 'otherness' and 'difference' circulate in (and are fundamental to) broader discourses of geopolitics and IR; in this sense, discourses of cybersecurity – and the positions outlined in this article – contain various types of digital danger emerging from the 'non-West': terrorists using the internet for radicalization, devious hackers from North Korea, hi-tech techniques of surveillance in China. But thinking about cybersecurity issues in terms of traditional geopolitical categories – developed/developing and so on – begins to look problematic in a world where all territories are being transformed by new technologies and where the sources of vulnerability become *deterritorialized*: threats can come from a 'problematic' zone of global politics but it might also come from a bedroom in the same town in your 'safe European home'. Innovations in technologies (and new uses of existing technologies) might continue to emerge from California and Silicon Valley – but they might also emerge in states anywhere around the planet.

Securitization theory warns us to be careful about the ways in which otherness can be drawn into broader geopolitical discourses of danger and difference. But what it can also alert us to is the tendency to write over the complexity and messiness of events and developments in global politics with visions of security and geopolitics that ignore the specific and particular characteristics of the worlds that are being researched and written about (see Hansen 2006). Hansen and Nissenbaum's article is a call to explore the complexity of cyber, to think more critically about what constitutes a catastrophe or digital disaster and the different problems that can be absorbed into the discourses of hypersecuritized threat. But what is clearer now is the need to explore the complexity of cybersecurity in different geopolitical and economic contexts around the planet, to become *granular* in our analyses, to explore the possibility that – while many cyber events emerge from the entangled, interconnected nature of events in the twenty-first century – there may also be new trends and developments in the ways that new technologies are used (and abused) in different contexts, to examine the new everyday security practices that might be experimented with in different states, to examine the specific vulnerabilities that might be emerging for individuals and communities in different places around the world. From the conflict over bloggers in Bangladesh, to the everyday security practices that Chinese citizens live with, to new types of crime in sub-Saharan African states, to the use of new technologies by Mexican drug cartels, new research on the global politics of cybersecurity needs to examine the local complexities and challenges faced not simply by states and corporations (the standard, 'official' approach to cybersecurity) but also by individuals and communities (the move that securitization theory prompts us to take), examining the tactics of states and non-state actors using digital strategies and techniques. The three positions outlined here can begin to open research questions to begin to examine the *global* contexts of cybersecurity and the various issues and challenges of securitization:

The Catastrophist: here the problems is to examine the potential for accidents and vulnerabilities (and what Rid would see as sabotage) – ranging from the relatively local and manageable to the more national and potentially catastrophic – that might emerge from the particular legal, political, economic and technological context; to examine the political and legal processes of technification that securitize issues or leave them in the realm of organised irresponsibility; to explore new types of crime that are possible due to trends in economy and technology (such as problems with 'mobile money' in states like Ghana or Nigeria, or new techniques of political and economic corruption).

The Techno Optimist: the problem is to explore the legal and political pressures that are attempting to shape the digital lives of citizens; to examine the techniques that might be used against the 'internal' others through new technologies of surveillance or abuse/ harm; to examine how violence and conflict is being transformed through new technologies (see, for example, Narrain 2017); to examine emerging tactics and trends that may be 'globalised' as useful techniques by states seeking to manage what they see as a the problematic digital 'mob'; or to examine new techniques of subversion that set out to shape the political landscape; and to explore the new possibilities for conflict prevention and resolution.

The Digital Realist: the challenge is to see how militaries around the planet – even the military forces that would be viewed as relatively 'undeveloped' and minor – are envisaging the use of new digital techniques technologies; to examine how they are dealing with the problems that – while not potentially 'catastrophic' – may result in operational and orga-nisational problems (espionage, subversion minor accidents or sabotage that may impact the functioning of an organisation).

So we need to remain open to what is happening in the digital lives of others, to the new vulnerabilities they confront, to the new forms of control that are deployed against them, to examine the trends in territories that might get ignored in our (imaginary) maps of digital geopolitics. But in the process of 'globalizing' these research questions, we should not lose sight of the need to think about the organized irresponsibility that we might find in the organizations and institutions that pride themselves as being the most 'advanced', 'rational' and 'cutting edge'.

Disclosure statement

No potential conflict of interest was reported by the authors.

References

Arquilla, J. 2012. "Think Again: Cyberwar." *Foreign Affairs*, February 27. http://foreignpolicy.com/2012/02/27/think-again-cyberwar/

Balzacq, T., ed. 2011. *Securitization Theory: How Security Problems Emerge and Dissolve*. London: Routledge.

Baudrillard, J. 1994. *The Illusion of the End*. Cambridge: Polity.

Beck, U. 1999. *World Risk Society*. Cambridge: Polity.

The Cabinet Office. 2010. *Securing Britain in an Age of Uncertainty: The Strategic Defence and Security Review*.

Calvety, M. D. 2011. "As Likely as a Visit from E.T." *The European*, January 7. http://www.theeuropean-magazine.com/133-cavelty/134-cyberwar-and-cyberfear

Cellan-Jones, R. 2017. "NHS 'Could Have Prevented' Wannacry Ransomware Attack." *BBC NEWS*, October 27. http://www.bbc.co.uk/news/technology-41753022

Clarke, R., and R. Knake. 2010. *Cyberwar: The Next Threat to National Security and What to Do about It*. New York: Ecco.

Coker, C. 2001. *Humane Warfare*. London: Routledge.

Dunn Calvety, M. 2008. *Cyber-Security and Threat Politics: US Efforts to Secure the Information Age*. London: Routledge.

Hansen, L. 2006. *Security as Practice: Discourse Analysis and the Bosnian War*. London: Routledge.

Hansen, L., and H. Nissenbaum. 2009. "Digital Disaster, Cyber Security, and the Copenhagen School." *International Studies Quarterly* 53: 1155–1175. doi:10.1111/isqu.2009.53.issue-4.

Hills, K. 2014. "Russian Move to Control Data Stokes Fears of the Balkanisation of the Internet." *Financial Times Weekend*, Saturday July 5/6, p. 10.

Jeffrey, Travis, dir. 2013. *Dragon Day*. United States: Burning Myth Productions.

Kelly, K. 2016. *The Inevitable*. London, UK: The Cabinet Office.

Narrain, S. 2017. "Dangerous Speech in Real Time: Social Media, Policing, and Communal Violence." *Economic and Political Weekly: Engage*, August 24. http://www.epw.in/engage/article/dangerous-speech-real-time-social-media-policing-and-communal-violence?0=ip_login_no_cache%3Da2d514cacfc04ca25be50c2bb148a93c

National Intelligence Council. 2012. "Global Trends 2030: Alternative Worlds." https://globaltrends2030.files.wordpress.com/2012/11/global-trends-2030-november2012.pdf

Pinkers, S. 2012. *The Better Angels of Our Nature*. New York: Allen Lane.

Quadir, S. 2016. "Bangladesh Bank Exposed to Hackers by Cheap Switches, No Firewall: Police." *Reuters*, April 22. http://www.reuters.com/article/us-usa-fed-bangladesh-idUSKCN0XI1UO

Rid, T. 2013. *Cyberwar Will Not Take Place*. London: Hurst.

Singer, P. W., and A. Friedman. 2013. *Cyberwar and Cybersecurity: What Everyone Needs to Know*. Oxford: Oxford University Press.

Valeriano, B., and R. Maness. 2015. *Cyberwar versus Cyber Realities*. Oxford: Oxford University Press.

Vatamunu, C. 2016. "Outnumbered, yet Strong: Artificial Intelligence as a Force Multiplier in Cybersecurity." *Bitdefender*, July 12. http://businessinsights.bitdefender.com/artificial-intelligence-cyber-security

Virilio, P. 2007. *The Original Accident*. Cambridge: Polity.

Work, B. 2015. "The Third U.S. Offset Strategy and its Implications for Partners an Allies." January 28. https://www.defense.gov/News/Speeches/Speech-View/Article/606641/the-third-us-offset-strategy-and-its-implications-for-partners-and-allies

Zetter, K. 2016a. "Inside the Cunning, Unprecedented Hack of Ukraine's Power Grid." *Wired*, March 3 2016. https://www.wired.com/2016/03/inside-cunning-unprecedented-hack-ukraines-power-grid/

Zetter, K. 2016b. "That Insane, $81 Million Bangladesh Bank Heist? Heres What We Know." *Wired*, May 17 2016. https://www.wired.com/2016/05/insane-81m-bangladesh-bank-heist-heres-know/

REPLY

The politics of securitized technology

Juha A. Vuori

This is a reply to:

Lacy, M. 2018. "Securitization and the global politics of cybersecurity." *Global Discourse* 8 (1): 100–115. https://doi.org/10.1080/23269995.2017.1415082.

In 'Securitization and the Global Politics of Cybersecurity', Lacy (2018) shows how cyber catastrophists, digital realists and techno optimists all have varying viewpoints in regards to the securitization of technologies. Each attitude towards the dangers posed by 'cyber-war' depends on its context, and such positions can be mixed and change within organizations. Lacy argues that we need to go beyond countering 'hypersecuritization' (Hansen and Nissenbaum 2009) of digital disasters to engage with 'organized irresponsi-bility' (Beck 1999) within the realm of technologized security. Indeed, Lacy's discussion of hypersecuritization and various imaginaries of digital disasters points to important facets of securitization and desecuritization dynamics within the realm of technological security practices. To my mind, this presents an even larger issue for investigating the politics of securitized technology both in the West and Non-West. Crucial here is how diffuse cybersecuritization interweaves with practices of dataveillance and censorship.

Indeed, computers and other communication technologies today are very common securitized spaces irrespective of whether you are in the West or not. This holds for both individual security in terms of malware and hacking, and for societal as well as state actors that are concerned with corporate espionage or gaining intelligence for purposes of state security. New communication technologies (NCT) are where the largest numbers of people encounter security and dataveillance practices in their everyday activities. The widespread use of these technologies provides both commercial and state actors with unprecedented opportunities to monitor and manipulate societal behaviour and opinion both in democratic and authoritarian political settings. This holds for both internal and external political actors. Indeed, the United States and a number of European states have complained about foreign manipulation of election campaigns and domestic politics, a concern previously raised mostly by authoritarian states in the 'non-West'.

Beyond deliberate propaganda and advertising purposes, the politics of technology has less apparent and intentional effects too. Crucially for the discussion at hand, studies that have explored both security articulations and the enactment of security techniques have emphasized how in addition to securitization in the exceptional manner of high politics, securitization can come about diffusely through techniques, technologies and practices (Huysmans 2014). Here, a by-product of state securitization of NCT is the circumvention of citizens' rights and protections against state infringements through cooperation of intelligence agencies that remains secret. In this way, the expansion of states' 'cyber capacities' in the form of mass surveillance, for example, undermines basic democratic rights such as privacy and confidential communication. As such, securitization in conjunction with the enactment of cybersecurity technologies and techniques modulate the limits of freedom and democracy (Huysmans 2014), or the thresholds of allowed/tolerated and prohibited in authoritarian settings (Vuori 2014). This shows how the politics of securitized technologies has a bearing on the conduct of conduct, but also how it concerns political orders and their core values.

This suggests the importance of exploring the politics of technology involved in security practice as well as security articulations. There is a need for further engagement with the relationship between political orders and the politics of technology around the world (Paltemaa and Vuori 2009). In the era of global information networks, algorithmic video and social media have produced a new logic for the circulation of security articulations (Andersen 2017). Yet, at the same time, some states still manage to have a keen grip on online censorship (Vuori and Paltemaa 2015, 2018). Both of these tendencies display the importance of laying out the interlinkages of dataveillance and security online, but also how they are operated in other technologies. In the realm of NCT, securitization is not only hyper – it can be very banal too. Both of these have political implications that need to be unpacked. As Lacy's discussion of global cybersecurity points out, we need to further examine the interrelations of securitized technologies and technological security securitization with core values of political orders and their visions of the political.

Disclosure statement

No potential conflict of interest was reported by the author.

References

Andersen, R. S. 2017. "Video, Algorithms and Security: How Digital Video Platforms Produce Post-Sovereign Security Articulations." *Security Dialogue* 48 (4): 354–372. doi:10.1177/0967010617709875.

Beck, U. 1999. *World Risk Society*. Cambridge: Polity.

Hansen, L., and H. Nissenbaum. 2009. "Digital Disaster, Cyber Security, and the Copenhagen School." *International Studies Quarterly* 53 (4): 1155–1175. doi:10.1111/isqu.2009.53.issue-4.

Huysmans, J. 2014. *Security Unbound. Enacting Democratic Limits*. London: Routledge.

Lacy, M. 2018. "Securitization and the Global Politics of Cybersecurity." *Global Discourse*. doi:10.1080/23269995.2017.1415082

Paltemaa, L., and J. A. Vuori. 2009. "Regime Transition and the Chinese Politics of Technology: From Mass Science to the Controlled Internet." *Asian Journal of Political Science* 17 (1): 1–23. doi:10.1080/02185370902767557.

Vuori, J. A. 2014. *Critical Security and Chinese Politics: The Anti-Falungong Campaign*. London: Routledge.

Vuori, J. A., and L. Paltemaa. 2015. "The Lexicon of Fear: Chinese Internet Control Practice in Sina Weibo Microblog Censorship." *Surveillance & Society* 13 (3/4): 400–421.

Vuori, J. A., and L. Paltemaa. 2018. "Chinese Internet Control over Social Media Discourse." In *Routledge Handbook of Chinese Discourse Analysis*, edited by C. Shei. London: Routledge.

Let's just say we'd like to avoid any great power entanglements: desecuritization in post-Mao Chinese foreign policy towards major powers

Juha A. Vuori

ABSTRACT

Previous studies on securitization in China have shown how security discourses can have various domestic political functions, how even security issues can be contested, and how China engages with the securitization moves of neighbouring states. Despite this growing literature, there is however no general view of desecuritization as a part of Chinese foreign policy towards the major powers. To fill this gap, the present article examines desecuritization in the foreign policy of post-Mao China. This discussion begins with the desecuritization of the Cold War, and then views how China has sought to prevent the securitization of China's rise in the US. This discussion contributes to the study of Chinese foreign policy maxims by providing it with insights seen through the lens of desecuritization.

Introduction

Much of the literature on desecuritization, or the dismantlement of security issues, has focused on the effects security practices or the absence of such have on domestic society (Wæver 1995; Buzan, Wæver, and de Wilde 1998; Hansen 2012). The focus has mainly been on the possibilities and normative desirability of defusing situations that are handled through a 'security rationale'. In such cases, from the viewpoint of 'tactics', social movements can use the language of desecuritization in order to deflect accusations of being a threat to national security or something else valued in society (Paltemaa and Vuori 2006). Indeed, antagonistic sides of a conflict usually blame one another, and depict themselves as not a threat.

In the case of China, previous studies on securitization, or the construction of security issues, have shown how security discourses can have various domestic political functions (Vuori 2008, 2011b), how even security issues can be contested (Vuori 2015; Topgyal 2016), and how China engages with the securitization moves of neighbouring states (Chin 2008; Wishnick 2008; Biba 2013; Danner 2014). As a result of such studies, we know quite a bit about how desecuritization moves and discourses have been used in domestic political contests, and how they are used in bilateral issues that are not at the top of the foreign policy agenda. What is still missing though is a discussion of desecuritization as a part of Chinese foreign policy lines in general and towards the major powers in particular.

To fill this gap in the literature, I examine Chinese desecuritization tactics at the international level. The most significant development here is the desecuritization of the Cold War macrosecuritization (Buzan and Wæver 2009) that structured and overlaid security dynamics in East Asia (Buzan and Wæver 2003), and where China played a key role. Beyond examining the process of dismantling such a major security frame, I explore how desecuritization has been used in China to pre-empt or contest moves towards presenting its post-Cold War rise as a threat. This kind of posture is quite evident in the foreign policy maxims of the People's Republic of China (PRC, China) since the late 1970s, and particularly after the end of the Cold War. Here, instead of viewing Chinese foreign policy maxims as a feature of a 'strategic culture' (Johnston 1995, 1996), or as an 'operational code' (Feng 2005; He and Feng 2013), these maxims are viewed as a tactic to avoid conflict, that is, a tactic to avoid the threshold of securitization. Such an overall stance has been deployed to create a peaceful or non-threatening reputation for China; indeed, a threat reputation would be damaging for an aspiring great power (Deng 2008, 102–103).

China's post-Cold War foreign policy maxims have previously been analysed through the viewpoints of reputation and the security dilemma (Deng 2006). The present article also contributes to this literature by investigating the use of these maxims through the securitization/desecuritization framework (Buzan, Wæver, and de Wilde 1998). While 'non-traditional' and 'traditional' studies of security are often presented as incommensurable, the applicability of the approach suggests that this may not always be the case. Most of the literature of critical studies of security in general and of securitization in particular has been focused on 'non-traditional' notions and issues of security (Kim and Lee 2011; Lupovici 2014). To view securitization and desecuritization as plays in politicians' 'playbooks' when they engage in political games in situations of security dilemmas is one way to allow securitization studies to study issues that have generally been left for 'traditional security studies'. Indeed, viewing securitization and desecuritization in this manner allows critical students of security to enter more traditional avenues of study.

The article begins with a brief review of the prominent ways to understand desecuritization. It then introduces the pre-eminent Chinese foreign policy maxims deployed during the Cold War. The analysis of desecuritization begins with the desecuritization of the Cold War, which is followed by a discussion of how desecuritization has been used to prevent the securitization of the rise of China during the Clinton, Bush, and Obama administrations. As the beginning of the Trump administration shows, China faces the greatest challenge yet to keep the 'China threat' discourse off of the official US security agenda.

The notion of desecuritization

The study of desecuritization is its own branch of Securitization Studies (Buzan, Wæver, and de Wilde 1998; Balzacq 2011). Securitization denotes the power politics involved in making issues ones of security. In other words, issues do not come with security labels, but gain the rights, duties, and other deontic aspects through social processes where speech acts of securitization play a major role. Talk is not cheap when it comes to security, as security speech produces antagonistic social realities and divides up opportunities and constraints accordingly.

Securitization theory was developed as part of the debates around the broadening and deepening of security notions in the late 1980s. The suggestion was that it would be possible to include a number of security 'sectors', such as military, political, societal, economic, and environmental security, without rendering everything as security. This was made feasible through a focus on the form of security speech, and by taking security as a status and modality. Indeed, 'one could "throw the net" across all sectors and all actors and still not drag in everything with the catch, only the security part' (Wæver 2011, 469). This 'security part' was the claimed existential threats to valued referent objects, and requested legitimacy for extraordinary measures in the defence of the referent (Vuori 2003). Different sectors of security engage varying threats, and security means different things to different societies, as the core fears of any group or nation are unique and relate to vulnerabilities and historical experiences (Wæver 1989, 301). As such, the state and society level is where most securitizations take place. Yet, there are also securitizations that are about grander referents, such as human civilization, or the planet. Such moves have received their own concept of macrosecuritization (Buzan and Wæver 2009; Vuori 2010).

As the literature on securitization theory has grown, so has the terminology in regards to various aspects of the political dynamics of security. One focus here has been the contestation of, and resistance to securitization (Balzacq 2015), either by more or less equal political actors (Vuori 2015), or between securitizing actors and the targets of securitization (Paltemaa and Vuori 2006). Such contests can also include co-securitization (Kim and Lee 2011). For the discussion at hand, the notions of reverse- and counter-securitization (Vuori 2011a; Stritzel and Chang 2015) are most relevant. Reverse-securitization discourses respond to other actors' securitization moves by reflecting them back at them in similar terms. By presenting their own identities in the same terms of the opponent, they try to become a 'matched pair' (Buzan and Wæver 2009) in the contest, and perhaps increase their social capital should such identities be accepted. Counter-securitization differs here in that in such a discourse, the opponents' securitization moves are not reflected back, but securitizing moves draw from inner discourses, identities, and cultural reservoirs. In the Chinese context, an example of this is the Falungong's securitization of the Communist Party (Vuori 2014).

Most crucial here though, is the notion of desecuritization that also plays the most common role in the contestation of security issues. As such, desecuritization is the negative corollary of securitization. Indeed, it has mainly been viewed as the unmaking of securitization (Huysmans 2006) that comes about either as a fading away of the issue (Behnke 2006) or through initiation with active moves (de Wilde 2008; Donnelly 2015). In this literature, desecuritization has largely been understood in terms of the deconstruction of collective identities in situations where relations between 'friends' and 'enemies' are constituted by existential threats (Roe 2004, 280). While the normative push of the original approach to desecuritization has been towards this kind of a situation, the literature on it has been criticized for eschewing politics (Aradau 2004), and biasing desecuritization when it is not necessarily morally better than securitization (Floyd 2011). Some view desecuritization as akin to securitization: for Floyd (2015), desecuritization is a set of actions that can be morally evaluated as a time-limited event, while Vuori

(2011a; 2011b; 2015) has treated desecuritization as a counter-move to securitization in processes of contestation and resistance. Others have favoured a return to the initial political purposes of the concept, like Hansen (2012) who has sought to recover the political status of desecuritization with an examination of the ontological and practical levels involved in empirical investigation of desecuritization processes. Here, Donnelly (2015) suggests that desecuritization moves can be conceptualized as both speech and other symbolic acts by examining how desecuritization moves can be accomplished after several decades of institutionalized securitization. Finally, Bourbeau and Vuori (2015) have suggested that desecuritization is not only about dismantling existing issues, but can also be actively used to retain a non-security status for an issue.

Originally, for Wæver (1995), desecuritization is a process by which security issues lose their 'securityness', and are no longer restrictive by nature. He has outlined three options for this: (1) simply not to talk about issues in terms of security, (2) to keep responses to securitized issues in forms that do not create security dilemmas or other vicious spirals, and (3) to move security issues back into 'normal politics' (Wæver 2000, 253). These options can follow objectivist, constructivist, or deconstructivist strategies in bringing about desecuritization (Huysmans 1995, 65–67). Indeed, the first discussions about desecuritization were about how it could be achieved (Huysmans 1995; Wæver 2000). In later development, the literature on desecuritization has focused on three sets of questions: what counts as desecuritization (identification of the phenomenon), why should there be desecuritization (ethics and normativity), and how can desecuritization be achieved (transformative practice) (Balzacq, Depauw, and Léonard 2015).

Most importantly for the present article, beyond conceptualizing desecuritization as an option or a strategy, it has also been viewed from the viewpoint of political actors (de Wilde 2008, 597), and their political moves in games of contestation and resistance (Paltemaa and Vuori 2006, 2011b; Vuori 2015; Stritzel and Chang 2015; Topgyal 2016). There can be desecuritizing actors who evade, circumvent, or directly oppose securitizing moves by, for example, emphasizing competing threats (de Wilde 2008, 597). Security policies aim at desecuritization (the solution to the threatening situation), but desecuritization can also happen independently from the actions of securitizing or desecuritizing actors: the original security problem may be solved, institutions may adapt through new reproductive structures, discourses may change (e.g. with the loss of interest or audiences), and the original referent object may be lost (de Wilde 2008). As empirical studies of securitization and desecuritization dynamics (e.g. Salter and Mutlu 2013; Lupovici 2014; Vuori 2015; Donnelly 2015) have shown, it is difficult to point to a definitive end-point for either securitization or desecuritization: political and social situations evolve.

Systematizing previous empirical studies of desecuritization, Hansen (2012, 529, 539–545) has identified four ideal-type forms for desecuritization. In regards to its issues of concern, namely the status of enmity and the possibility of a public sphere, when a larger conflict is still within the realm of possibility, but when a particular issue is presented with terms other than security, we have an instance of (1) 'change through stabilization'; when another issue takes the place of a previously securitized issue, we have (2) 'replacement'; when the originally phrased threat is resolved, we have (3) rearticulation; and finally, when potentially insecure subjects are marginalized through depoliticization, we have (4) 'silencing'. Bourbeau and Vuori (2015) add to these 'pre-emptive desecuritization through rebuttal'. For Wæver (2000, 254), securitization can be pre-empted or forestalled through silencing. For Bourbeau and Vuori (2015), desecuritization can also be used actively to avoid the escalation of a contention.

Indeed, as the securitization literature on securitization/desecuritization dynamics points out, political actors have a menu of choice when they encounter a security discourse: they can adopt or translate it into their own policies, try to transform the discourse with concomitant implications for other actors, they can keep the issue on the agenda in non-security terms with politicization, or they can aim take the issue completely off the agenda through desecuritization. Each of these is a different type of political move that allows for different kinds of room in the games great powers play, and each has different kinds of political costs (e.g. raising the stakes of the issue to a principled level, various kinds of security dilemmas as well as reputation and discursive costs). Such plays can happen on a number of levels, including the most encompassing referent object of macrosecuritization and macrodesecuritization (Buzan and Wæver 2009).

Armed with the above five 'models' of desecuritization, we can now begin the examination of how they have appeared in Chinese foreign policy.

Chinese foreign policy principles and the cold war

Before analysing China's post-Mao foreign policy maxims from the point of view of desecuritization it is good to provide some contrast to them through a brief review of the development of the main foreign policy principles of the People's Republic since its establishment in 1949. From a western standpoint, the PRC of the Cold War may seem a key part of the monolithic Soviet bloc. This however is far from the realities of Chinese foreign policy.

The Cold War overlaid much of the security dynamics around the world, and it structured many lower level securitizations (Buzan and Wæver 2003). Formative speeches and documents in both the Soviet Union and the US after the Second World War already showed the formation of this bipolar constellation between the victors of the war (Gaddis 2005, 30–31). There could be no peace among the hostile camps of socialism and capitalism, whereby 'nearly every nation' had to 'choose between alternative ways of life' (Truman [1947] 1963, 178–179). 'New Cold War history' suggests (e.g. McMahon 1994; Gaddis 2005; Lüthi 2008) that the macrosecuritization structure allowed smaller powers, at times, to set the agenda of the camps on both sides of the conflict: clients were able to present their patron superpower with the securitization argument that they could not afford the fall of this or that regime. President Eisenhower's ([1954] 1960, 383) influential metaphor of falling dominos captures this logic quite well: 'You have a row of dominos set up, you knock over the first one, and … the last one … will go over very quickly. So you could have … a disintegration that would have the most profound influence'. In view of this logic, such 'dominos' could influence those with a vested interest in the particular domino not to fall.

Although not a small power by any account, China too was able to use the macrosecuritization constellations of the Cold War to its own advantage, and had a major impact on them. Although it did not appear so at first, China was a key player in the Cold War. Indeed, China became 'a target of influence and enmity for both' camps (Nathan and Ross 1997, 13). A key factor here was China's rhetoric of world revolution, which 'dramatically enhanced the perception of the Cold War as a battle between "good" and "evil" on both sides' (Chen 2001, 3–4). In effect, China became a force multiplier for the macro-moves of the superpowers.

China entered the Cold War in the Soviet camp in order to secure the 'fruits of victory', which became crucial referents of Chinese security discourse. Accordingly, Chinese views in the late 1940s (e.g. Liu 1948; Mao 1949) clearly structured the world into two opposing camps, which supports the structuring power of the early securitizations of the era. Yet, while macrosecuritizations can label and may dominate security discourse, China's alignment in the Cold War actually demonstrates their vulnerability: it has even been argued that 'no other event during the Cold War contributed more to changes in perceptions of the Communist powers than did the rise and fall of the Sino-Soviet alliance' (Chen 2001, 49). For example, US perceptions of Mao's China ranged from optimistic views of Mao as an Asian Tito, to China being a monolithic satellite of the Soviet Union, to finally an ally in the triangular politics of the Cold War (Christensen 1996; Scott 2007).

Like China's position in the Cold War constellation, Chinese foreign policy principles have been contested since their initiation during the Cold War (Chen 2001). After the establishment of the People's Republic 1949, China 'leaned to one side' (一边倒, yībiāndǎo) in the two-camp (两个阵营, liǎng ge zhènyíng), Cold War structure of world politics (Mao 1949, 292). Beyond this pro-Soviet stance, China's first premier Liu Shaoqi promoted the view that China should actively support all liberation struggles in the 1950s. In this view, China should be an anti-imperial force in the world. This 'hard stance' was contested by China's foreign minister Zhou Enlai, who promoted the view that China should build a 'zone of peace' around its borders, which would allow China to concentrate on the consolidation of its domestic order (Shao 1996). According to this view, China should work together with the 'third power' of 'oppressed peoples' in the 'intermediate zone' between the two poles of the Cold War.

By the 1950s, Zhou's line won over Liu's harder stance, and the 'five principles of peaceful co-existence' (和平共处五项原则, hépíng gòngchǔ wǔxiàng yuánzé) became the leading diplomatic principle for establishing foreign relations for the People's republic after the Asian-African Conference in Bandung 1955.[1] This initial success for a 'peaceful' foreign policy did however not end the contestation of China's foreign policy line. In the radicalization of Chinese domestic politics in the 1960s, and after Lin Biao had been promoted into the position of defence minister in 1959, Mao's theory of world revolution became a major part of China's official foreign policy line. Lin (1965) followed Mao's theory of guerrilla warfare. On the international level, this meant that the post-colonial developing nations represented the 'countryside' of the world while the industrial nations represented the 'cities'. The countryside would eventually envelop the cities, which would lead to a world revolution. China should support all 'freedom fighters' in the world. While this radical rhetoric did not match China's pragmatist foreign policy behaviour (van Ness 1970), when combined with the turmoil of the cultural revolution this radical rhetoric isolated the people's republic from most of its foreign relations.

During the 'polemics' between the Chinese and the Soviet Communist Parties in the 1960s, it was quite evident that both Soviet and Chinese securitizations were pulling away from the two inclusive universalist macrosecuritizations of the Cold War (Chen 2001; Lüthi 2008). Furthermore, Mao linked the revisionism he identified in the Soviet

Union to that which he also securitized domestically: not even the success of the revolution could guarantee that Chinese ideological differences were in the past – they could only be solved through class struggle. Accordingly, Mao identified and securitized a great danger for Communism: whether the emergence of Khrushchev's revisionism will be prevented 'is an extremely important question, a matter of life and death for our Party and our country' (The Polemic 1965, 478).

China's turn away from the Sino-Soviet alliance did however not mean that China leaned to the other side. Instead, China began to 'hit with two fists', i.e. waged a struggle against both the imperialist superpower and the social imperialist superpower, and looked for company from the 'intermediate zone' between them. Indeed, anti-American rhetoric retained its strength in China even during the heights of the Sino-Soviet split when the Soviet Union was formally declared as China's greatest enemy (Barnouin and Yu 1998, 98); the notion of 'peaceful evolution', promoted by John Foster Dulles as the best way to combat socialist regimes, remained among the top threats in Chinese discourses right up to the end of the Cold War. The US however turned out to be the lesser evil when Mao began a rapprochement with Nixon and improved Sino-US relations as a balance against the USSR.

Indeed, in the late 1960s, the Sino-Soviet split was so severe that a full scale war seemed possible due to increasing border skirmishes (Lüthi 2008). The possibility of the realization of the spectre of a Soviet threat Mao had utilized for a decade (Christensen 1996; Lüthi 2008) allowed China to shift its foreign policy stance. In this situation Mao realized the problems of 'fighting with two fists', and promoted the opening up of relations with the United States. Nixon's famous trip to China in 1972 was a sign of victory for Zhou Enlai's pragmatic foreign policy line (Burr 1999).

This victory did however not mean the end of conflictual principles in China official views on foreign relations. In 1974 Mao's principle of the 'intermediate zone' was finalized into the 'theory of the three worlds', which was stipulated by Deng Xiaoping to the United Nations in 1974. Like the theory of the intermediate zone, the theory of the three worlds divided the world into three segments: the first world that consisted of the US and the Soviet Union, the second world that consisted of developed industrial countries, and the third world that consisted of developing nations. In this theory, China would always be part of the third world, and never vie for its leadership.

Yet, Mao had not shied away from conflictual foreign relations. This was evident in his radical principles but also in some of his foreign policy actions like bombardment of Quemoy in 1958 (Christensen 1996). Mao was willing to provoke conflict within the Cold War when it seemed to serve his domestic purposes. In post-Mao China, the situation has mostly been different (except in the case of Taiwan, and the 'punitive war' with Vietnam in 1979). Once Deng Xiaoping had consolidated his leadership grasp, he promoted foreign policy principles that were in accordance with the now late Zhou Enlai's views of a zone of peace: China would need a peaceful international environment in order to concentrate on its domestic development and construction. In the 1980s these principles seemed to work well as both relations with the Soviet Union and the United States were better than never before. Deng (Deng [1985] 1993, 126–129) even noted that China was under the least military threat in its history.

Macrodesecuritization and the end of the cold war

Sino-Soviet relations began to mend in the 1980s with the removal of a number of political obstacles and with the intensification of the conflict between the US and the Soviet Union (Wishnick 2001); the reduction of tensions across the border lead to the largest arms reduction of the Cold War. Yet, it is only with the fall of the Soviet Union that we can see an overall desecuritization in the form of rearticulation (Hansen 2012, 542–544) taking place in Sino-Russian relations. For the socialist macrosecuritization of the Cold War though, the transitions away from socialist orders in Europe and collapse of the Soviet Union meant the loss of its referent object (de Wilde 2008).

The Sino-Soviet split had largely been waged in ideological terms, and had been driven by Mao (Lüthi 2008). With Mao's passing, China shifted once more to a more pragmatist line in its foreign pronouncements. There were moves towards rearticulating the Sino-Soviet relationship on both sides. In his speech in Tashkent, Brezhnev acknowledged China as a socialist state, opposed the two China policy of the US, promised not to threaten China, and offered negotiations on the border issue (Wishnick 2001). In turn, China no longer demanded a common front against the Soviet hegemony. Deng also emphasized China's non-aligned security policy position, and its independent foreign policy of peace (Wu 2001). In effect, China no longer hit with either fist. Gorbachev continued the line of improving relations in China, which culminated in his state visit in 1989.

In the aftermath of the end of the Cold War, Deng Xiaoping continued along the line of not taking the lead in international affairs. He summed this principle up in 24 Chinese characters in November 1991: China's maxim was to 'observe calmly, secure our position, cope with affairs calmly, hide our capabilities and bide our time, be good at maintaining a low profile, and never claim leadership'. Such principles meant that China should not engage in international conflicts. China should work towards 'world multipolarization' (世界多极化, shìjiè duōjíhuà) (Deng 1990). This was exemplified with China and Russia forming a 'strategic partnership' in 1996. China and Russia even shared the same 'threat package' of 'terrorism, separatism, and religious extremism' (the 'three evils') within the Shanghai Cooperation Organization (Jackson 2006, 310) – a form of securitization that is distinctly apart from those of the Cold War. These are strong indicators of how the two states have managed to reform their identities away from the Sino-Soviet antagonism. In the overall state relations then, we can see a rearticulative desecuritization tactic at play on both sides: ever since the early 1980s, China's policy towards the Soviet Union (and later Russia) shifted from antagonism to one of collaboration and negotiation rather than reciprocal securitization. Instead, there has been a shared threat package since the late 1990s.

Accordingly, the fall of the Soviet Union meant the end of Chinese block politics in Cold War terms. Instead, China has promoted a 'fair international order' and 'world multipolarity' (Deng 2008). Such maxims have aimed to keep China away from the securitization threshold of other states, and detach China from antagonisms. China does not appear to favour a return to antagonistic macro-security constellations with other major powers. Even in the war on terror, China aligned with the US (Wayne 2008).

The Cold War has also been actively desecuritized when there have been estimations of a return to such sustained conflicts. For example, in the context of rising tensions between Russia and the EU, due to the Ukraine crisis, a comment in the People's Daily

(27 February 2014) emphasized that 'The political, economic and security theories that belonged to the Cold War era still dominate many people's minds nowadays. […] [O]nly through breaking the shackles of the Cold War mentality can we avoid unnecessary confrontation.' In the Asian context of the US 'pivot' and discussions of a new cold War in Asia (Keck 2013; Legvold 2014), Chinese reactions have voiced the need to 'cast away the Cold War mentality' (People's Daily 22 April 2014). Comments such as these indicate that China aims to keep the Cold War macrodesecuritized, and the rising China off the security agendas of great powers.

Rebutting the China threat

In the post-Cold War situation, China found itself in a new situation: Russia had half the power resources of the Soviet Union while China kept increasing its own. The ideological macrosecuritization structure was also gone (Buzan and Wæver 2009). China was on the rise in international politics. This raised worries in many parts of the world, especially after the violent crackdown on its own citizens in 1989. Assertive moves in the South China Sea and on Taiwan increased impressions of a bellicose China. Prominent Chinese military figures spoke of China's need to expand its maritime defences and 'living space' guided by principles such as 'sea as national territory' (海洋国土, hǎiyángguótǔ) and 'survival space' (生存空间, shēngcún kōngjiān). Even coastal defence (近海防御, jìnhǎi fángyù) was transformed into offshore defence (近洋防御, jìnyáng fángyù). This situation fuelled the flames of the 'China threat theory' in the US.

The presentation of China as a threat to the US has its origins in 1992 (Deng 2006, 192; 2008). This discourse presented China as a military and economic threat to the US (see e.g. Bernstein and Munro 1997; Timperlake and Triplett 1999; Mosher 2000). These aspects of military and political security were soon joined by societal aspects, as China as the last major socialist state was presented as an affront to liberal-democratic values. This 'China threat theory' predicted that an economically and militarily strengthening China that presented increasing territorial claims, and had an authoritarian political order would increase its demands and eventually challenge the international order, i.e. the US, on a global level.

The China threat discussion fed a critical response in China, which was most discernible in nationalist circles. The 'patriotic education campaign' launched in response to the events of 1989 in China had already amplified the pre-existing nationalist sense of injustice in world affairs in regards to China's experiences and current position (see e.g. Hughes 2006, 73–76; Wang 2008). There had been a clear change of tune in the nationalist discourse: while still in the 1980s nationalists had criticized the backwardness of Chinese culture, science, technology, and economy (e.g. the 'River Elegy' television series), in the 1990s the US China threat theory was tackled head on. This was explicit in the publication of books such as 'China can say no' (Song et al. 1996; see also Li et al. 1996), which aroused lots of attention abroad as well. Such nationalist texts admitted China's weaknesses, but at the same time they condemned the 'baseless demonization of China' in the West, particularly in the US, and thereby the justification to subjugate China. In turn, these nationalist writings were shunned outside China, and were used as evidence of a China threat (e.g. by Bernstein and Munro 1997). Thereby the two national 'threat literatures' fed each other, and served domestic functions of identity reproduction (cf. Callahan 2005, 708–712). As Callahan (2005, 712) notes, the China threat rebuttal texts are problematic for their authors in the sense that they keep reproducing the very threat discourse they are rebuking, a point which has been pointed out in the 'normative dilemma of writing critical security' debate within securitization studies (Vuori 2011b).

Beyond the 'nationalist' response, Chinese analysts had picked up on the US China threat theory (中国威胁论, *Zhōngguó wēixiélùn*) by the mid-1990s (see Yee and Storey 2000; Deng 2006). They directly addressed the securitization claims of US counterparts (e.g. Bernstein and Munro 1997): titles such as 'True threat comes from those trumpeting "China Threat"' (Da 1996) and '"China Threat" theory groundless' (Wang 1997) exemplify the interaction between unofficial securitization moves in the US and mirrored desecuritization moves in China. Such articles can be viewed as an interactive desecuritization discourse that targets the claims made in the securitization moves that have targeted China as a threat (see e.g. Yee and Zhu 2000).

Many Asian states have their own China threat discourse (Yee 2000) and China has reacted to them as well. Discourses in Japan and Taiwan have been most poignant here (Deng 2006, 187). An interactive securitization/desecuritization dynamic is also at work in China's positions on the issues of Chinese migration to Russia's far east being securitized in Russia as part of the 'China threat' (see e.g. Lukin 2000; Wishnick 2008), the securitization of human smuggling across the Taiwan Strait (Chin 2008), the issue of transboundary rivers (Biba 2013), and the island dispute with Japan (Danner 2014). China has deployed desecuritization in all of these issues too.

In the biggest game in town though, both US China threat securitization moves, and Chinese nationalist responses were exaggerative: instead of the multi-polar world desired by Chinese foreign policy, 'unipolarity' seemed to be more prevalent in view of the military might of the US displayed first in the Gulf war of 1991, and later in Kosovo 1999. Irrespective of China's military modernization programme since the 1980s, the People's Liberation Army lagged far behind US capabilities (Shambaugh 2003). Thereby military assertion was not a viable option for China in the 1990s. This was also discernible form unofficial and official responses to the securitizing discourse of the China threat in the US as well as from China's foreign policy actions since the late 1990s: China's emphasis on multilateral diplomacy (e.g. being the head of the Shanghai Cooperation Organization), activity in international organizations (e.g. joining the World Trade Organization), and other deeds to strengthen complex interdependence (e.g. the world's largest foreign currency reserves) were unprecedented in China's previous foreign policy behaviour (Johnston 2003).

Reaction to the China threat theory was not limited to popular writers or political analysts: major figures of the China political leadership took part as well. Both Li Peng and Jiang Zemin commented directly on the views that expressed China as a threat in the late 1990s: 'China will not pose a threat to any other nation, nor will it invade or oppress other countries' (Li 1996; see also Xinhua 1994; People's Daily 2000); 'A developing and progressing China does not pose a threat to anyone. China will never seek hegemony' (Jiang 1997); 'A Developed China will play a positive role in maintaining world peace and stability and will by no means constitute a threat to anybody' (Jiang 2000). As if harking back directly to the cottage industry of US books on the threat of China, both Li and Jiang proclaimed that China did not strive for hegemony, and that China would never be a threat to any nation. High level representatives disclaimed the

China threat, like for example General Chi Haotian ([1996] 2002, 64) who remarked that 'there are still some people around the world who keep spreading the fallacy of the "China threat"'. Even the first National Defence White Paper (1998) proclaimed that China sought to 'lead a peaceful, stable, prosperous world into the new century'. Similarly, the 15th Party Congress emphasized 'handling relations among great powers' (处理大国关系, chǔlǐ dàguó guānxi), where China would work towards building peace (all the while China's regional behaviour was considered quite expansive in the mid-1990s). Subsequent White Papers by the Hu and Xi administrations have continued this cooperative 'operational code' (Yang and Keller 2017).

The securitization discourse of the China threat had stemmed from mainly private actors in the US. For example, President Clinton had campaigned on a strong anti-China stance but by his second term he had taken a more pragmatist stance on China and in his last China speech called for engagement of China with an open hand rather than a clenched fist. The mainly private moves however resulted in desecuritization moves by both private and public actors in the PRC. Such moves worked towards countering and disclaiming the threat claims present in securitization moves. While this was done by even the most prominent Chinese politicians, and was present in White Papers, the foreign policy maxims remained the same. In the 2000s, desecuritization discourse would be inserted into them as well.

Desecuritization has however not been the only move put forth in China. When US securitization moves have been on the non-state level, there has been an opportunity to do respective reverse-securitization moves by similar Chinese actors, in a similar way as in disputes with Japan (Danner 2014). Here, the US was presented as a threat to China, and particularly as 'a thief crying "stop the thief"' (贼喊捉贼, zéihǎnzhuōzéi). Even some official statements have echoed such views. For example, China's first White Paper on National Defence (1998) has a taste of reverse-securitization, albeit in an implicit fashion as to its targeted threat: 'hegemonism and other power politics remain the main source of threats to world peace and stability. [...] Some countries, by relying on their military advantages, pose military threats to other countries, even resorting to armed intervention.' The mirroring effect has also been evident in articles by the People's Daily (2002): 'the "theory of the China threat" has been spreading like a pestilence [...] in fact, [the] real threat comes from the creator of the 'theory of threat'.

Desecuritizing China's rise

The 1990s were a difficult decade for Sino-US relations. It seemed as if China was being propped us as the next big competitor for the US in the post-Cold War era. This was the case in US academic discussions as well. Political scientists such as Samuel Huntington (1996, 313–316) and John Mearsheimer (2001) presented China as the key competitor state for the US in either civilizational or real political terms. The presidency of George W. Bush also began in dire circumstances: the spy plane incident of 2001 was the first international crisis of the Bush administration. However, talk of 'Cold War 2' was soon replaced with the war on terror after events of September 11th. China became an immediate partner in this global macrosecuritization, and the US reciprocated with an unofficial presidential visit in October, and eventually by adding the East Turkistan Independence Movement onto the UN terrorist organization list (Wayne 2008).

Even though the China threat discourse was tuned down in the US, China continued to rebut it, and institutionalized its own position. In late 2003, the foreign policy idea of 'peaceful rise' (和平崛起, hépíng juéqǐ) (Xinhua 3 November 2003) was hotly promoted and briefly became the leading slogan of the new Hu Jintao administration (Zheng 2005; Deng 2006; Glaser and Medeiros 2007). It is as though the maxim of peaceful rise would be a direct rebuttal of the US China threat discourse. Many of the securitization moves of the China threat discourse were premised on theories and beliefs of international relations, which suggest that rising powers eventually lead to conflict, and even major war.[2] The foreign policy slogan of peaceful rise explicitly counters this avenue of thought: it is as if the maxim had been developed to work against theories of hegemonic wars. Thereby it can be read as a tactic that aims to keep China off the acute security agenda of concerned states. Indeed, Chinese observers have been attuned to both non-state and state discourse (Deng 2008, 113), and the stance aims to limit such views to the non-state level. Indeed, China has itself deployed non-state actors in the securitization of its island dispute with Japan, which has subsequently been desecuritized by official actors (Danner 2014). The principle of 'peaceful rise' argues that China is not a threat to other states' security, although China's 'comprehensive national strength', that consists of economic, political and military elements, and China's capabilities to project it even militarily, are increasing. If the securitization discourse in the US would break out of the 'private sector', and be adopted by public securitizing actors, this could lead to containment policies against the PRC. In this context, the official maxim can be read as a move to avoid the China threat discourse to become official US policy; the concept of peaceful rise of the 2000s seems to be a 'pre-emptive desecuritization move' (Bourbeau and Vuori 2015).

By the summer of 2004, the initially very active study of the new notion of peaceful rise died down as it was deemed too optimistic, and even counterproductive (Deng 2006, 200): even peaceful rise could be read as a threat by those whom China was gaining on. As the peaceful rise principle was shot down, the Hu Jintao administration adopted the slogan of 'Peaceful Development' (和平发展, hépíng fāzhǎn) in 2005 (Information Office 2005), and the maxim of a 'Harmonious World' (和谐世界, héxié shìjiè).[3] While not as explicitly in response to political theories of hegemonic wars, these two principles still contain the same notion: China's increased strength should not be considered as a threat as China is working towards peace and harmony. Such maxims seem to be aimed at keeping China's relations with major powers on a desecuritized footing.

Holistic security and China as a responsible international actor

China has not remained oblivious to global security discourses. In the post-Cold War period, China has emphasized that it is working under a 'new concept of security' (Deng 2008). The new concept is a departure from previous notions in that what China now pursues is, to a large extent, the security of its 'sustained development', or its 'comprehensive national strength' on a range of battlegrounds (inter alia in military, political, economic, and technological areas). Sustained development is seen as a guarantee, or even a necessity, for the other objectives of national security of a more traditional type. Indeed, in his statement after the first meeting of the Central National Security Committee, Xi Jinping emphasized that 'China must pay attention to both development and security, because only a prosperous country can have a strong military, which in turn can protect the country' (China Daily 15 April 2014). Sustained development then becomes both a security objective and a means for security. Indeed, according to the revised Party constitution (*Constitution of the Communist Party of China* 2017): 'The Party shall pursue a holistic approach to national security and resolutely safeguard China's sovereignty, security, and development interests.'

As China has become more involved in global governance, it has emphasized itself as a 'major and responsible country' that works towards 'a community with a shared future for mankind' (Xi 2017). Major projects like the 'belt and road' initiative, and activity in global governance continue to present China's rise as an unthreatening development. Such efforts have not been without their successes. For example, under Barack Obama, the US and China found each other begrudgingly in the issue of climate change (U.S.-China Joint 2014), as they had with the war on terror under Bush (Wayne 2008). Obama (e.g. White House 2015) also stated many times that the 'the United States welcomes the rise of a China that is peaceful, stable, prosperous, and a responsible player in global affairs'. Such statements show how China's foreign policy dictums have been adopted by other major powers.

On the Chinese side, Xi too has kept pace with American theories of power transition. He has explicitly denied the existence of a 'Thucycides's trap', put forth by Graham Allison (2017). The notion refers to the stresses that result from one power declining and another gaining strength, which has many times lead to wars between major powers. For Xi (Xinhuanet 2015) though, 'There is no such thing as the so-called Thucydides trap in the world. But should major countries time and again make the mistakes of strategic miscalculation, they might create such traps for themselves.' To avoid such miscalculation, China seeks 'non-conflict, non-confrontation, mutual respect and win-win cooperation' (Xinhuanet 2015) in its foreign policy with the US – in other words, to produce stabilized desecuritization (Hansen 2012).

The election of Donald Trump has brought with it perhaps the greatest challenge yet for maintaining this kind of desecuritized state of affairs in Sino-US relations. Indeed, while Trump has made several gaffes with regards to the established diplomatic practices, the greater issue is with the world-view of Trump's advisor Stephen Bannon where China is presented as expanding at the cost of the Judeo-Christian West. Accordingly, in march 2016, Bannon predicted that 'We're going to war in the South China Sea in five to 10 years […] there is no doubt about it' (Bannon 2016). Indeed, it is as if the authors of the 1990s China threat literature were now directly advising the president. In such a situation, China faces the stark probability that previously unofficial securitization speech may become official policy. As with foreign minister Wang Yi, desecuritization is viewed as the rational line here: 'Any sober-minded politician, they clearly recognize that there cannot be conflict between China and the United States because both will lose, and both sides cannot afford that' (Guardian 2017). Luckily for China, Bannon was included in those dismissed from the Trump Whitehouse in 2017.

Conclusions

As the above has shown, desecuritization speech in post-Mao China has taken on many forms, yet it has been fairly consistent towards other major powers since the mid-1980s, and followed developments in international affairs. Desecuritization as rearticulation was how relations with the Soviet Union were mended in the 1980s. Soon after, the macro-desecuritization of the Cold War together with the effective loss of the referent object on one side redefined the world view of the entire international order and brought a definitive end to ideological forms of security speech towards other states, even though ideology still informed China's domestic security discourse. Furthermore, the desecuritization of the Cold War has been actively maintained even in more recent tensions, such as the soured relations between Russia and Europe after the annexation of Crimea in 2014.

In the case of Sino-US relations after the Cold War, China has directly rebutted securitization moves that have been part of the so called China threat discourse. The aim seems to have been to restrain such moves to the level of private actors and keep them away from official policy statements. Such rebuttals work towards maintaining stabilized desecuritization in the relations. The Trump administration appears to be providing the stiffest challenge for this stance to date, despite the exit of the most prominent proponent of securitizing Sino-US relations.

Looking at China's foreign policy dictums through the lens of securitization/desecuritization shows how this approach that has mainly been applied to study domestic politics and 'new' security issues can also be successfully deployed to investigate 'traditional' security issues as well as interactions between states. Indeed, the framework is applicable to the study of diplomacy and foreign policy. At the same time, the case of China provides desecuritization studies with an empirical case of desecuritization that is engaged in actively, and in order to maintain a non-securitized state of affairs among major powers.

Notes

1. The five principles were first mentioned in the 1954 'Agreement between the Republic of India and the People's Republic of China on trade and intercourse between Tibet Region of China and India', and they consisted of: (1) mutual respect for sovereignty and territorial integrity, (2) mutual non-aggression, (3) non-interference in each other's internal affairs, (4) equality and mutual benefit, and (5) peaceful coexistence.
2. For a critical review of the applicability of various models on power-transition and major war to the Chinese case, see Chan (2008). Allison (2017) has been the most recent scholar to point out the dangers of the power shift in China's favour.
3. See e.g. http://www.china.org.cn/english/features/UN/142408.htm.

Disclosure statement

No potential conflict of interest was reported by the author.

References

Allison, G. 2017. *Destined for War: Can America and China Escape Thucydides's Trap?* Boston: Houghton Mifflin Harcourt.
Aradau, C. 2004. "Security and the Democratic Scene: Desecuritization and Emancipation." *Journal of International Relations and Development* 7 (4): 388–413. doi:10.1057/palgrave.jird.1800030.
Balzacq, T., Ed. 2011. *Securitization Theory: How Security Problems Emerge and Dissolve.* London: Routledge.
Balzacq, T., ed. 2015. *Contesting Security: Strategies and Logics.* London: Routledge.

Balzacq, T., S. Depauw, and S. Léonard. 2015. "The Political Limits of Desecuritization: Security, Arms Trade, and the EU's Economic Targets." In: *Contesting Security: Strategies and Logics*, edited by T. Balzacq, 104–212. London and New York: Routledge.

Bannon, S. 2016. "Breitbart News Daily," March 10. https://soundcloud.com/breitbart/breitbart-news-daily-lee-edwards-march-10-2016.

Barnouin, B., and C. Yu. 1998. *Chinese Foreign Policy during the Cultural Revolution*. London and New York: Kegan Paul International.

Behnke, A. 2006. "No Way Out: Desecuritization, Emancipation and the Eternal Return of the Political - A Reply to Aradau." *Journal of International Relations and Development* 9 (2): 62–69. doi:10.1057/palgrave.jird.1800070.

Bernstein, R., and R. Munro. 1997. *The Coming Conflict with China*. New York: Alfred A. Knopf.

Biba, S. 2013. "Desecuritization in China's Behaviour Towards Its Transboundary Rivers: The Mekong River, the Brahmaputra River, and the Irtysh and Ili Rivers." *Journal of Contemporary China* 22 (84): 1–23.

Bourbeau, P., and J. A. Vuori. 2015. "Security, Resilience, and Desecuritization: Multidirectional Moves and Dynamics." *Critical Studies on Security* 3 (3): 1–16. doi:10.1080/21624887.2015.1111095.

Burr, W., ed. 1999. *The Kissinger Transcripts. The Top-Secret Talks with Beijing & Moscow. A National Security Archive Book*. New York: New Press.

Buzan, B., and O. Wæver. 2003. *Regions and Powers*. Cambridge: Cambridge University Press.

Buzan, B., and O. Wæver. 2009. "Macrosecuritization and Security Constellations: Reconsidering Scale in Securitization Theory." *Review of International Studies* 35 (2): 253–276. doi:10.1017/S0260210509008511.

Buzan, B., O. Wæver, and J. de Wilde. 1998. *Security: A New Framework for Analysis*. Boulder, CO: Lynne Rienner Boulder.

Callahan, W. A. 2005. "How to Understand China: The Dangers and Opportunities of Being a Rising Power." *Review of International Studies* 31 (4): 701–714. doi:10.1017/S0260210505006716.

Chan, S. 2008. *China, the U.S., And the Power-Transition Theory: A Critique*. London: Routledge.

Chen, J. 2001. *Mao's China and the Cold War*. Chapel Hill and London: University of California Press.

Chi, H. [1996] 2002. "U.S.-Chian Military Ties." In: *Chinese Views of Future Warfare*, edited by M. Pillsbury, 61–67. Honolulu: University Press of the Pacific.

Chin, J. K. 2008. "Human Smuggling and Trafficking in the Taiwan Strait: Security Predicament or Political Dilemma?" In: *Security and Migration in Asia: The Dynamics of Securitisations*, edited by M. G. Curley and S.-L. Wong, 100–119. London and New York: Routledge.

China Daily. 2014. Xi stresses importance of national security, April 15. http://www.chinadaily.com.cn/china/2014-04/15/content_17436440.htm

Christensen, T. J. 1996. *Useful Adversaries: Grand Strategy, Domestic Mobilization, and Sino-American Conflict, 1947-1958*. Princeton: Princeton University Press.

Constitution of the Communist Party of China. 2017. http://news.xinhuanet.com/english/download/Constitution_of_the_Communist_Party_of_China.pdf.

Da, J. 1996. "True Threat Comes from Those Trumpeting 'China Threat'." *Beijing Review*: 7–8, November 11–17.

Danner, L. K. 2014. "Securitization and De-Securitization in the Diaoyu/Senkaku Islands Territorial Dispute." *Journal of Alternative Perspectives in the Social Sciences* 6 (2): 219–247.

de Wilde, J. H. 2008. "Environmental Security Deconstructed." In: *Globalization and Environmental Challenges: Reconceptualizing Security in the 21st Century*, edited by H. G. Brauch, Ú. Oswald Spring, C. Mesjasz, J. Grin, P. Dunay, N. C. Behera, B. Chorou, P. Kameri-Mbote, and P. H. Liotta, 595–602. Berlin and Heidelberg and New York: Springer.

Deng, X. [1985] 1993. "Speech at an Enlarged Meeting of the CMC." In: *Selected Works of Deng Xiaoping*. III vols. Beijing: People's Publishing House.

Deng, X. 1990. "Guoji Xingxi He Jingji Wenti." In: *Deng Xiaoping Wenxuan*, 353–356. 3 vols. Beijing: Renmin Chubanshe.

Deng, Y. 2008. *China's Struggle for Status. The Realignment of International Relations*. Cambridge: Cambridge University Press.

Deng, Y. 2006. "Reputation and the Security Dilemma. China Reacts to the China Threat Theory." In: *New Directions in the Study of China's Foreign Policy*, edited by A. I. Johnston and R. S. Ross, 186–216. Stanford: Stanford University Press.

Donnelly, F. 2015. "The Queen's Speech: Desecuritizing the Past, Present and Future of Anglo-Irish Relations." *European Journal of International Relations* 21 (4): 911–934. doi:10.1177/1354066115570157.

Eisenhower, D. D. [1954] 1960. Dwight D. Eisenhower: 1954 : containing the public messages, speeches, and statements of the president, January 1 to December 31, 1954. Ann Arbor, Michigan: University of Michigan Library.

Feng, H. 2005. "The Operational Code of Mao Zedong: Defensive or Offensive Realist?" *Security Studies* 14 (4): 637–662. doi:10.1080/09636410500468818.

Floyd, R. 2011. "Can Securitization Theory Be Used in Normative Analysis? Towards a Just Securitization Theory." *Security Dialogue* 42 (4–5): 427–439. doi:10.1177/0967010611418712.

Floyd, R. 2015. "Just and Unjust Desecuritization." In: *Contesting Security: Strategies and Logics*, edited by T. Balzacq, 122–138. London: Routledge.

Gaddis, J. L. 2005. *The Cold War. A New History*. New York: Penguin Books.

Glaser, B. S., and E. S. Medeiros. 2007. "The Changing Ecology of Foreign Policy-Making in China: The Ascension and Demise of the Theory of 'Peaceful Rise'." *China Quarterly* 190: 291–310. doi:10.1017/S0305741007001208.

Guardian, The. 2017. "China Plays down Steve Bannon's Predictions of War with US." https://www.theguardian.com/us-news/2017/feb/07/steve-bannon-china-plays-down-predictions-of-war-with-us-wang-yi.

Hansen, L. 2012. "Reconstructing Desecuritisation: The Normative-Political in the Copenhagen School and Directions for How to Apply It." *Review of International Studies* 38 (6): 525–546. doi:10.1017/S0260210511000581.

He, K., and H. Feng. 2013. "Xi Jinping's Operational Code Beliefs and China's Foreign Policy." *The Chinese Journal of International Politics* 6 (3): 209–231.

Hughes, C. R. 2006. *Chinese Nationalism in the Global Era*. London: Routledge.

Huntington, S. P. 1996. *The Clash of Civilizations and the Remaking of World Order*. New York: Simon and Schuster.

Huysmans, J. 2006. *The Politics of Insecurity. Fear, Migration and Asylum in the EU*. London: Routledge.

Huysmans, J. 1995. "Migrants as a Security Problem: Dangers of Securitizing Societal Issues." In: *Migration and European Integration: The Dynamics of Inclusion and Exclusion*, edited by R. Miles and D. Thärenhardt, 53–72. London: Pinter.

Information Office of the State Council of the People's Republic of China. 1998. *China's National Defence in 1998*. Beijing: Waiwen chubashe.

Information Office of the State Council of the People's Republic of China. 2005. White Paper: China's Peaceful Development Road. http://unpan1.un.org/intradoc/groups/public/documents/APCITY/UNPAN023152.pdf

Jackson, N. J. 2006. "International Organizations, Security Dichotomies and the Trafficking of Persons and Narcotics in Post-Soviet Central Asia: A Critique of the Securitization Framework." *Security Dialogue* 37 (3): 299–317. doi:10.1177/0967010606069062.

Jiang, Z. 1997. "Speech by President Jiang Zemin at the Public Gathering to Celebrate Hong Kong's Return." *Beijing Review* 40 (27–38): 27–30.

Jiang, Z. 2000. "Together to Build a China-U.S. Relationship Oriented Towards the New Century," September 8. http://www.cfr.org/publication.html>?id=3803.

Johnston, A. I. 1995. *Cultural Realism: Strategic Culture and Grand Strategy in Chinese History*. Princeton: Princeton University Press.

Johnston, A. I. 2003. "Is China a Status Quo Power?" *International Security* 27 (4): 5–56. doi:10.1162/016228803321951081.

Johnston, A. I. 1996. "Cultural Realism and Strategy in Maoist China." In: *The Culture of National Security*, edited by P. Katzenstein, 216–268. New York: Columbia University Press.

Keck, Z. 2013. "Why Asia Should Welcome a US-China Cold War." *The Diplomat*, August 8.

Kim, S.-H., and G. Lee. 2011. "When Security Met Politics: Desecuritization of North Korean Threats by South Korea's Kim Dae-Jung Government." *International Relations of the Asia-Pacific* 11 (1): 25–55. doi:10.1093/irap/lcq015.

Legvold, R. 2014. "Managing the New Cold War: What Moscow and Washington Can Learn from the Last One." *Foreign Affairs* 93 (4): 74–84.

Li, P. 1996. "The Impact of China's Development and the Rise of Asia on the Future of the World." *Beijing Review* 39(40): 6–11.

Li, X., K. Liu, L. Xiong, W. Zhu, S. Han, J. Wu, A. Shi, and M. Wang. 1996. *Yaomohua Zhingguo De Beihou*. Beijing: Zhongguo shehui kexue chubanshe.

Lin, B. 1965. "Long Live the Victory of People's War!." In: *Commemoration of the 20th Anniversary of Victory in the Chinese People's War of Resistance against Japan*. Beijing: Foreign Language Press.

Liu, S. 1948. "On Internationalism and Nationalism." *Renmin ribao*, November 7.

Lukin, A. 2000. "Russian Perceptions of the China Threat." In: *China Threat: Perceptions, Myths, and Reality*, edited by H. Yee. Surrey: Curzon Press.

Lupovici, A. 2014. "The Limits of Securitization Theory: Observational Criticism and the Curious Absence of Israel." *International Studies Review* 16 (3): 390–410. doi:10.1111/misr.2014.16. issue-3.

Lüthi, L. M. 2008. *The Sino-Soviet Split. Cold War in the Communist World*. Princeton and Oxford: Princeton University Press.

Mao, Z. 1949. "On the People's Democratic Dictatorship." In *Selected Works of Mao Tse-tung*, Vol. I – V. Peking: Foreign Languages Press.

McMahon, R. 1994. *The Cold War on the Periphery. The United States, India, and Pakistan*. New York: Columbia University Press.

Mearsheimer, J. J. 2001. *The Tragedy of Great Power Politics*. New York and London: W. W. Norton.

Mosher, S. W. 2000. *Hegemon – China's Plan to Dominate Asia and the World*. San Francisco: Encounter Books.

Nathan, A. J., and R. S. Ross. 1997. *The Great Wall and the Empty Fortress - China's Search for Security*. New York: W.W. Norton and Company.

Paltemaa, L., and J. A. Vuori. 2006. "How Cheap Is Identity Talk? A Framework of Identity Frames and Security Discourse for the Analysis of Repression and Legitimization of Social Movements in Mainland China." *Issues and Studies* 42 (3): 47–86.

People's Daily Online. 2000. *Li Peng on International Situation, China's Domestic Policies*, June 27. http://en.people.cn/english/200006/27/eng20000627_44039.html

People's Daily Online. 2002. *'Theory of Threat' Is Groundless, Erroneous: Analysis*, June 6. http://en.people.cn/200206/06/eng20020606_97261.shtml

People's Daily Online. 2014. *Drop Cold War mentality on China's cyber security*, April 22. http://en.people.cn/90780/8606087.html

People's Daily Online. 2014. *Time to put to rest the Cold War mentality*, February 27. http://en.people.cn/98649/8550976.html

Roe, P. 2004. "Securitization and Minority Rights: Conditions of Desecuritization." *Security Dialogue* 35 (3): 279–294. doi:10.1177/0967010604047527.

Salter, M. B., and C. E. Mutlu. 2013. "Securitisation and Diego Garcia." *Review of International Studies* 39 (4): 815–834. doi:10.1017/S0260210512000587.

Scott, D. 2007. "China Stands Up." In *the PRC and the International System*. London and New York: Routledge.

Shambaugh, D. 2003. "Modernizing China's Military." In *Progress*. Berkeley & Los Angeles & London: University of California Press.

Shao, -K.-K. 1996. *Zhou Enlai and the Foundations of Chinese Foreign Policy*. New York: St Martins Press.

Song, Q., Z. Zhang, B. Qiao, Q. Gu, and Z. Tang. 1996. *Zhongguo Keyi Shuo Bu: Lengzhan Hou Shidai De Zhengzhi Yu Qinggan Jueze*. Beijing: Zhonghua gonshang lianhe chubanshe.

Stritzel, H., and S. C. Chang. 2015. "Securitization and Counter-Securitization in Afghanistan." *Security Dialogue* 46 (6): 548–567. doi:10.1177/0967010615588725.

The Polemic on the General Line of the International Communist Movement. 1965. Peking: Foreign Language Press.

Timperlake, E., and W. Triplett. 1999. *Red Dragon Rising: Communist China's Military Threat to America*. Washington, DC: Regnery.

Topgyal, T. 2016. "The Tibetan Self-immolations as counter-securitization: Towards an Inter-unit Theory of Securitization." *Asian Security* 12 (3): 166–187. doi:10.1080/14799855.2016.1227323.

Truman, H. S. [1947] 1963. *Public Papers of the President of the United States: Harry S. Truman, 1947*. Washington: Government Printing Office.

U.S.-China Joint Announcement on Climate Change. 2014. http://www.whitehouse.gov/the-press-office/2014/11/11/us-china-joint-announcement-climate-change.

van Ness, P. 1970. *Revolution and Chinese Foreign Policy: Peking's Support for Wars of National Liberation*. Cambridge: University of California Press.

Vuori, J. A. 2003. "Security as Justification: An Analysis of Deng Xiaoping's Speech to the Martial Law Troops in Beijing on the Ninth of June 1989." *Politologiske Studier* 6 (2): 105–118.

Vuori, J. A. 2008. "Illocutionary Logic and Strands of Securitisation: Applying the Theory of Securitisation to the Study of Non-Democratic Political Orders." *European Journal of International Relations* 14 (1): 65–99. doi:10.1177/1354066107087767.

Vuori, J. A. 2010. "A Timely Prophet? The Doomsday Clock as a Visualization of Securitization Moves with a Global Referent Object." *Security Dialogue* 41 (3): 255–277. doi:10.1177/0967010610370225.

Vuori, J. A. 2011b. *How to Do Security with Words – A Grammar of Securitisation in the People's Republic of China*. Turku: University of Turku.

Vuori, J. A. 2014. *Critical Security and Chinese Politics: The Anti-Falungong Campaign*. London and New York: Routledge.

Vuori, J. A. 2011a. "Religion Bites: Falungong, Securitization/Desecuritization in the People's Republic of China." In: *Securitization Theory: How Security Problems Emerge and Dissolve*, edited by T. Balzacq. London: Routledge.

Vuori, J. A. 2015. "Contesting and Resisting Security in post-Mao China." In: *Contesting Security: Strategies and Logics*, edited by T. Balzacq, 29–43. London: Routledge.

Wæver, O. 2011. "Politics, Security, Theory." *Security Dialogue* 42 (4–5): 465–480. doi:10.1177/0967010611418718.

Wæver, O. 2000. "The EU as a Security Actor - Reflections from a Pessimistic Constructivist on Post-Sovereign Security Orders." In: *International Relations Theory and European Integration: Power, Security & Community*, edited by M. Kelstrup and M. C. Williams, 250–294. London: Routledge.

Wæver, O. 1989. ""Conflicts of Vision – Visions of Conflict'." In: *European Polyphony: Perspectives beyond East–West Confrontation*, edited by O. Wæver, P. Lemaitre, and E. Tromer. London: MacMillan.

Wæver, O. 1995. "Securitization and Desecuritization." In: *On Security*, edited by R. D. Lipschutz, 46–86. New York: Columbia University Press.

Wang, Z. 1997. "'China Threat' Theory Groundless." *Beijing Review* 40(28): 7–8.

Wang, Z. 2008. "National Humiliation, History Education, and the Politics of Historical Memory: Patriotic Education Campaign in China." *International Studies Quarterly* 52 (4): 783–806. doi:10.1111/isqu.2008.52.issue-4.

Wayne, M. I. 2008. *China's War on Terrorism: Counter-Insurgency, Politics and Internal Security*. London and New York: Routledge.

White House, the. 2015. "Remarks by President Obama and President Xi of the People's Republic of China in Joint Press Conference," September 25. https://obamawhitehouse.archives.gov/the-press-office/2015/09/25/remarks-president-obama-and-president-xi-peoples-republic-china-joint.

Wishnick, E. 2001. *Mending Fences: The Evolution of Moscow's China Policy from Breznev to Yeltsin*. Seattle: University of Washington Press.

Wishnick, E. 2008. "The Securitisation of Chinese Migration to the Russian Far East: Rhetoric and Reality." In: *Security and Migration in Asia: The Dynamics of Securitisation*, edited by M. G. Curley and S.-L. Wong, 83–99. London and New York: Routledge.

Wu, B. 2001. "The Chinese Security Concept and Its Historical Evolution." *Journal of Contemporary China* 10 (27): 275–283. doi:10.1080/10670560124748.

Xi, J. 2017. "Secure a Decisive Victory in Building a Moderately Prosperous Society in All Respects and Strive for the Great Success of Socialism with Chinese Characteristics for a New Era." Delivered at the 19th National Congress of the Communist Party of China, October 18. http://www.xinhuanet. com/english/download/Xi_Jinping's_report_at_19th_CPC_National_Congress.pdf.

Xinhua. 1994. "Li Peng Denies China Threat," January 2.

Xinhua. 2003. "Boao Forum: Chinese Official Says China Important to Asian Development." FBIS-CHI-2003-1103, November 3.

Xinhuanet. 2015. "Full Text of Xi Jinping's Speech on China-U.S. Relations in Seattle," September 24. http://news.xinhuanet.com/english/2015-09/24/c_134653326.htm.

Yang, Y., and J. Keller 2017. "An Operational Code Analysis of China's Defense White Papers: 1998-2015." Paper presented at the 2017 ISA in Baltimore. doi:10.1007/s11366-017-9524-5.

Yee, H., ed. 2000. *China Threat: Perceptions, Myths, and Reality*. Surrey: Curzon Press.

Yee, H., and F. Zhu. 2000. "Chinese Perspectives of the China Threat: Myth or Reality?" In: *China Threat: Perceptions, Myths, and Reality*, edited by H. Yee. Surrey: Curzon Press.

Yee, H., and I. Storey. 2000. "Introduction." In *China Threat: Perceptions, Myths, and Reality*, edited by H. Yee. Surrey: Curzon Press.

Zheng, B. 2005. "China's 'Peaceful Rise' to Great-Power Status." *Foreign Affairs* 84 (5): 18–24. doi:10.2307/20031702.

China and discourses of desecuritization: a reply to Vuori

Mark Lacy

This is a reply to:

Vuori, J. 2018. "Let's just say we'd like to avoid any great power entanglements: desecuritization in post-Mao Chinese foreign policy towards major powers." *Global Discourse* 8 (1): 118–136. http://doi.org/10.1080/23269995.2017.1408279.

Desecuritization can be a means of taking an issue out of a realm filled with geopolitical and national anxieties – over dangerous otherness, catastrophic threats to the identity and security of the nation, the emergence of fears that require new security practices in every life – and to place the problem into a frame where there can be more measured and constructive responses to the problem. The risk of hypersecuritization – of exaggeration, moral panic and the political exploitation of threat – is reduced as the problem is delinked from simplistic understandings of danger and politics, the 'spectacularization' of security. But one of the many uncertainties on China and desecuritization that Juha Vuori's (2018) paper leaves us with is this: are the desecuritizations of Chinese foreign policy discourse outlined in the paper a strategy of deception? Is the desecuritization of discourse a reflection of the capabilities and desires in the *current* state of play? With regard to China should we not be looking at the *infrastructure* that is being constructed alongside these discourses that attempt to desecuritize foreign policy discourse? While you do not have to buy into the traditional realist account of international politics in terms of inevitable paths to insecurity, conflict and competition, it doesn't take much to begin to form ideas on what the longer term plans for China are or what they sense is the type of world they will be operating in: one policymaker/security analyst working in the military realm mentioned to me in a wide ranging conversation – if you want to see how China is preparing for the coming century look at what is going on in the shipbuilding yards.

So while it may be the case that China is going to re-imagine great power politics in the coming century, to set out to do things differently, to innovate in the realm of diplomacy and foreign policy, to build an alternative approach to how great powers operate across the planet, it might also be the case that it is now caught up in a process that will lead to dangerous tipping points as other states watch its actions – regardless of desecuritized foreign policy discourse: the tragedy of great power politics, as the realist of international politics would say.

So it might be the case that while the discourses of foreign policy maybe desecuritized, on the ground and in the labs and research centres the infrastructure of war and security – the drones, the cyberweapons, the ships, planes and tanks – are being designed and redesigned for war and conflict in the 21st century: of course, China can deploy desecuritized language while it builds and prepares for the inevitable and inescapable future conflicts. At the same time, it could be argued that China deploys the language of desecuritization – carefully outlined in this essay – because its primary security concerns are currently less about controlling distant territories via military force or becoming entangled in messy and costly interventions overseas – especially when economic influence is a more beneficial strategy – and more about maintaining order and control at home. Colonizing overseas territories through traditional techniques is less important than maintaining what Paul Virilio describes as *endo-colonization* of society at home: refining the arts of social and political control to manage the internal disruption and disorder that could emerge in coming years. It might be the case that the security politics of China remains focused on endo-colonization: the interesting (and possibly disturbing) innovations will not be new approaches to geopolitics and war but the new techniques for governing and managing populations, the new technologies and biopolitical policies that may or may not spread to or influence other governments approach to control, the everyday security practices from the hypersecuritizations that emerge from the anxiety of governing a large, complex society, where the fear is of the otherness and disorder within. But there is nothing inevitable about a China that repeats the foreign policy strategies of other great powers.

But the balance of internal/external security objectives may shift in time; China may – as an emerging 'Great Power' – get drawn into external conflicts. Nationalist desires may begin to establish themselves more aggressively in the foreign policy discourses: the language of foreign policy will evolve as the strategic environments evolve – home and abroad. At some point the tension between desecuritized foreign policy discourse and the material infrastructure of an emerging 21st century military superpower may become too untenable and precarious to uphold. In another wide ranging discussion among military analysts and policymakers, one 'practioner' from the army mentioned his concern about what would happen when/if we reached the tipping point when the United States felt it had been overtaken militarily, economically and technologically by China. Years before Trump came to power, he was concerned about the type politics and policy that would take hold in such a moment. This essay leaves us with the question about how good all sides would be at negotiating the potential for conflict to come at such a tipping point – and whether the language of desecuritization is a superficial strategy of deception or a reflection of a deeper awareness of the problems of great power politics, of negotiating international politics in a manner that avoids the type of conflict that destabilised the world in previous centuries.

Disclosure statement

No potential conflict of interest was reported by the authors.

Securitization, mafias and violence in Brazil and Mexico

John Gledhill

ABSTRACT
The elites of Latin American societies, founded on genocide of indigenous peoples and the Atlantic slave trade, always manifested anxiety about mixed race 'dangerous classes' and used violence to 'keep them in their proper place'. Contemporary depictions of poor people and migrants as threats to the rest of 'society' replicate securitisation discourses associated with neoliberal capitalism elsewhere in the world. Latin America also replicates much of the North Atlantic world in the way centre-left governments adopted public security policies embodying the same logic, despite their pretensions to mitigate social inequality and racism. Moves back to the right multiply the contradictions: fiscal austerity, attacks on wages and social entitlements and abandonment of national sovereignty over resources fail to solve economic problems but increase inequality, motivating regimes lacking political legitimacy to resort to the criminalization of social movements and militarization of internal security. Using Brazil and Mexico as examples, and considering border security as well as internal security, this paper also shows how political mafias promote the rise of criminal mafias in a securitized environment in which public guardians of order contribute to the escalation of violence but may also see themselves as victims of the system they serve.

Introduction: a politics of social threats and criminalization

The Copenhagen School's account of securitization is attractive to anthropologists because it offers a social constructivist approach. Nevertheless, although it clearly makes sense to ask which social actors have greater power to define an issue as one of security, anthropologists generally seek to add a bottom-up perspective to state-focused, top-down models (Goldstein 2010, 492–3), taking up a critique already made within the Copenhagen School itself that top-down perspectives marginalize the voices of the poor, indigenous people and women (Hansen 2000). This is not simply a matter of thinking about how a diversity of audiences react to securitization discourses propagated by governments, mass media visual images or social media that focus on propagating hate, xenophobia and fake news. We need to think about how the lived experience of social actors, including subaltern actors, shape how they think about issues of 'security' and how their stances influence what happens in practice when more powerful actors securitize social issues. Taking a view from below enables us to extend Wæver's insistence that whilst the Schmittian foundations of securitization theory (exception, emergency and decision) are central to understanding what secur- itization does, decisions are reached 'by people in a political situation' (Wæver 2011, 478, note 2). Adding concern for social situations to the focus on politics, views from below expand understanding of the logics of securitization and its unintended consequences, as this paper aims to show.

Anthropologists are also concerned about ethnocentrism. The Copenhagen model of securitization and desecuritization assumes a 'normal politics' in the Western liberal tradition, making Latin America a particularly interesting region for exploring 'securitiza- tion in the non-West'. Its independent nation states adopted liberal constitutions, but formal declarations of the equality of all citizens before the law became instruments for deepening injustice in societies in which the rights of some categories of people remained foundationally unequal (DaMatta 1991). The elites of nations founded on the genocide of indigenous peoples and the Atlantic slave trade display a predisposition to securitize social problems because they have a long tradition of anxiety about mixed race 'dangerous classes' and using violence to 'keep them in their proper place'.

The centrality of corruption and clientelism in the 'normal', including democratic, politics of Latin American societies might also seem to distance them from the West. Yet, it has never been easy to distinguish Latin American political practices from those of European countries such as Italy, and the claims of the United States to represent a paragon of liberal democratic values can certainly be questioned. Much of what I am going to discuss in this paper not only reveals the negative impacts of the power of the global North on the global South, but also the existence of common tendencies that transcend this division of the world. Understanding securitization processes anywhere requires an understanding of context, and of how, as Goldstein puts it, 'global discourses are adopted, manipulated, transformed, and deployed in quotidian interactions and events' in particular places (Goldstein 2010, 492). But I begin my discussion from the premise that all securitization processes have something in common: they define certain categories of people as 'existential threats' to the rest of society.

This paper is about the consequences of that, including ways in which measures justified in the name of fighting crime and violence can result in the propagation of crime and violence. My focus is on Latin America's two largest countries, Brazil and Mexico, and three contexts of securitization. In Brazil, I discuss the policing and mass incarceration of people who live in large irregular settlements, called *favelas* in Rio de Janeiro, and more frequently the (urban) 'periphery'[1] in São Paulo and in Salvador, Bahia, the country's original capital city and third largest metropolis. In Mexico, I consider what happens to international migrants and refugees crossing the country's securitized south- ern border with Guatemala and northern border with the United States. Finally, I examine the rise and suppression of armed local self-defence units that followed the deployment of the military in internal security tasks in the Mexican state of Michoacán, a region that became a zone of criminal sovereignty.

Federal troops are also being increasingly deployed in policing operations in Brazil, even though the enforcement arm of Brazil's police is itself organized as a corporation subject to military discipline. Brazil's military police are a legacy of dictatorship, con- ceived as a local support to the army. The use of soldiers who are not trained as police is fraught with hazards. Ironically, Mexican soldiers convicted of human rights violations have claimed the status of victims on these same grounds of lack of training. But both Brazil and Mexico exemplify a broader tendency towards the militarization of regular police forces as they are deployed to repress not only organized crime but broader categories of people that securitization declares a 'threat', including protest movements that are criminalized for their resistance to fiscal austerity that undermines public education and health care, attacks on wages and worker protection, socially exclusionary urban development, abandonment of land reform and national sovereignty over resources and environmental destruction.

A common thread running through my case studies is that entire populations of people tend to be criminalized, both by the state and by other classes in the social worlds that they inhabit. In the case of undocumented immigrants in the United States, academic studies have long shown that popular perceptions of immigrant criminality are false (Reid et al. 2005). Since it is a crime simply to be in the USA without papers, and work can only be secured by means that will also be deemed illegal if the worker is caught in a raid, undocumented migrants have greater incentives than ever not to risk losing their jobs and ability to raise their families by committing any other kind of misdemeanour, since this now guarantees immediate deportation. Young people who entered the United States as children are especially vulnerable, and being 'illegal' places them in a situation of everyday insecurity and abjection (Gonzales and Chavez 2012). Legal residents and citizens also suffer from the stigma created by securitization because non-Latinos assume that they too are 'illegals'. Obama and Trump's deportation drives are not, however, about 'protecting the public' from criminals: they are about giving the impression of responding to the economic problems and identity crises afflicting not only the white working class but also much of the US middle class, the result of the socio-economic polarization and precarianization produced by financialized neoliberal capitalism. Trump in fact received a substantial number of votes from Latinos who did not fear deportation but did have other anxieties. We will not discover the deeper social and political logics of securitization in the official pretexts used to justify it, but this example underscores the need to understand how lived experience shapes political choices.

It is true that there are drug traffickers within the urban communities that I studied in Brazil, but those directly involved in criminal activities are a small minority (Barcellos and Zaluar 2014). These are socio-economically differentiated populations, but all their members are subjected to a common racialized class stigmatization by outsiders, which their criminalization by securitization discourse exacerbates. It is these stigma-tized populations, and not members of other classes, that experience the highest levels of victimization at the hands of criminals, whose material support and 'protection' tend to be selective and combined with various forms of coercive imposition and threats of violence (Penglase 2009). Nevertheless, repressive policing of these communities often leads their residents to conclude that the criminals are the lesser of two evils compared with the agents of the state, who all too often prove corrupt, racist, and given to exercising their violence in arbitrary ways, through extra-judicial killings of people who are not involved in the criminal world and high tolerance of 'collateral damage' when engaged in armed confrontations with real criminals. Criminals do often 'help' residents in need and offer a more predictable everyday presence than police who only appear, shooting, when they have specific targets to apprehend (Machado and Leite 2007).

Similar reactions followed military operations in rural communities in Michoacán, but when the criminals' extortion and violence made a mockery of their claims to 'protect', citizens organized to protect themselves against them rather than depend on official security forces in which they lacked confidence.

Once a population is defined as a source of 'threats', its members tend to be treated by soldiers and police with a lack of respect that makes building trust impossible. This is true even in Salvador, where policing of the urban periphery is done by officers who themselves live in similar neighbourhoods and tend to be black or dark skinned mixed-race, just like the people they police. Transformed into agents of the state, but subject in their everyday lives to the same kind of racialized class hierarchy as everyone else, police, just like 'respectable' working class families in the peripheral neighbourhoods, are engaged in an everyday struggle for the 'respect' that their society often denies them when they are out of uniform. When they beat up a young black man who protests at being subject to a truculent stop and search and call him a 'monkey', a slur understood as racist by black Bahians, police are responding to a refusal to respect their persons as well as their authority. In so doing, they make use of a licence to violate human rights that is anchored in the way that whole communities are turned into 'suspects' and denied full citizenship by the process of securitization. Police killings of young black men in Salvador remain as disproportionately high today as they were at the start of the millennium (Paes Machado and Noronha 2002), despite new campaigns against racism by both government and grassroots movements. The year 2016 produced the highest national violent death rate in Brazilian history, inflected by a racial bias that reawakened activist talk of a 'genocide' of black youth.

To understand the social effects of securitization fully, we need to understand what is specific about the social relations of each society in which it is occurring. As Caldeira (2002) observed, the apparent paradox of the policing of the urban periphery in Brazil is that many residents simultaneously complain about police abuse and accept that the police have a right and a duty to kill criminals. *Bandido bom é bandido morto* (a good criminal is a dead criminal) is not just a middle-class perspective. What lower class citizens refuse to accept is a 'lack of respect' for 'honest workers' (Cardoso 2014). The self-help-orientated prosperity theology of Pentecostal churches and extension of the ethos of neoliberal market society under Workers Party (PT) governments, which encouraged banks to give consumer credit to everyone, fostered more individualized and fragmented 'popular classes'. Although neighbourliness and a spirit of community remain more characteristic of favelas than formal working-class neighbourhoods in which everyone puts bars on their windows, and neighbourliness is minimal in the fortified vertical condominiums in which the upper classes live, solidarity within poorer communities today has definite limits.

Drivers of securitization and the hidden agendas of new policing models in Brazil

Both Brazilian and Mexican cities exemplify a neoliberal model of urbanization driven by financialization (Sassen 2012). Real estate speculation and construction, including modernization of mass transit systems, building of shopping malls, gentrification and the creation of safe and attractive spaces for tourists, are the leading sectors of the urban economy. Hosting the World Cup and the Olympics made Rio de Janeiro a special case, because public works associated with the sporting mega events required the forced removal of favela residents on a larger scale, but similar tendencies are also visible in Salvador.

For decades, favelas were left to their own devices not simply because public housing programmes were inadequate and rents in regularized zones of the cities too high, but because the votes of their residents could be mobilized at election time by politicians who promised to help with service provision. Neoliberal urbanism has made displacement of poor citizens from central zones of cities more likely. In Rio, a new policing strategy for favelas, based on the installation of permanent Pacificatory Police Units (UPPs), made it possible to force residents to pay for water, electricity and other services, increasing the profits of privatized utility companies (Freeman 2012). Initially, the new policing strategies did reduce levels of violence, so living in favelas became more attractive to outsiders and rents rose. Increases in costs forced poorer residents to leave for more dangerous places further from the city centres and sources of jobs. Combined with forced removals that also relocated displaced families far away from the city centre, these processes have had a profound impact on the social geography of Rio de Janeiro (Faulhaber and Azevedo 2015). This form of urban transformation is a classic example of 'accumulation by dispossession' (Harvey 2007). The main winners are the property developers. There are some favela residents who see the upgrading of their neighbourhoods as a positive development, but those who were forcibly relocated have ended up losing their 'capital' in the form of self-built homes and sociable communities.

Although the police units were given a different name (Community Security Bases) in Bahia, the PT government of that state replicated Rio's UPP model. The promise was that the new policing strategies would be based on community or 'proximity' policing that would ensure that honest residents would be treated with respect. The installation of permanent police bases would reduce both the levels of lethal violence associated with drug gang turf wars and the considerably larger number of 'collateral damage' deaths caused by sporadic police incursions into the neighbourhoods. The work of the new police bases in this 'pacified' environment would be complemented by new social development programmes in which the police themselves would participate (Fleury 2012).

I did find some Military Police soldiers in Bahia who were strongly committed to this new paradigm (Gledhill 2015, 91–107). Highly class conscious, they insisted that even if tranquilizing the middle classes was the principal political motivation for the policy, it could and should be used to guarantee the poor themselves greater security in their everyday lives. Yet the culture of the police corporation and the wider power relations in which it is embedded militate against such aspirations. Without a radical reform of Brazil's police system, based on a dysfunctional division of labour between the 'ostensive' military police corporation and a no less violent civil police investigative branch, 'proximity policing' seems doomed to fail to realise its potential.[2] My own ethnographic research in Salvador illustrates some of the problems. When residents complained about the 'truculence' of police stop and search operations, the base commander responded, in an authoritarian tone, that they should take classes in how to 'react' to stop and search. In 2016, the residents convened a public meeting to protest the regular violation of their human rights by police. The representative of the state government human rights secretariat agreed that there was cause for grave concern, but there have still been no effective investigations even into extra-judicial killings by police in this community. The base commander is adept at human relations and strategies to 'win hearts and minds'. His base has developed health care, educational, social and cultural programmes, many focused on children. This would be positive were it not for the fact that state government and municipal resources have been taken away from the community's many successful but politically independent grassroots NGOs, whilst partnerships with Salvador's federal university have been replaced by arrangements with academically questionable private institutions run by US companies. But if Bahia, a state still governed by the PT, although Salvador's city government is in the hands of a right-wing party, has produced mixed results, Rio has proved a disaster. The Brazilian Democratic Movement Party (PMDB) state government's exploding financial deficit meant that there was no money for social programmes, the traffickers counterattacked, frustrated police committed every abuse in the book and even previously 'pacified' favelas such as the famous City of God had become war zones again by the time of the Olympics.

None of this violence had the slightest impact on the security of visitors and tourists, safe in newly rehabilitated and gentrified parts of the city. Yet the hidden agendas of favela securitization became even more apparent after the Olympics. It became clear that there was insufficient money to provide new homes for all the families that had been evicted or even to pay them rent subsidies while they waited. Most had never wanted to be shipped off to the edge of the city, in what was in effect a process of 'social cleansing', but one group from the Alemão favela complex decided that they had no practical choice but to return to where their demolished homes had been and try to start again. As soon as they reoccupied the land, the police from the local UPP base attacked men, women and children, plus community journalists trying to record events, refusing negotiation. As an activist from the landless movement supporting the reoccupation put it, 'you could see in their eyes that these police hate us' (Sudré 2016). For their part, many Rio police now say forget 'proximity policing', we are engaged in a war.

Although securitization reinforces the idea of war, there is a powerful subjective basis for police feeling this way. Being police is genuinely dangerous, not simply on the job but also during off-duty hours, since criminals regularly kill police if they identify the victim's profession during an armed assault. Police complain that the public do not appreciate the risks that they take in their service and that they are unfairly stigmatized by mass media more interested in reporting their mistakes than their achievements. Increasingly frustrated by the threat austerity poses to their pay and pensions, it is not difficult to find police who recognise that public security policies are class-biased and describe themselves simultaneously 'warriors' and 'victims' in an unjust society.

As Graham (2011) has shown, militarization of policing is typical of securitized neoliberal cities[3] throughout the world, including the United States. What Brazilian policing has in common with policing in countries such as the USA and France (Fassin 2013) is that catching criminals and bringing them to justice is of secondary importance to keeping lower class people of colour in their proper place in society, at the bottom and as segregated from elites as their menial service worker roles permit. Yet securitization not only fails to suppress crime, but also contributes to the development of mafia-style crime networks, a perverse consequence that is readily intelligible in terms of the political and capitalist drivers of the securitization process.

Unspeakable connections between securitization and crime

I will begin with migrants and refugees, in a context in which that distinction now has little meaning. Thanks to massive US investments in security technology and a compliant Mexican government, Mexico's once porous southern border in Chiapas became the first line of border defence of the United States under Obama. The fact that the everyday violence of states, gangs and transnational organized crime have been driving ever increasing numbers of women and, often unaccompanied, children across that border is a consequence of the kinds of societies and governments produced by US Cold War interventions in Central America, reinforced by vigorous promotion of mining and energy projects by US and European transnational capital in that region (Vogt 2013; Corvo 2014). The consequences of Obama's deportation policy for Central American refugees, made even more inhumane by new rules and procedures introduced by Trump, is that more and more people never make it to the USA. This makes them vulnerable to victimization and exploitation by members of the Mexican security forces as well as criminal networks, with which federal as well as local security agents often work hand in glove. Exploitation of migrants and refugees trapped in Mexico includes generalized extortion, child slavery and sex-trafficking of women (Casillas 2011). Mexico's government has declared that it will not accept Trump's new policy of deporting non-Mexican undocumented migrants and refugees into Mexican national territory, nor pay for his infamous wall. Yet by deepening a militarization of internal security whose disastrous consequences are now beyond debate, Mexico continues to dance to a tune composed in Washington.

It might seem odd that Brazil needs to bring in troops given that it has a militarized police force. But it is state governments that are responsible for both the military and civil police under Brazil's federal constitution. Federal troops have been used to reinforce the efforts of state government security forces in Rio since 2007, putting poor communities under a state of siege under the pretext of guaranteeing the security of visitors attending sporting mega-events (Alves and Evanson 2011). This policy was fostered by the supposedly 'pro-poor' federal governments led by the Workers Party. But since Brazil's elite ousted the last elected PT president, Dilma Rousseff, through a 'constitutional' coup in 2016, federal troops have been deployed more frequently throughout the country, because police have been unable to cope with a mounting series of problems.

The purpose of the coup, consolidated through a generalized state of exception, was to push through a neoliberal austerity package so radical that even the International Monetary Fund judged it unacceptably socially regressive, coupled with an unprecedented attack on worker's rights, privatization of public enterprises and surrendering of sovereignty over national resources to foreign capital. Police themselves became protesting victims of the cuts to public finances, although when not on strike, which is a radical step since military police strikes are considered mutiny,[4] they continued to carry out orders to repress social movements and demonstrations against the regime. But the crisis of Rio de Janeiro's UPP programme brought troops back to the favelas and onto the streets of the city more generally, whilst the need to send in the army with increasing frequency also reflects longstanding contradictions in public security policies, particularly the unintended consequences of a US-style policy of mass incarceration. Prison numbers escalated throughout the years of PT national governments, a measure of the extent to which their widely praised anti-poverty programmes did not transform the underlying conditions that motivated Wacquant (2009) to associate the development of the 'penal state' with neoliberalism. Yet much of the impetus behind mass incarceration came from state governments controlled by other parties, notably São Paulo, bastion of the Party of Brazilian Social Democracy (PSDB), which also followed the US tendency of the time to promote private prisons. The contradictions of São Paulo's public security policies gave birth to a powerful criminal network.

Conditions in Brazil's gaols are inhuman and degrading. Almost 650,000 inmates occupy a space designed for 360,000. This reflects routine incarceration for trafficking of drug users who only possessed tiny quantities beyond what they consumed for resale, and the fact that 40% of inmates have yet to have their cases heard by a judge. The year 2017 produced a manifest crisis. Prison riots in different parts of the country involved massacres of inmates by prisoners belonging to a different criminal faction, which replicated the spectacular violence associated with Mexico's drug cartels: victims were tortured and decapitated.

Gaoled criminals responded to appalling conditions by organizing themselves. The First Command of the Capital (*Primeiro Comando da Capital*, PCC) emerged in the prisons of São Paulo after military police massacred 111 inmates in the Carandiru penitentiary in 1992, but subsequently extended its reach far beyond São Paulo. The PCC is organized into divisions: these include a division for enforcing discipline and determining punishments based on the PCC's normative order, not only within prisons but in the many communities controlled by the PCC outside; another for providing material and legal support for prisoners and their families; and others for managing the PCC's portfolio of economic activities, which extend from drug trafficking and bank robbery through collecting protection money to laundering the proceeds of crime through legal businesses. In economic terms the PCC is now a clandestine business corporation, but the authorities are challenged to identify its 'leaders'. Although its original leadership was hierarchical and violent, Biondi (2016) argues that the PCC evolved into a decentred network organization quite distinct from a state or capitalist firm. There is still an organizational hierarchy of authoritative positions, but different members are empowered to occupy them at different moments of time, through processes that are consensual and deliberative in nature, in line with an ethos that emphasises the equality of all who prove themselves worthy of trust and respect, whilst at the same time accepting the need to make decisions and enforce discipline.

The PCC has two categories of affiliation, 'brothers' and 'cousins'. Those who choose to accept its invitation to 'commit themselves to crime' are 'baptised' as 'brothers' in a ritual reminiscent of those of the Sicilian mafia. The ritual is more than show: it is an effective way of extending PCC rhyzomic networks in space, to other prisons and other regions. Another perverse consequence of the UPP's original drive to capture and imprison leading drug traffickers in Rio's favelas is that gaoled members of Rio's Red Command (*Comando Vermelho*, CV) organization, losing ground in the favelas, strengthened their own hegemony in gaols that they could control, while continuing to direct allies outside. Various other regional organizations have emerged in response to PCC expansion beyond its original territory, seeking to maintain control of cross-border drugs and arms trafficking in their own regions. These include the Family of the North, allied to the CV, which initiated the violence of 2017 by killing 56 PCC inmates in a prison in Manaus. This was a state prison that had been turned over to private sector administration. The state government made such a mess of dealing with the consequences of the massacre that federal troops were sent in to restore order and keep violence off the streets.

It is impossible to understand the growth of criminal networks in either Brazil or Mexico without understanding the role of politicians. First, politicians are not just passive recipients of bribes. The spotlight in Brazil recently has been on the bribes paid by Brazilian engineering and construction companies such as Odebrecht to politicians of all parties and even foreign heads of state in return for contracts, part of which provided illegal funding for election campaigns. But politicians in Brazil and Mexico also seek out relations with criminals to help them win elections and finance clientelism, as well as for the personal pay-offs they get for offering protection. In Mexico, cartel gunmen have been used by both the state and mining interests to eliminate local opposition to natural resource extraction. Criminals offer a means for transnational companies, governments and individual political actors to make a violence of which they are the intellectual authors 'deniable'. Second, backstage political deals with criminal organizations help governments keep security crises under control. In the case of São Paulo, there have been periodic outbreaks of violence on the streets related to breakdowns in everyday pacts between police and the PCC in the communities of the urban periphery. The worst violence of all, in 2006, resulted from the PCC leadership ordered killings in response to police efforts to extort money from them by threatening their families (Fernando, Dodge, and Carvalho 2011). The PCC killed 48 police. The police retaliated by killing 120 people. But these wars are ultimately not convenient for either the state government or the police.

Although this is repeatedly denied, the PCC increased its influence outside the prisons because the PSDB elite of São Paulo, much denounced in Brazil's corruption scandals, made backstage deals with the organization in the interests of furthering governability, police on the streets found that accommodations made their working lives easier, and there were also considerable economic benefits in these arrangements. The order imposed on the urban periphery by the tribunals of the PCC has resulted in a lower homicide rate than in other metropolitan cities, suppression of petty and sexual crimes and an end to lynching (Feltran 2008; Willis 2015). For a time, the PCC maintained a truce with the Red Command in Ceará state that had similar positive consequences for residents of poor communities. The bloody consequences of the breakdown of this pact are now apparent. There are structural differences between the two organizations, because the PCC controls the lion's share of São Paulo's drug traffic whereas Rio's trafficking is fragmented, with violent clashes between local gangs for control over territory. CV expansion still depends more on violence than the subtler means by which the PCC has constructed a crime organization with a diversified portfolio of legal and illegal sources of profit.

There are limits to criminal governance, as my own ethnography of the rise and demise of a PCC 'order of crime' in Bahia demonstrates (Gledhill 2015, 67–76). There are obvious measures that the authorities could take to reverse the growth of criminal networks, along with the violence that competition between them sooner or later brings to the streets as well as the gaols, starting with prison reform and ending with definitive solutions to the country's problems of poverty and inequality. Yet the politicians driving post-coup Brazil towards social regression are taking the country down a different road.

Cartel land

As a comparative case, Mexico's experience is hardly encouraging.[5] Collaboration between drug traffickers and the Mexican state dates back to the 'dirty war' in Guerrero, a major production zone for marijuana and heroin (Gledhill 2015, 113–30). The Mexican army crushed Guerrero's guerrilla insurgency through a strategy of pre-emptive violence against the peasant population that might support them, used in counter-insurgency wars in other parts of the world at that time. In many ways, contemporary violence in Guerrero is a legacy of a counter-insurgency war that never really ended. But the contemporary situation also differs from the past in some respects, because of inter-related transformations of the Mexican state and the world of crime.

The development of organized crime in Mexico underwent a steep change after Mexican cartels assumed responsibility for trafficking Colombian cocaine to the US market, along with Mexican-produced marijuana, heroin and methamphetamines, whose use also exploded on the domestic Mexican market. Mexican cartels became transnational organizations reaching down into Central and South America, expanded their business into Europe, and are now encroaching on the Chinese heroin trade on the US East Coast with a cheaper product that looks like Chinese 'white' heroin rather than the traditional Mexican 'black' product. But they did not stop at drugs. Illegal mining, with some of the minerals traded with Chinese intermediaries for chemicals used in methamphetamine production, became as profitable as narcotics. Cartel portfolios also include illegal logging and siphoning off oil from the pipelines of the national oil company. The most important change of all was diversification from trading in illegal commodities into generalized mafia-style operations based on extorting money from businesses, including transnational companies. Poorer citizens must also pay up in regions where these mafias take control of local government.

Politics is again central to these changes. A corporate state system run for 70 years by a single political party became a more competitive party system within a neoliberal framework of governance. Neoliberal economic policies contributed to the growing power of organized crime in rural areas by impoverishing the extensive peasant sector that existed alongside commercial agribusiness after Latin America's most important land reform. The scale of land reform is a major difference between Mexico and agribusiness-dominated Brazil. With new mining concessions to transnational companies adding to other environmental problems, the architects of Mexican neoliberalism envisaged an accelerating exodus of rural labour to the cities, and encouraged land concentration and foreign agribusiness investment.[6] Yet official plans remained silent on the alternative that the criminal economy could provide for rural people. This is not surprising in the light of the role that drug money came to play in Mexican politics.

The neoliberal faction that hijacked the Institutional Revolutionary Party (PRI) at the end of the 1980s disarticulated a corporatist regime whose rent-seeking, corruption and extortion had provisioned a pervasive web of patron–client relations. Privatization of state enterprises and fiscal and administrative decentralization cut off many established sources of political plunder, but neoliberalism has increased rather than reduced the scale of clientelism in Mexican political practice (Müller 2016). In a more competitive political field there are more actors building their networks under the banner of different parties. The state itself has become 'feudalized' through competition between different factions and cliques. Money from organized crime has become integral to the Mexican way of doing politics across the party-political spectrum, and if today's criminals needed any lessons on how to extort money from the population, they only needed to look at the old PRI regime for practical inspiration.

In 2001, a year after Mexico's illusory 'transition to democracy' began with the National Action Party's Vicente Fox beating the PRI's candidate for the Presidency, Sinaloa cartel boss Joaquín 'Shorty' Guzmán escaped from prison in Guadalajara with an ease that many interpreted as proof that Fox's government had decided that the best way to deal with the cartel problem was to allow one organization to become dominant. Guzmán combined violently eliminating competition with efforts to broker peace with other crime organizations, but dividing up the country into co-existing spheres of operation under Sinaloa hegemony did not prove viable. Suspicion that the commanding heights of the national security apparatus were also on Guzmán's payroll continued throughout PAN president Felipe Calderón's catastrophic effort to use the military to end inter-cartel violence from 2006 to 2012 (Hernández 2012). Calderón's pursuit of the US 'War on Drugs' strategy of 'taking out cartel kingpins' produced more violence because of conflicts over succession to leadership and greater regional fragmentation of criminal groups. It resulted in well over 100,000 deaths and disappearances (Jorge 2017), but left local government in Calderón's own home state of Michoacán more firmly under the control of organized crime than ever. The violence continued unabated after PRI president Enrique Peña Nieto succeeded Calderón, maintaining the same security strategy and rejecting pleas for drug decriminalization. But Peña's government earned further opprobrium for its response to the forced disappearance of 43 students in Guerrero in 2014 and a series of mass extra-judicial executions by security forces.

In 2014, Peña sent a close political associate, Alfredo Castillo, to Michoacán as special federal Commissioner for Security and Integral Development. Castillo was tasked with dismantling the Knights Templar (*Caballeros Templarios*) cartel. *Templario* backing had become crucial for electoral success in the state, and by this stage the cartel not only directly controlled many of its municipal governments, but had deeply penetrated the state government. Yet although the *Templarios* had become the dominant criminal force regionally, they were under growing pressure from the expanding Jalisco New Generation Cartel, whose leaders include the nephews of the founders of the Millennium cartel, Michoacán's first local organization (Maldonado Aranda 2013). Millennium's hegemony had been ended by a new generation of local *narcos* who established the Michoacán Family (*La Familia Michoacana*), and the *Templarios* emerged through a leadership split within *La Familia*. These newer Michoacán cartels were like the Brazilian PCC in enjoining their members to follow a code of conduct, in this case based on a mix of heterodox Christianity and US self-help principles. The *Templarios* introduced more elaborate initiation rituals to consolidate their Mexican 'brotherhood of crime'. Yet what motivated the federal government to intervene in Michoacán was not the power of a cartel but the growth of armed resistance to it that the state did not control.

Local *autodefensas* (self-defence groups) appeared in different places for different reasons. Some were formed by indigenous and poorer mestizo citizens. Others emerged in places where commercial farmers had grown tired of paying extortion money and having land stolen by the *Templarios*. All the *autodefensas* insisted that they were acting because government had failed to act. But some were not what they seemed. Several *Templarios* founded *autodefensas* because they saw that their cartel's days were numbered and wanted a place in the coming new order. Some groups were armed and possibly clandestinely organized by New Generation. In the event, Commissioner Castillo 'pacified' the state by negotiating backstage deals with the criminal elements within the *autodefensa* movement while persecuting the more honourable and popular *autodefensa* leaders, who were seen as a threat to the continuity of the political class's 'normal' ways of engaging in the business of politics. Castillo insisted that *autodefensas* had to accept conversion into a state-controlled uniformed 'rural defence force', which gave them a licence to extort. Castillo's strategy did not end drug-trafficking or illegal mining. It simply allowed these activities to pass into new hands.

The Commissioner is now long gone, to prove an equally controversial National Commissioner for Sport, but the legacy of his intervention is that Michoacán is a battleground for local fragments of the previously dominant cartel fighting for control over localities against each other and New Generation. The new governor elected in 2015 may have hoped that time would allow New Generation to re-establish a stronger but more discrete kind of order. But that order has yet to materialize. Narco-violence is now occurring in towns that were previously relatively safe places, even if their commercial and civic improvement over the past thirty years was heavily based on laundering drug money.

Conclusion

In this paper, I have tried to move beyond a model of discourses aimed at audiences towards a more complex account of how different kinds of social actors adopt stances that may shift over time and are often characterized by ambiguity. In certain circumstances the rule of crime may prove preferable to the rule of the state, despite popular support for killing criminals, in some circumstances citizens may seek to resolve their own security problems by defying state claims to a monopoly of legitimate violence, and in others, illustrated by the PCC in the urban periphery of São Paulo, justice systems administered by criminals may even prove capable of reducing violence.

I have also shown that the United States government is more than an audience to which Latin American securitization moves attend. The US government has actively shaped border securitization and Mexico's 'war against drugs', with exceptionally perverse consequences, and exported a model of 'punishing the poor' through mass incarceration. The conversion of the Michoacán *Templarios* into a full-fledged mafia was aided by President Calderón's acceptance of US policy, which encouraged counter-productive repressive military operations in rural communities. The specific nature of the national state and society is, however, still important. For both Mexico and Brazil, I concur with the perspective of Goldstein (2012) on Bolivia: the problem has never really been the complete absence of the state, but the nature of its sporadic violent presence and its agents' failure to treat people with respect. Securitization's construction of entire populations as sources of 'threats' to the rest of society exacerbates these problems.

But securitization is not simply a response to the 'threats' that provide its justifications. It has deeper class agendas. These reflect general tendencies in financialized neoliberal capitalist development and the way that neoliberal solutions to problems of capitalist accumulation increase inequality and undermine the economic security of growing numbers of people. Countries such as Brazil and Mexico express these contradictions in a particularly violent way because of the nature of their elites and the ways in which these elites maintain themselves in power. One of the consequences of the way political power was maintained under neoliberal regimes in Latin America was that organized crime became increasingly politically useful. Violent death in Brazil and Mexico has reached levels associated with countries at war. The everyday violence of the criminal world seems unending in its elaboration of horror, exemplified in brutal femicides as well as torture and decapitation of male victims.

A final perverse consequence of securitization in these two countries is the transformation of the state's own ordering agents into criminals. The especially violent Zetas cartel in Mexico was founded by former special forces officers. In Brazil, former, and in some cases serving, police, encouraged by unscrupulous local politicians, created paramilitary mafias called *milicias* in poor communities, driving out the drug traffickers but then subjecting its residents to multiple kinds of extortion. In 2010, *milicias* controlled 422,000 people in Rio de Janeiro favelas, not much fewer than the 557,000 residents of favelas controlled by Rio's three criminal networks, and much more than the 142,000 residents included in the UPP programme at that time (Barcellos and Zaluar 2014, 3–4). Despite the stir caused by representative Marcelo Freixo's Parliamentary Commission of Inquiry into the *milicias* – celebrated in José Padilha's second *Elite Squad* movie – it was the traffickers, not the *milicias*, that lost ground in the following years. Such outcomes become all too predictable when understood in terms of the durable structures of racialized class power and the logic of a 'normal' politics dominated by corruption, clientelism, rent-seeking and mass media manipulation.

Notes

1. Periphery here has a social rather than spatial connotation. Irregular settlements are not necessarily located on city outskirts and may be immediately adjacent to middle- and upper-class residential areas.
2. My research did find some support in the ranks for demilitarization of the corporation, but serving military police who argue the case for demilitarization publicly have often been subjected to sanctions of imprisonment and dishonourable discharge.
3. Smith (2002) defined the 'new urbanism' of the neoliberal capitalist era, from Barcelona to São Paulo, in terms of the leading role of real estate interests in capital accumulation and dominance of capitalist production of space over social reproduction. Its goal is to make the city 'safe' for the middle classes by privatizing public space and enabling those who can afford it to buy private security services, whilst criminalizing the poor, facilitating the socially exclusionary redevelopment and gentrification of working class areas. In 2017, the Federal Bureau of Investigation escalated the logic of securitization blighting the lives of poor Afro-Americans by identifying 'Black Identity Extremism' as a *terrorist* threat. The agency justified

this claim by citing rising numbers of retaliation shootings of police by ghetto residents, but its effect is to criminalize the Black Lives Matter protests against killings by police.

4. There were police strikes in Bahia in 2012 and 2014 (Gledhill 2015). Police wives spearheaded a 2017 stoppage in the state of Espiritu Santo, whose governor persisted in implementing a particularly harsh austerity package.

5. Although I do not have space to pursue that comparison here, Mexican and Brazilian prisons present very similar problems.

6. It was also assumed that migration to the USA would provide a 'safety-valve', preventing rural–urban migration from reaching proportions that would create insuperable problems, while providing valuable dollar remittance income to the national economy. But net migration from Mexico to the United States was already in decline before Trump took office. Should Trump's anti-immigrant agenda be carried through fully, Michoacán's state government estimates that a million Michoacanos might be forced to return to a 'homeland' in which some have never lived as adults.

Acknowledgements

The author gratefully acknowledges the support of a Leverhulme Trust Major Research Fellowship for some of the research reported in this paper, but he alone is responsible for the conclusions drawn from it.

Disclosure statement

No potential conflict of interest was reported by the author.

Funding

The author gratefully acknowledges the support of a Leverhulme Trust Major Research Fellowship for some of the research reported in this paper.

References

Alves, M., and P. Evanson. 2011. *Living in the Crossfire: Favela Residents, Drug Dealers, and Police Violence in Rio de Janeiro*. Philadelphia, PA: Temple University Press.

Barcellos, C., and A. Zaluar. 2014. "Homicides and Territorial Struggles in Rio De Janeiro Favelas." *Revista de Saúde Pública* 48 (1): 94–102. doi:10.1590/S0034-8910.2014048004822.

Biondi, K. 2016. *Sharing This Walk: An Ethnography of Prison Life and the PCC in Brazil*. Chapel Hill, NC: UNC Press Books.

Caldeira, T. P. R. 2002. "The Paradox of Police Violence in Democratic Brazil." *Ethnography* 3 (3): 235–263. doi:10.1177/146613802401092742.

Cardoso, M. 2014. "Respect, Dignity and Rights. Ethnographic Registers about Community Policing in Rio de Janeiro." *Vibrant* 11 (2): 47–72.

Casillas, R. 2011. "Redes visibles e invisibles en el tráfico y la trata de personas en Chiapas." In: *Migración y seguridad. Nuevo desafío en México*, edited by N. A. Canto, 53–71. Mexico City: Casede.

Corvo, A. C. 2014. "Poderes viejos y vecinos nuevos: la disputa por los recursos naturales en el norte de Quiché." Accessed 15 April 2014. https://comunitariapress.wordpress.com/2014/07/14/poderes-viejos-y-nuevos-vecinos/.

DaMatta, R. 1991. *Carnivals, Rogues, and Heroes: An Interpretation of the Brazilian Dilemma*. Notre Dame, IN: University of Notre Dame Press.

Fassin, D. 2013. *Enforcing Order: An Ethnography of Urban Policing*. Cambridge: Polity.

Faulhaber, L., and L. Azevedo. 2015. *SMH 2016: remoções no Rio de Janeiro olímpico*. Rio de Janeiro: Mórula Editorial.

Feltran, G. D. S. 2008. "The Management of Violence on the São Paulo Periphery." *Vibrant* 7 (2): 109–134.

Fernando, R. D., R. E. F. Dodge, and S. Carvalho. 2011. *São Paulo sob achaque: Corrupção, crime organizado e violência Institucional em Maio de 2006*. São Paulo: Justiça Global and Harvard University.

Fleury, S. 2012. "Militarização do social como estratégia de integração-o caso da UPP do Santa Marta." *Sociologias* 14 (30): 194–222. doi:10.1590/S1517-45222012000200007.

Freeman, J. 2012. "Neoliberal Accumulation Strategies and the Visible Hand of Police Pacification in Rio de Janeiro." *Revista de Estudos Universitários* 38 (1): 95–126.

Gledhill, J. 2015. *The New War on the Poor: The Production of Insecurity in Latin America*. London: Zed Books.

Goldstein, D. M. 2010. "Toward a Critical Anthropology of Security." *Current Anthropology* 51 (4): 487–517. doi:10.1086/655393.

Goldstein, D. M. 2012. *Outlawed: Between Security and Rights in a Bolivian City*. Durham, NC: Duke University Press.

Gonzales, R. G., and L. R. Chavez. 2012. "'Awakening to a Nightmare.'Abjectivity and Illegality in the Lives of Undocumented 1.5-Generation Latino Immigrants in the United States." *Current Anthropology* 53 (3): 255–268. doi:10.1086/665414.

Graham, S. 2011. *Cities Under Siege: The New Military Urbanism*. London and New York: Verso Books.

Hansen, L. 2000. "The Little Mermaid's Silent Security Dilemma and the Absence of Gender in the Copenhagen School." *Millennium* 29 (2): 285–306. doi:10.1177/03058298000290020501.

Harvey, D. 2007. "Neoliberalism as Creative Destruction." *The ANNALS of the American Academy of Political and Social Science* 610 (1): 21–44. doi:10.1177/0002716206296780.

Hernández, A. 2012. *Los señores del narco*. Mexico City: Grijalbo.

Jorge, C. A. 2017. "2007-2016: La violencia cobró más de 208 mil vidas." *Proceso* 2015: 10–13.

Machado, L. A. D. S., and M. P. Leite. 2007. "Violência, crime e polícia: o que os favelados dizem quando falam desses temas?" *Sociedade e Estado* 22 (3): 545–591. doi:10.1590/S0102-69922007000300004.

Maldonado Aranda, S. 2013. "Stories of Drug Trafficking in Rural Mexico: Territories, Drugs and Cartels in Michoacán." *European Review of Latin American and Caribbean Studies* 94: 43–66.

Müller, M.-M. 2016. *The Punitive City: Privatized Policing and Protection in Mexico City*. London: Zed Books.

Paes Machado, E., and C. V. Noronha. 2002. "A Polícia Dos Pobres: Violência Policial Em Classes Populares Urbanas." *Sociologias* 4 (7): 188–221. doi:10.1590/S1517-45222002000100009.

Penglase, B. 2009. "States of Insecurity: Everyday Emergencies, Public Secrets, and Drug Trafficker Power in a Brazilian Favela." *PoLAR: Political and Legal Anthropology Review* 32 (1): 47–63. doi:10.1111/plar.2009.32.issue-1.

Reid, L. W., H. E. Weiss, R. M. Adelman, and C. Jaret. 2005. "The Immigration–Crime Relationship: Evidence Across US Metropolitan Areas." *Social Science Research* 34 (4): 757–780. doi:10.1016/j.ssresearch.2005.01.001.

Sassen, S. 2012. "Expanding the Terrain for Global Capital." In: *Subprime Cities*, edited by M. Aalbers and S. Sassen, 74–96. New York: John Wiley & Sons.

Smith, N. 2002. "New Globalism, New Urbanism: Gentrification as Global Urban Strategy." *Antipode* 34 (3): 427–450. doi:10.1111/anti.2002.34.issue-3.

Sudré, L. 2016. "RJ: 'A polícia estava com ódio', diz militante do MTST sobre despejo no Complexo do Alemão." Accessed 6 April 2014. http://www.carosamigos.com.br/index.php/cotidiano/8046-rj-a-policia-estava-com-odio-diz-militante-do-mtst-sobre-despejo-no-complexo-do-alemao

Vogt, W. A. 2013. "Crossing Mexico: Structural Violence and the Commodification of Undocumented Central American Migrants." *American Ethnologist* 40 (4): 764–780. doi:10.1111/amet.12053.

Wacquant, L. 2009. *Punishing the Poor: The Neoliberal Government of Social Insecurity*. Durham and London: Duke University Press.

Wæver, O. 2011. "Politics, Security, Theory." *Security Dialogue* 42 (4–5): 465–480. doi:10.1177/0967010611418718.

Willis, G. D. 2015. *Killing Consensus: Police, Organized Crime and the Regulation of Life and Death in Urban Brazil*. Berkeley: University of California Press.

REPLY

Sovereign implications of securitization work

Simon Mabon

This is a reply to:

Gledhill, J. 2018. "Securitization, mafias and violence in Brazil and Mexico." *Global Discourse* 8 (1): 139–154. https://doi.org/10.1080/23269995.2017.1406679.

One of the most popular TV shows of recent years has been Netflix's *Narcos*, a series aimed at documenting – albeit with creative license – the rise of Pablo Escobar. The show depicts the growth of the cocaine industry, amidst the efforts of governments and their agencies – notably the American Drug Enforcement Agency – to prevent the regional distribution of the drug. Of course, a by-product of this is a consideration of the social and economic impact of the drug trade on life across Colombia. John Gledhill's article *Securitization, mafias and violence in Brazil and Mexico* does not focus explicitly upon Colombia, but a number of themes are similar to those addressed in *Narcos*. Gledhill's argument, in a nutshell, is that violence serves a regulatory role within society, stemming from economic conditions emerging from neoliberalism; moreover, that political elites have capitalized on changing societal power relations as a means of ensuring their survival within an increasingly securitized environment.

Gledhill's argument, whilst not necessarily a traditional approach to securitization provides fascinating insight into life in Brazil and Mexico, wherein structural factors shape the capacity of agency to operate. It also focuses upon the nature of political and social life that is shaped by the market forces of neoliberalism but a zone in which a range of domestic actors also seek to exert influence. In doing this, the article raises questions about the nature of political organization broadly, which, in turn, raises a number of issues for approaches to securitization. A Weberian understanding of a sovereign state bestows a legitimate monopoly of violence upon ruling elites, yet the erosion of such a monopoly has serious consequences for authority and political hierarchies. From the level of violence across South America, arguing such a position is easily done. Moreover, with this breakdown, there are clear repercussions for securitization theory, with an apparent linear structure of securitizer and audience. Amidst the fragmentation of political authority, this linear process is broken among competing audiences and a number of different sources of authority and power.

Political life is a key part of Gledhill's article, which, in turn, provokes a number of issues for the application of securitization. As with much of the recent literature on securitization, it is with the concept of the audience that the article finds the most traction. For Gledhill, securitization in South America serves as a means of regulating life, amidst rising criminality which the author suggests is a direct manifestation of neoliberal agendas. With this in mind, the author sets out to reveal more about the social relations of each society. In doing so, the article evokes ideas of sovereignty and broader under- standings of territoriality. Within this, securitisation efforts frame criminality as an existential threat to social - and societal - dynamics and it is typically those hardest hit by neoliberal agendas that are the victims of such moves. In a nod toward the work of Giorgio Agamben, whose ideas of the *state of exception* (2005) and *homer sacer* (1999), the article sets out the conditions within which life becomes marginalized, with all traces of political meaning removed. It is in such conditions that we can see the successes of securitization processes.

Where Gledhill diverts from conventional approaches concerns the multiplicity of actors involved in a multidirectional set of securitizing process(es) and, broadly, within political life itself. It is here where Gledhill's application of securitization is at its most useful: by shedding light on the internal dynamics of Brazilian and Mexican societies, securitization helps to reveal how political life is regulated and by whom, moving beyond the conventional understandings of power within state structures. In doing this, Gledhill's approach makes an important contribution to debates on the internal machinations of sovereignty, moving away from Weberian understandings of institu- tions and a legitimate use of force, to reveal the multiplicity of actors involved in violence and the regulation of life.

Whilst this may seem to many to be the predilection of Security Studies or of Policing, broadly, there is a more much existential and ontological concern at play. Indeed, the article seeks to unpack the social relations of society and the 'hidden agendas' that are shaping life in *favelas* and urban environments. This is important within the age of neoliberalism as it is the urban environment that brings people together as a site of political life but also contestation; the struggle to regulate urban life is a struggle to regulate politics broadly. This struggle, of course, is dangerous, not only to those whose life is marginalized but also to police and individuals involved in regulation beyond formal institutions.

It is with this that Gledhill's article offers a great deal. Securitization has typically sought to understand the logic behind, and framing of, particular issues as existential threats to security. These have typically occupied a central, and visible, space within a state's calculations, playing upon existing, latent fears of society. In Gledhill's piece, latent and manifest structures are revealed, along with the multidirectional process of securitization. The use of securitization initially appears counterintuitive, yet proves invaluable as a mechanism to reveal structural dimensions within society. Thus, with Gledhill's argument, we see how securitization theory can be used as a mechanism to engage with political life more broadly.

Disclosure statement

No potential conflict of interest was reported by the author.

Index

Note: Page numbers followed by 'n' refer to endnotes